AN IRISHMAN ON THE
THIN GREEN LINE

AN IRISHMAN ON THE
THIN GREEN LINE

Patrick D. Goggin, Capt.,(rtd)

SOMERVILLE PRESS

Somerville Press Ltd,
Dromore, Bantry,
Co. Cork, Ireland

First published 2013
by Somerville Press Ltd

This is a book of my memories, experiences, analyses of situations, opinions on people and ideas. Any errors or omissions are regretted. I am not an historian or political philosopher. I ask questions. Readers will arrive at their own conclusions. These opinions are my own and are not offered as being the official political or military beliefs, ideas or opinions of the Defence Forces. The title of this book is intended to convey the fact that it is about me, not an academic review of the Army.

Designed by Jane Stark
Typeset in Adobe Garamond
seamistgraphics@gmail.com

ISBN: 978 0 9573461 8 5

Printed and bound in Spain
by GraphyCems, Villatuerta, Navarra

*I wish to dedicate this book
to my Army comrades,
who made my story,
and my wife and family,
for whom it was written.*

Contents

Acknowledgements 9

Prologue 10

PART ONE: PREPARATIONS 13

1 Dingle Doings
    a.   The Peacock's Tail 14
    b.   Political Irish Stew 20
    c.   The Monks 25
    d.   The Dingle *Dáil* 30

2 Almost a Soldier
    a.   In the Green 34
    b.   Old Sweat? 36
    c.   Career Decision 39

3 The Cadet School
    a.   Arrival 44
    b.   On the Range 49
    c.   Departure 52

PART TWO: OPERATIONS 59

4 Infantry Officer
    a.   Embarrassments 60
    b.   The Officer Corps 64
    c.   Stand by my Men 66
    d.   One of the Best 69
    e.   The Fall 74
    f.   Postings 77
    g.   Platoon Commander 82
    h.   Warriors 88
    i.   Sport 92

5 Stormy Weather
    a.   The 1950s 97
    b.   Field Exercises 103
    c.   Internment 110
    d.   A Career Asset 113
    e.   God's Army 119
    f.   Border Patrol 122

6 Military Low-life
    a.   Military Theatre 128
    b.   Military Characters 130
    c.   Military Weddings 133
    d.   Military Staff-work 136
    e.   Military Dancing Years 138

7 World War Three?
    a.   The Observer Corps 142
    b.   PSO to ACS 147
    c.   Looming Trouble 149
    d.   Neutrality 151

8 The Military College
    a.   The Command and Staff School 156
    b.   Night Patrol 158
    c.   'Brigade Commander' 160
    d.   Tests 162
    e.   Certificates 165

9 Peace in Cyprus
    a.   The Trumpet Sounds 168
    b.   The Office 172
    c.   International Comrades 176
    d.   KIA 178
    e.   Life on the Island 180
    f.   Assignments 183

10 War in Ireland?
    a.   Back in the Green 189
    b.   Second in Command 191
    c.   To Reason Why? 195

PART THREE: REFLECTIONS 199

11 A Late Vocation Civilian

    a.   Off Parade. 200

    b.   Military Diary. 208

    c.   Home Base 212

12 The Profession of Arms

    a.   Officers and Gentlemen?. 219

    b.   A Soldier's Soldier 223

    c.   Mess Life. 226

    d.   Clothes and the Man. 228

    e.   A Soldier's Friend 230

    f.   Days of Wine and Roses 232

    g.   Our Military Tradition – a Shared Inheritance?. 240

Epilogue 249

Appendix A   Clippings. 256

Appendix B   Some of the Books in my Life 257

Appendix C   Cadet Class 1950-52 269

Acknowledgements

This book is the result of a suggestion from the agent Jonathan Williams and the publisher, Andrew Russell, opening a door for me. Having completed the writing, which I enjoyed, I hesitated at the idea of putting myself centre stage, but Andrew held the door open and I received invaluable help from Jane Russell in the editing and Jane Stark for the book design and photographs (with assistance on the photographs from my son-in-law Ian McColl).

I thank my wife Muriel for her patient encouragement over the years and my daughters Jennifer, Erika and Ursula, my sons-in-law Martin, Assie and Ian, as well as my grandchildren Rebekah, Ally, Jordie, Zach, Stephanie and Megan for being there – for being my reasons for writing this book.

I also thank my ex-Cadet School classmate, Colonel Michael Moriarty, author of *An Irish Soldier's Diary*, for his thorough reading of the script. My other ex-classmates were, I believe, a significant influence over the years as well as the commanding officers and orderlies, who defined my world.

It is worth recording also the help available from the staff of the Military Archives, but the real sources of this book are no longer with us – my parents, who did so much for me, but mainly encouraged me to read, think and arrive at my own conclusions.

Prologue

This is the story of a military pilgrim's progress and a bird's eye view of the Army holding the thin green line. It is a soldier's hacking of the path of military duty through the tangled undergrowth of Irish political beliefs in the mid-twentieth century, when, according to some politicians and Christian Brothers, the truth was known and need not be questioned.

It is also the story of the social and military ups and downs, warts and all, of a young officer in the mid-century, and the important people in his life: his CO and his orderly. While the 'downs' will come under the spotlight, I will also make the most out of my few 'ups', while aiming at Garret Fitzgerald's standard of explaining 'one's own contemporary motivation with as little abuse of hindsight and as much avoidance of self-justification as possible' – recognising 'that memory is a fickle guide'.

While accepting that memory is indeed a 'fickle guide', that is what I am offering for the judgement of the reader. This is a book of my memories, takes on situations and people, and analyses of political ideas. This is not being offered as an academic treatise. It is therefore spared the sprinkling of reference numbers. The quotations and conclusions are from my experience and are all open to question.

This book was written over twenty years, based on notes in my files going back at least forty. Whatever about anything else, my central philosophy has not changed, its aim an Ireland at peace, John Hume's 'Agreed Ireland', accepting all who live on this island as equally Irish, all happy with Tone's 'common name of Irishman'. It was intended to be a lived, on-the-ground view of the military factor in Irish life, but it developed into one Irish Everyman's story of life in the second half of twentieth-century Ireland, with its changing attitudes to our received ideas about religion and the officially approved versions of history as well as our 'national aim' of the 'restoration of the Irish language'.

The New Ireland into which I was born was struggling to emerge into the sunlight of Independence. The Civil War wounds were still raw. Two years before I arrived we could boast about the Shannon Scheme, but the year before I was born saw the embarrassment of a Protestant, Trinity College graduate, being rejected by Mayo County Council despite being appointed as librarian by the Local Appointments Commission. This was to be the view of Ireland as seen through the prism of my place in the ranks, but it became clear to me that there are civilians also manning part of the thin green line. These are the politicians and academics, who insist on truth rather than self-serving claptrap, that set out to fulfil the task of our generation – to clarify and challenge our inherited concepts in political philosophy.

It also became obvious as I moved through the book, that an essential element was the cultural well from which I drew my ideas. Therefore, my family, touching both sides of the 'national question' and Dingle in the time of my youth, became significant factors. I had tried to find my military feet in FCA boots. I had searched for light in the archaic world created by the Christian Brothers within school walls decorated with a map of a huge island of Ireland in splendid separatist isolation guarded by portraits of the 1916 leaders seemingly just succeeding in holding back tears of sincerity.

I hope that this book will strike some memory bells for those who lived through that time of change and provide insight into the second half of twentieth-century Ireland for those who came after. I also hope that it will be of some use to the young people who are now contemplating a military career in the twenty-first century.

I had gained a Cadetship after 600 had been interviewed for the thirty-two places. Today it seems that there are nearly three thousand applicants. After two years in the novitiate of the Cadet School of the Military College I was awarded the President's Commission. I had to return to the Military College for my 'Infantry School' and my 'Command and Staff School' courses at intervals, but it is the comrades of those two years in the Cadet School that remain one of the principal military social components of an officer's life, with, as in our case, class reunions over half a century.

My job was to lead men in the defence of my country. But, how well were we fitted as an army for this task? What kind of an army were we? I had had ex-Free State Army commanding officers and soldiered with ex-'Temporary Officers' from the Emergency. The number of Cadet School graduates was small at the time.

On what did we ground our fortitude, described by General Sean McKeown, when he was our Cadet-master, as 'mental robustness'? To what military tradition did we look for inspiration in the '*Bearna Baol*'? What, for instance, about those soldiers, who had fought and died in Irish regiments of other armies for hundreds of years? Had they anything to do with us? Or did we just start from nothing in 1913? Was our military tradition merely a paramilitary one and were we now an IRA in uniform?

Yet our situation is not without hope or signs of progress. President Mary McAleese joined with Queen Elizabeth to honour the memory of the Irish soldiers in the First World War. The North's Deputy First Minister, Martin McGuinness, who has recently worked so well for peace, in an Easter address, has urged his supporters to engage with Unionists and increase their efforts to achieve true reconciliation. Also, at long last, John Redmond and his constitutional nationalists are being officially commemorated.

The words of a one-time President of the Military History Society of Ireland, Sir Charles Petrie, are apt: 'I should have regrets, I only have memories'.

Part One

PREPARATIONS

1

Dingle Doings

a. The Peacock's Tail

I had intended to begin this book with me on a bus, either the bus from Dingle to the FCA Camp in Tralee or the bus from Dublin to the Cadet School in the Curragh. But it became clear to me, as I progressed, that a vital part of understanding my response to the situations, big and small, national and personal, with which I was faced, was where I had come from, and the people who had helped to form that response.

As in the mid 1950s and late 1960s, when storm clouds gathered and we were threatened with subversion from within our gates, from what well did we draw strength? Is it formed by nature or nurture, or a combination of both?

The first source is obviously the family. Mentally searching now for the seeds of my social, intellectual and character formation, I must go back to Dingle and the home where I grew up.

Osbert Sitwell's idea of the spread peacock's tail of our ancestry, where we refer only to the shining green spots, ignoring the humbler feathers in between, was stood on its head in the Ireland of my youth. People searched frantically for any sign of a jailbird hero to boast about and ignored any ancestor, who failed to fit in with de Valera's frugal land of 'men of no property'.

My maternal great-grandfather's Victorian work title, Chief Clerk, of a large builders' providers, presumably sounded just right, worthy and respectable, and would have pleased de Valera, had he been there.

According to my mother however, he did not seem to contribute his managerial skills very much at home. She rarely asked him for explanations as he insisted on precise connotations and denotations of definitions at all times, when all she wanted was a quick answer. My maternal grandmother was a nurse, professionally trained in the Rotunda, who 'threw out' the herbal cures that my great-grandmother had believed in. My grandmother was what was called a 'Jubilee' nurse for the Town of Dingle, recruited by the Queen's Institute for District Nursing.

My family was a typical Irish stew of dollops from both sides of the 'Irish Question' happily coexisting. My mother's boasted 'Fenian drop' came from my grandfather, Patrick Foley. We were told that the first meeting of the West Kerry Land League was held in our house. My grandfather was a devoted follower of Parnell.

Things cannot have been too bad if, ten years before my mother was born, General Sir Redvers Buller, acting as special commissioner of the RIC in Kerry, declared that the people saw 'the Land League as their salvation', that 'nobody did anything for them before it was founded'. He felt safe enough to travel on a jaunting car, no cavalry escort, as reported by *United Ireland*.

'Foley Brothers, Masons' would now be described as 'building contractors'. But is it fair to ask today, why, if he was this great Republican, how come he got valuable contracts from the landlord? We still had six of his houses by the time I arrived, which we let for rent. The problem was that the rent remained at the level it was set at the end of the previous century, while we were responsible for the current cost of repairs and general maintenance.

My name Patrick came from him. Stories shadowed my grandfather's memory like seagulls over a returning fishing boat. One was that he could have been a rich man if he had only lifted his bowler to the landlord's agent, known as 'the Captain'. As a family we loved books and stories. We were told that my grandfather underwrote the cost of a boat for a fisherman. A story however, that I totally rejected privately, was that a bank manager in Mexico was responsible for the loss of some of my grandfather's money. Even as a child I felt that

15

that was stretching credulity too far. Curiously enough, I discovered later that his first cousin had in fact been in Mexico, presumably in connection with his writing.

My paternal grandfather, David Goggin, had a farm. The David in my name came from him. We have a photograph of him in his formal black suit and hat standing proudly beside an early Christian standing stone on his land in Riasc. He had 'rescued' it with the help of a friend from the National Museum. As a family we seem to take great pleasure in being photographed standing beside it.

I remember my grandmother in severe high-necked black with a brooch at the neck in the fashion of Queen Victoria. She must have been a somewhat demanding, complaining person, because when I was small, I repeated to her what I had overheard my mother say to my Aunt Katy. I do not remember seeing any indication that she saw any reflection of herself in my: 'Woe, woe, nag, woe'.

My maternal grand-uncle, Maurice Griffin, was a co-founder of the *Kerryman*. My mother had acted as his personal assistant (reference material, filing the *Times Literary Supplement*, etc.) until it was suggested that her more stylish sister, Aunt Hanna, deserved the opportunity.

In a short time, however, Aunt Hanna met and married Uncle Pat. Patrick Flynn had just returned from South Africa, where he had an interest in diamond mines, to run a pub in Tralee. His daughter, my cousin Marie, eventually married a South African doctor, who had been a member of the famous heart team. Uncle Pat's main distinction was his use of a South African word that sounded like 'footsac', which seemingly is the South African equivalent of 'F off'.

However, the friendly assistance of a major-general in the Free State Army and a government minister helped my mother to get a post office 'to keep her going temporarily'. It lasted for half a century. My uncles Joe and Brendan helped her to run it as clerks/postmen. They also contributed significantly to my informal education. Brendan did so as a poet and Joe as a sportsman with gun and rod. My Aunt Katy ran the house with the help of a maid and a young children's maid when I was small. The latter, to my embarrassment, once, home from America, came looking for me, when I was out with my 'gang'. I was terrified that she might hug me in public.

My Uncle Joe also acted as rent collector for the remaining houses built by my grandfather. Uncle Brendan was Dingle correspondent for the *Kerryman* ('Dingle Doings'column) but he was also a poet in his spare time. Some of his poems appear in the book of local poetry, *Ancient Town of High Renown*. Some lines give an idea of how local history was part of their mental furniture.

> '*Reenbeg's Hill looked grey and steep*
> *Where sailors of the Armada sleep.*'

and,

> '*Mount Brandon holds last rays of day*
> *Where Brendan used to retire to pray.*'

My first political memory was being taken by my father to look at the picture of Parnell, the dead Chief, surrounded by ivy leaves, in a ground floor window, on a day of commemoration. To put it into its historical context, my father was born just five years after Captain O'Shea named Parnell in his divorce. That picture of Parnell normally hung in my bedroom.

In Senior Infants in the Convent, Sr Kevin once asked:

'What holy pictures have you in your house?'

'The Holy Family, St Patrick and St Parnell,' I said.

Although our school politics then largely consisted in praying for General Franco, in Spain, fighting the 'Reds', who, I assumed, were Red Indians. We knew nothing about the 200,000 men who died in combat or of the 200,000 men, women and children who also perished, nor of the Catholic clergy's encouragement of Franco's atrocities.

In 1930s Dingle the main excitement was the burning and rebuilding of the local cinema, the 'Phoenix'. This was eventually owned and run by my friend Michael O'Sullivan, who ran the widely famed Film Festivals. Michael is sadly no longer with us, but the cinema is still being run by the family.

In later years Parnell and the other saints were still there but, for me, as well, there was nothing incongruous in a full colour plate of a nineteenth-century British cavalry officer stuck between the fighting generals of the Second World War. My bedroom was on the third floor. The ground floor was the Dingle Post Office. Skylights on the sloping ceiling overlooked Strand Street, which still has a warm yellow glow in my mind in memory of childhood sunshine. I remember the cheerful scraping and brushing as my father and neighbours prepared for the Corpus Christi procession. All co-operated: an echo of the ancient '*meithal*' system. Passers-by waved a cheery 'God bless the work'. Civic guards and postmen, as befitting uniformed servants of the State, offered encouragement, while a bus conductor, who was also a county footballer, with a shotgun and a duck, returns from a country run.

In and from this small room, on a small street, I lived intellectually in my world. For me, and for my family, neither the Malaya States (Uncle Tom) nor South Africa (Uncle Pat) nor even the Indian Ocean (my father, Maurice) seemed too far away. There were doctors at both ends of the street in houses, which also had businesses on the ground floors. One was a chemist's shop. The other was a marvellous emporium, where 'wellies' vied for attention with salted ling and Guinness. Their son Joe was my childhood friend. His three sisters graduated from Trinity. In those days that made them different. Archbishop John Charles McQuaid, in his instructions for Lent in 1947 had set out an uncompromising view that 'the Church forbade parents to send a child to any non-Catholic school, whether primary or secondary, or continuation or university'. In our house we liked people to be different. My mother's favourite quotation:

> '*Be not like dumb driven cattle;*
> *Be a hero in the strife.*'

The 'Troubles' in Dingle seem to have been reasonably civilised, at least until the Civil War when things turned nasty. Despite my mother's boasted 'Fenian drop', she spoke highly of a British Army officer she knew at the time. It seems that, once, when he heard of some problem, he headed out with his handful of men to sort it and said nothing to the 'Tans' who would have started a war, which would have disturbed the peace of the town.

There were fourteen men of the 2nd East Lancs Regiment stationed in Dingle in 1920: being an important town it was allotted one more than Valentia Island's thirteen. In *Kerry's Fighting Story*, published by the *Kerryman* in the 1940s, the chivalry of the Dingle IRA was illustrated. After an ambush, the lorries were burned, the arms were taken but of thirteen soldiers who surrendered, six wounded, after first aid, were sent to Dingle Hospital.

But things turned nasty in the Civil War. The train from Limerick to Tralee was derailed, killing the driver and the fireman. The IRA from Lispole, a village on the road between Dingle and Tralee, burned down two valuable properties in Dingle that had been handed over by the British. This was despite a local delegation led by Fr Finucane, who pleaded to save the buildings: the local RIC Barracks and the Coast Guard Station. The echoes of this unrest were still heard in the Ireland that was waiting for my arrival. De Valera took power but dissidents remained, with whom he had to deal in his turn.

In the year before I was born the ugly spectre of sectarianism surfaced, when a young Protestant graduate of Trinity College, appointed as a librarian, by the Local Appointments Commission, in Co. Mayo, was opposed by the County Council. It was said that this was because she did not have a full knowledge of Irish and that it had nothing to do with her religion or university.

In those years also communism and fascism were in the background, with some delegates to the Fine Gael (United Ireland) party's first *ardfheis* wearing blue-shirt 'uniforms'.

The *Kerryman* had survived attacks from the 'Tans' before my arrival (when it was 'blacked' for a time) and threats from the IRA in my lifetime, neither having any influence on its editorial policy. The editor rejected a threat from the IRA and published an anti-IRA column by Con Houlihan.

My grand-uncle Maurice was centre stage in many family stories, especially of his ongoing row with Mr Tom O'Donnell, MP. I cannot remember being told the subject of this difference of opinion, but the story had it that Uncle Maurice (as he was called at home) contributed to Mr O'Donnell's departure from the chairmanship of the Tralee and Dingle Railway and being replaced by the Republican Austin Stack.

I was nearly five years old when the first scheduled air service between Dublin and London was offered, leaving Baldonnel Airport after a blessing by the Army Air Corps chaplain. But there were dark shadows over the Ireland of the time that did not seem to be a real concern to the majority of its citizens. One was the nearly 80,000 living in abject poverty, confined to one room tenements in Dublin. The other, that was to loom very large in later years, as reported by Peter Tyrrell in his book *Founded on Fear* was the unbelievable brutality in the industrial schools.

The other cause of concern in the 1930s was the 'Economic War' when we withheld the land annuity payments to Britain and faced the retaliatory trade tariffs. This caused severe problems for farmers like Uncle Mike, bringing a collapse of agricultural prices.

However, according to *Kerry's Football Story* the Kerry team won the All-Ireland and had a very successful tour of America, in the year I was born. This must have lifted spirits, at home at least.

That was the Ireland of the early 1930s that, I assume, welcomed me.

b. Political Irish Stew

The first Goggin in the family came to the area as a Chief Petty Officer of the Sea Fencibles at the time of the Napoleonic scare, about the time that they built the Martello tower for James Joyce in Sandycove. In the scheme of defence of the West Coast, Dingle was the Sea Fencibles District HQ. The Fencibles were not just a Local Defence Force/Militia: they could be sent anywhere in the Empire.

He met, fell for and married, Vice-Admiral Sylvarius Moriarty's niece. This is why my grandfather's tomb, the only tomb apart from the Admiral's, was allowed to 'ruin' (my wife's word) the ruins of the old church at Kilmalkedar. Recently, however, it was sunk into the floor. I pointed out to my grandchildren on a visit that they were standing by the tomb of their great-great-grandfather.

I have a hazy memory as a child of some Gardai in attendance at a funeral there. I cannot remember why, whether it was to ensure something or prevent something. I understand that ours was the only other family allowed to be buried in that church. The judgement of the family that lived beside the graveyard and that had looked after it for several generations was taken as having legal status.

The Admiral fought in major battles of the American War of Independence and ended his days as OC the Naval Dockyard in Haulbowline. On a visit to Haulbowline I had hoped to find some documents but there were no records from that long ago. However, my brother Bernie found some papers in London.

Dingle was the Sea Fencibles District HQ with a series of Signal Stations on headlands on the look-out for French invading ships. One of these was where we had an LOP (Look Out Post) during the Emergency. My father used to get me to ring the amused volunteer on duty there in order to tell the green uniformed Santa what I wanted for Christmas. I can imagine his surprise when my request once was for a rifle. The amused soldier asked: 'What kind of a rifle?'

'An Army one not a cowboy one,' my father told me I replied.

My father had served as a radio officer towards the end of the First World War on troopships of the British Indian Line. The highlight of his war was the sinking of a submarine which, being French, and an ally, would now be described as a 'blue on blue'.

He was proud to know Tom Crean, the famous Antarctic explorer. When I was about six years of age we visited the South Pole Inn in Annascaul. I remember sitting in a car and seeing someone like an Indian Chief dancing and yelping around me. I read afterwards that Tom Crean was a great comic performer as well as a good sailor, who entertained the explorers when spirits were low.

My father was recalled in the Second World War for a commission in the RNVR (Royal Naval Volunteer Reserve), as an instructor, but my mother shot down this potential adventure. She also showed herself to be the more adventurous by accompanying me on a flight in an open cockpit plane during a Flying Circus visit to Dingle, which got me reported in the *Kerryman* as 'Dingle's youngest pilot' at seven years of age.

Choosing Fianna Fáil as the purest 'republican' party was presumably to demonstrate that he was at last really back home. His contribution to the local *cumann* included sitting over scotch and sodas in Benner's Hotel listening to de Valera's stories, while the real canvassing went on around the town, where 'Dev' would have been a disaster, because he insisted on listening seriously to people.

As well as Irish, my father had reasonable Spanish. Brendan Behan came into the office one day and made a request in Spanish. My father answered without indicating any surprise. Behan, seemingly not amused, left in a huff.

His brother, Uncle Tom, Chief Inspector, ex-RIC, served as OCPD (Officer in Charge of the Police District) of Kuantan, Pahang, in the Federated Malaya States. A fluent Irish speaker and constitutional nationalist, by the time he left in 1907, the RIC, mainly Catholic, marching to mass on Sunday, had achieved a certain grudging respect in their local communities, carrying out normal police duties. The RIC does not get 'a good press' in nationalist histories, but were spoken of very highly by Mr John Dillon, MP, in parliament, when he recalled that they had protected him from attack by a crowd of about 200 armed Orangemen, at a political meeting in the North. Some ex-RIC helped in the formation of the new Garda Síochána.

There seems to be a softening of the memory, however, when the GAA set up a commemorative headstone to mark one of those present at the meeting when the organisation was founded, Thomas St George McCarthy, District Inspector RIC. Chris Ryder made a case in *The Irish Times* that now 'at a time of mutual recognition and forgiveness', it would be unforgivable if the memory of the RIC continues to be excluded from the process of reconciliation'.

Happily in 2012 two retired members of An Garda Síochána organised a commemoration of the RIC attended by over 150 relatives and friends, as part of our healing process in a decade of inclusive commemorations. As Conor Brady wrote in *The Irish Times* 'for more than ninety years the RIC has been consigned to a loser's role in history', and 'that this commemoration is a heartening step in acknowledging our many-stranded past'.

Larger than life, Uncle Tom never considered himself a problem. He became fluent in Malayese and made friends with the local Chinese minority, and we assumed, as a party piece for us, he would eat my mother's curry with chopsticks. He never married but had an eye for the ladies. He christened a striking looking maid 'Greta' (as in Garbo) explaining that it was because of her beautifully posed hands. A lady doctor in Switzerland took his fancy for a time, but the only result of this was a most unexpected picture of snow-capped mountains in our sitting room.

In his letters he wrote of how he 'maintained the traditions of the RIC in suppressing bribery'. The story goes that he could have come home a *nawab* if he had accepted half the bribes he was offered for 'administrative difficulties' in a boat coming ashore on a particular day. The local 'movers and shakers' just thought him to be eccentric because they were merely following custom and simply landed the boat somewhere else, on a very long coastline.

Among his papers are letters from the Bishop's House looking for advice, from people on a rubber estate thanking him for help during a flood and from the Commissioner of Police awarding him a 'record of commendation for his excellent work'. He was appointed a Peace Officer and conducted important cases. He was awarded the Imperial Service Medal by King George V. (Silver with red-blue-red ribbon). In those days according to our constitution, we continued as members of the British Empire (i.e. pre-1937) and *Dáil* deputies swore allegiance to the king as head of the empire.

A top class shot, with cups to prove it, we still have the skin of a tiger he shot (minus the whiskers that I cut off as a child) now rejoicing in the name of 'Tim the Tiger' for visiting grandchildren, the boys asking when, how and where he was shot, the girls wanting to know why. Sadly there are now only about 600 left of Tim's relations in the Malayan sub-species of tiger. Uncle Tom presumably must share the blame.

Retired, in town to spend his dividends, flower in buttonhole, swinging his Malacca cane, he would land himself and his driver on my mother for a meal. This cane is still in a twenty-five pounder artillery shell case at home. A silver-topped black one, that my father carried in uniform, was with it until a friend of our daughters, when small, broke it. Now nearing its hundredth birthday, it is still sadly in two pieces in a press waiting to be fixed. Regardless of the planned meal, my mother always put on a special curry for him with her own chutney. The driver would eat in the kitchen with the maid and the 'Rajah' (my mother's name for him) would entertain at table with his adventures and his rules. Especially his rules, for instance, all toy weapons (in other words all my toys) had to be put out of sight.

He once brought me a brown velvet suit and a yellow silk shirt, in which I had the standard 'one hand on chair' photograph taken. On being asked by my pal Joe's mother where I got it I said 'China' and was warned about being cheeky. He had to retire early due to ill-health. One of my last memories was of a maid bringing up tea and biscuits for the nurse when my father called her back to put a white cloth on the tray. As a little pitcher with big ears I heard a man saying, 'typical of Maurice'. His funeral was reported in the *Kerryman* as 'the biggest seen on the peninsula for years' and that 'he spoke Irish with fluency' and was 'a supporter of the language and all it connotes'.

We were very pleasantly received with a welcoming coffee, on a visit to the Police HQ in Kuantan in what is now, of course, Malaysia, by Wan Abd Ghani Bin HJ Wan Salim, DSP, the then holder of the appointment. He very kindly asked for a picture of Uncle Tom to hang in the Police Club. We have a picture of him in his pith helmet (solar topi) and sword, backed by his turbaned warriors.

These were the principal characters in our family drama, living on now in family folklore. The sad thing is that by the time we reach the photograph on the mantelpiece stage, for our grandchildren, these characters will have slipped over the social horizon.

This section is offered as a rough 'field sketch' indicating the general social and political background from where I came and the source of much of my world-view. However 'the past is another country' and by the time that my brothers were growing up our world had changed.

The houses left over from my grandfather's building days were on the same small rents since his time and we were still responsible for costly maintenance. In those, still early, days of the new state, all laws seemed to be against the 'landlords' even if those landlords were ordinary people just making a living.

My brothers coming at a later stage in our family history, would have their own interpretations of the family saga. Colman is now retired as a Lieutenant Colonel, having held the appointment of Army Psychologist. Bernie is a retired publisher, a naturalist and active in An Taisce.

However, I did things that they did not do, like shooting a grey-haired old lady who sold fish out of a bucket at the corner of the Colony. I do not remember why I felt that it was my duty to rid the town of her, but it was a disaster. I went marching back complete with cowboy hat, sheriff's badge and my two guns swinging in my holsters. The cap-gun, however, misfired and a bit flew into my eye, at which she was all concerned about me. I have never before revealed this operation.

Our house is now part of Garvey's shop. But if Dustin the Turkey ever gets the Dart to Dingle, he will be a most disappointed turkey if he expects to find my Dingle: the tramp steamers landing coal for Latchfords; Jack Kennedy's 'Model T' lorry rattling past Dick Mack's pub; the Crimean War tunes of Charlie Flannery's 'fife and drum band'; the sparks flying in Barry's Forge. Gone are Nell Grandfield's home-made ice cream and Katie Sarah's Bull's Eyes.

Exeunt omnes: 'Oh brave Old World that had such people in it.'

c. 'The Monks'

Like everyone else in Dingle my education, up to Senior Infants began in the Convent. My memories are pleasant. I won a prize in a fancy-dress competition in a morning suit with a card saying 'Not an Inch' on my top-hat, as some politician. (I have no memory of who or what was his problem.)

My other claim to fame was when, with my pal Vivian Sheehy, we did a minuet in suitably French fancy clothes as part of the Nuns' annual concert. Our previous year's performance was an early Irish Riverdance. Vivian had a song with the lines:

> *'All soldiers love the leg of a duck,*
> *Every Sunday morning the officer wakes them up.'*

My *Bumper Book for Boys* military knowledge gave me the certainty that the officer did not wake them up, the Bugler did and the Sergeant. Feeling superior was enough. I did not need to say anything.

Sr Kevin put me on the big drum in the school band. We played on the stage in the cinema:

> *'If you're Irish, come into the parlour,*
> *There's a welcome there for you'*

only to hear complaints from some that we were playing a British Army recruiting song. However, despite my musical success with the big drum, I must have been a considerable wear on Sister Bernard, who did her best to teach me the piano. This was one of my father's disappointments, having gone to the trouble of having a piano winched up from the street and taken in a sitting-room window. He seemed to have a hope that I would be a hit at parties, when I grew up.

Boys eventually graduated from Senior Infants to the first class in the Christian Brothers Primary School. The Christian Brothers in Dingle were known as 'The Monks'. The Primary School was 'downstairs' on the ground floor and the Secondary School was 'upstairs'. The Victorian social connotations of these terms seemed curiously apt in those pre-O'Malley days in Irish education when the State accepted that the fate of the majority was to remain 'downstairs' and that its potential future leaders would be found among the minority 'upstairs'. When I was eventually moved 'upstairs' I found that I liked a line in the prescribed text: *'Arma virumque cano'* ('of arms and the man I sing'). I saw it as a link between our grey world and the glory days of the Roman Imperium. I was always on the side of the Romans against the Barbarians (Glory, Glory, Rome United): as indeed, on the side of the Austro-Hungarian Empire against the rebel Hungarians. I did not know then that Dingle had a close connection to the Hapsburg Empire through some of its leading local families. I knew however about the Rice house as part of a plan to save Marie Antoinette. Uniting people under one flag seemed nobler to me than raising many flags in conflict.

I was quite happy watching the chalk-laden sunbeams, coming through the high Gothic windows, warming the grainy desks. Yet, the 'leather' was in daily use for failure to work at lessons. 'Whacks' on the hand were doled out in a cool, matter of fact manner. Rarely more than one at a time, they were as much part of the day as the Kerry showers, forgotten outside the gates. I do not remember seeing 'whacks' for bad behaviour: they did not seem necessary, the certainty of the consequences must have been sufficient.

Keen on us passing examinations and getting jobs; their mistake was, as Charles McCarthy put it, the enthronement of 'archaism' and the 'practice of latter-day ancestor worship.' They attempted to recreate a world of 'a virtuous Gaelic past'. On entering the school gates we left the real world behind in the sounds of a town going about its business and stepped on a stage for a very serious pantomime: an agricultural world, curiously peopled by saints and scholars, who seemed to spend their time passing and blessing each other, in Irish.

We did all our subjects through Irish, including science and Latin. Yet, we left the Irish language behind us, like a football strip after playing a game, when we went out the school gates, back into the real world. In my six years, I never heard a word of Irish exchanged between students outside the school. I have no reason to believe that things are different anywhere else, even in the new *Gaelscoileanna*.

Today, it is very hard to believe that professional *gaelgoiri* and politicians hoping to score, do not know this. Yet Minister O'Cuiv pretended that the answer to the restoration of the language is in more education through Irish. I speak and still love the language but I am not aware of any desire among the people to give up the international language that allows them, for instance, to listen on TV to the Presidents of Afghanistan, Pakistan and the USA discussing matters of importance to our security. It is the most widely spoken second language in the world and today an economic asset.

Bribery, (then £5 per annum for Irish speaking families), bullying and compulsion seem to have been accepted like the weather. It seems to be the pretence, for example, that it is necessary to use tons of paper to print translations of legislation to be read by a person or persons unknown that is turning most people off. We participated in rituals, intoning mantras in our stage language. Like *'gan teanga gan tir'*, despite the evidence of our eyes that we had a country, even though nobody seemed to want to throw out English and become Irish speaking.

In the eighteen years I spent growing up in Dingle, whereas I heard the occasional exchange of greetings in Irish between visitors from the West of the town, I never heard a conversation in Irish between two Dingle people. It might seem strange to city people, but we were very conscious of being townspeople and referred to any place outside the town as 'the country'. Things are perhaps somewhat different now with droves of professional *gaelgoiri* arriving. The school was like a mini-*gaeltacht* in the town and its lack of influence on the town makes me wonder if it echoes the effect of the national *gaeltachts* on the country. Yet, within its walls, we were in a different world, where the truth was known and therefore was not to be questioned.

The beatification of Irish Revolutionaries would make excellent psychological training for fanaticism, where the views of the ordinary people did not count. The 1916 leaders eyed us critically from their places on the walls. They defended a map of Ireland that showed what a huge and important country it was: all on its own in the middle of a blue sea, with, perhaps, a ghostly hint of the Mull of Kintyre in white.

This must have reinforced the geographical nationalism of some, who would be opposed by others, who had spent their school-days looking at a bigger map which included the other island of this archipelago, confirming for them the physical truth of the union.

I was entertained by 'An Irishman's Diary' in the *Irish Times*, by Dick O'Riordan, on the 'fierce nationalistic environment' in O'Connell School, in 1961, where 'the Rising was always sacred and central to OCS culture'. He struck an amused memory cord in me as he wrote of the brother's 'vision of a triumphant Gaelic Ireland that would emerge through the will of God and the Christian Brothers'.

'Would you believe that the Dublin Jackeens jeered the men of 1916?' I remember a brother would say, with a wide aggressive smile, at the enormity of this crime, that, as Christians, we could only consider with the patience and tolerance for which we were famous.

The whole class would have to pause and dutifully look at each other, putting on what they hoped were smiles of disbelief. I felt that a certain eyebrow raising was called for on the grounds that some of the Jackeens might have been hurt or had fathers or brothers fighting for their lives against the 'gallant allies' of the rebels, but for some reason my own eyebrows remained flat.

However, a lay history teacher, Tom Lundon, asked other questions: 'Imagine yourselves in Dingle in smoking ruins, what would your fathers say?'

We knew, however, that he was not 'anti-national' (God forbid). Listening to our national story in UCD in the early sixties as told by Professor Robin Dudley Edwards, I recalled the flavour of his words.

O'Riordan also wrote of the fact that Paddy Finucane, the RAF ace, who died fighting Hitler, was never mentioned. This brought back another memory.

Once when I brought in a copy of the *War Illustrated* and talked about the Dingle men who had fought with the Eighth Army in North Africa, I was advised to: *faigh brat na Sasanach*.

In practical terms however, the contribution of the Brothers was recognised as the town's necessity, with few local jobs for youth.

English was my favourite subject. I have a happy memory of a whack for not 'admitting' that an essay was copied. Val admitted to copying a paragraph and was excused for his honesty, whereas I refused because mine had not, in fact, been copied. It was my vision of a United States of Europe, but I was flattered by the judgement.

I loved and still love the sound of Irish but mainly the older texts with their alliterative cadences like *'Bodach an Chota Lactna'*. I treasure it as an invaluable gateway to the land of our forefathers.

My Latin produced good marks on tests but also earned the occasional whack for chancing my arm, as translating *'virgo lacerato'* as 'having lacerated himself with a maiden'.

Brother Barry, the Principal, like Brother O'Doherty before him, was an honest, witty and decent man who believed in 'Irish Ireland'. They tried to create a truly green world as envisaged by the millenarian poets in 1916.

We marched to confession once a month, an indignity much resented among the seniors. Marching up Main Street, with my class-mate Paddy Betts, whose father was the manager of the National Bank, taking advantage of a protruding corner of the bank building we would disappear inside to play croquet in the back until it was time to go home.

This vanishing trick was not my only act of daring rebellion. We were forbidden to walk down the front steps from the monastery. We were supposed to go out on the Barrack Height. I ran down the forbidden steps at least three times in the six years.

d. The Dingle Dáil

In jungle clearings and the hearts of great cities, at lonely rustic crossroads and coffee tables in front of Greek tavernas, timeless little groups of men meet and exchange human concerns. Dingle had its share of these informal *Dáils*: one was at the 'chemist's corner' of Strand Street.

They enjoyed the flow and rumble of voices blending in a stream of idle chatter that swirled with the breeze down the three streets that formed a 'Y' junction.

Men hung around between finishing work and going to the pub or the cinema. Some sat on the window ledge, others stood looking down one or other of the streets and a few always stood listening outwards, as if expecting to hear some distant music, or thunder.

On those pre-television days, on returning from a walk with my pal Bob Hurley and the dogs, we liked to stand and listen for a while. We walked every day after school, regardless of the weather. The dogs had to get their walks and so did we, even if it was only as far as the boathouse in Cooleen in the rain, where we would sit on an upturned boat and plan. Major agreements were finalised in that location: an important one was that all blondes would be Bob's, all brunettes mine. The fact that we rarely got talking to them did not matter. We worshipped them from afar.

We had now both fallen for the same girl, who used to cycle home from the Convent every day. We would meet her and, one on each side of the bicycle, walk her out the Mail Road as far as the Racecourse. She was blonde, but I had torn up that agreement. She never indicated a definite preference, but must have been amused or bemused enough to put up with our attentions. It was a most unusual situation for us because, instead of the normal competition, we found ourselves saying things like:

'She allowed you to carry the bike longer than me.'

'Well, she kept looking at you while she was talking.'

The Nuns got to hear of it and they had a priest talk to her in the school. The news was also conveyed to Brother Barry who told us that he was going to get a picture painted of the two of us and the bike. He loved it. We believed that if there was anything known about it and us in the town the *Dáil* would have it, so we checked on our way home one day, taking up a position on the fringe.

A passing elderly priest holding his hat against the wind was saluted. A man said: 'Salute your priest, salute your doctor, salute your teacher', repeating a line from a homily directed at school children, on the previous Sunday, who had been the subject of some censure. The authoritarian image of the church was being found unacceptable to men, some who had spent time in England or America. Their fathers had stories of priests

31

trying to prevent local dances as their grandfathers had of scattering cross-roads *ceilis*.

No word was said of these things, the *Dáil* went temporarily silent; but new ideas, while not yet articulated, were deeply felt.

The silence was broken by a one-line poet: 'Silent O Moyle be the roar of thy waters.'

Then, with a shift of position from seat to footpath, finding new beauty: 'Silent, sez he, O Moyle, be the roar of thy waters.'

'I saw a Joaney-scruggle flying over a while ago and she was looking very *craite,*' said one.

Nobody knew how to take this bit of news.

'And silent, there sez he, O Moyle, boy, be the roar of thy waters,' offered the poet.

An attempt to introduce a serious note by a reference to the 'BORDER MUST GO' slogan painted on a local wall failed. It was 1949 and a Republic had been declared.

Arguments had flowed in the papers as to how the Coalition arrived at that decision. Was it a result of a fit of Costello (then Taoiseach) pique after a dinner in Canada, or an attempt to mollify the 'green' McBride element of the government?

The British response of the 'Ireland Act', re-affirming the position of Northern Ireland, had produced thunderous, pained speeches in the *Dáil*. A 'National Anti-Partition Campaign' was launched. But the ordinary people of Ireland did not get very excited about it. Men and women from Dingle could still go to England and be normal citizens. Mr Atlee had prevented an attempt to have Irish people designated as foreigners.

Inevitably, however, a small minority saw the possibility of re-introducing the ideology of 'physical force' and re-awakening the dormant IRA as a means of achieving the campaign's objective, once again with the apparent encouragement of politicians. The virus of militant republicanism in our political culture had been faithfully preserved by teachers, politicians, writers in the *Irish Press* and 'historians'.

Aiseirghe posters screamed: 'ARM NOW TO TAKE THE NORTH'.

'There's talk of the lads (the IRA) starting up again,' said one in a half-hearted tone.

The comment died in the evening air.

I wondered if I should have felt guilty holding on to my British Commonwealth stamp album, even though I had one page for the USA and one for Germany?

A backbencher reminded the house of the Dingle team's recent performance. In those days the Kerry Team seemed to have two colours the 'Green and Gold' of Kerry and the 'Red and White' of Dingle. Men like Paddy 'Bawn' Brosnan, Timineen Deas, Gega O'Connor and Bill Dillon.

A man with a yellow handkerchief in his top pocket, carrying three books from the Carnegie Library and accompanied by a local spinster, with whom he was considered to be friendly, distracted the *Dáil*, stunned by the multiplicity of targets.

There was no reference to us or the bike.

2

Almost a Soldier

a. In the Green

The bright sun of morning shone and the little hills behind the town stretched two green arms around the sparkling harbour as if holding the sunlight in liquid form, as I boarded the bus for the FCA Summer Camp. I had dressed in my uniform earlier under the gaze of grave military leaders on the wall beside my bed. Clippings from a 1943 *Illustrated* magazine: Montgomery and Eisenhower glaring at Rommel and Von Runstedt; with, as centrepiece, a full colour plate, from a very old copy of *Chums*, of an officer of the First Life Guards carrying a straight sword, which I knew was most unusual for the Cavalry. I liked knowing that.

I was not armed with a sword now, straight or otherwise, but I was in uniform, making a lot of impressive military noise banging size eight hob-nailed boots on the ringing flagstones. The boots were obviously too big, but I had read about route marches and I was not going to get caught with boots too tight. I had broken them in, as I knew old soldiers did, by banging around the town in the summer sun, with soaped socks, to the amusement of any who heard me.

I now had my own rifle, a possession that made me feel a different person the minute I lifted it in my arms. Uncle Joe had been a sergeant in the LDF (Local Defence Force). I had practised with his rifle even before I could hold it by placing it on a cushion on a table and aiming at a mark: getting the 'tip of the foresight in the centre of the U of the back-sight'. My rifle was a veteran of the First World War, complete with wind-gauge, but to me it was all I wanted. Uncle Brendan had also been a volunteer in the LDF, during the emergency, invariably appearing in uniform on the saluting base with de Valera and army officers for ceremonial parades, in his capacity as a war correspondent in the Dingle theatre of war for the *Kerryman*.

The camp was in Ballymullen Barracks in Tralee, once the Depot of the Royal Munster Fusiliers. My hut contained a social mixture including middle-aged labourers on their 'alkaholiers' and young clerical students in sober black 'civvies'. I liked the word 'civvies', confirming my new warrior status. 'I'm going to change into civvies,' I would say in the evenings.

On my first morning something unbelievable happened. The Company Sergeant responsible for us, a tall, rangy, harassed, red-faced, regular NCO, shouted:

'I'll never get all you fucking lot over to breakfast on time. One of you will have to march this hut to the dining-hall. Any NCO? Anyone will do. Here you (pointing to me) march these hoors over to breakfast.'

I was momentarily paralysed in the spotlight but I had attended enough FCA parade nights to be familiar with the commands 'get fell in' and 'quick march'. So, before I had time to be nervous, I found myself shouting the magic words, getting in a quick 'halt' outside the dining-hall just in time before they happily fell out. I could have retired then.

As it happened, I had to be called into breakfast by a comrade:

'Hey, are you coming in or what?'

The rest of the morning was spent under a clear blue sky, drilling on a real barrack square and delighted that my heavy boots banged down when and where they should.

My enthusiasm saw me through the TOETs (Tests of Elementary Training) in the first week and, as a result, I found myself 'dug-in' in the dining-hall on fatigues. There was an 'old sweat' (already on his third camp), who spent some time taking up different positions in the dining-hall and I wondered why.

'Oh', he said, 'I'm counting how many windows I can be seen through in each place, so I can pick a spot to have a bit of a honk.'

I did not approve of this, though, as the week progressed, I took other bits of his advice. I was always conscious of the necessity for balance, for discretion, remembering how I avoided overdoing it on Thursday afternoons on the sports-field.

'Never be seen without a bucket or a brush', he advised me, 'or better still, both.'

We floated like green ghosts from billet to dining-hall to canteen on our magic carpets of buckets and brushes, totally ignored by the stern-eyed NCOs. Officers were dead easy: we just had to stop and salute them, their half-hearted response indicating that they did not really see us behind the protective wall of the implements.

I asked my mentor: 'I suppose anytime anybody looks closely at us we had better start filling our buckets or brushing?'

'Oh, for God's sake, no. Then they'll know you're dodging and they'll either move you or find something for you to do. No, just stand there looking stupid and that gives them a chance to show how clever they are and they'll just shout at you. Be prepared to be shouted at several times a day if you want to hold on to this cushy berth.'

He looked at me, judging my hesitating acceptance of his advice. 'On the other hand, if you really want to score, if you have been seen by the same NCO a few times already, start cleaning your brush. Just stand it on its handle,' he said, swinging his brush in the air in a practised drill movement, and grasping it firmly with his left hand, he began to pluck straws out of the bristles with his right.

b. Old Sweat?

Ballymullen Barracks might have been new to me, but I had lots of relations in Tralee. My Uncle Paddy was the editor of the *Kerryman* and my Uncle Pat had a pub in Edward Street. I had spent some weeks on holidays in Tralee every year.

I was always interested in things military. Once on a visit, when I was a little boy, the Artane Boys Band was entertaining the crowd for a football match. I asked my cousin Ita (highly sophisticated, she called everything 'topping'), 'Who are the boys in the uniforms playing drums?'

'Oh, they're orphans,' she replied.

When I got home I said to my bemused parents:

'If I were an orphan I'd play the big drum.'

Following my interest in uniformed service, some time afterwards, I tried to join the boy-scouts, even getting a notebook and drawing the '*Bi Ullumh*' (Be Ready) badge on the first page. But I was not accepted because I was too young. Now, at fifteen years of age, except for a stay in the Metropole Hotel in Cork, for my Aunt Noreen's wedding, this camp was my first time out from under the friendly roofs of family or relations.

I visited my cousins most evenings. Knowing me, they were only slightly puzzled by my arrival in a greatcoat on a summer's evening, but the problem was that while my loose FCA blouse type tunic did not fit in the regimental way that I would have liked, the greatcoat did.

One night, on arrival back at barracks, I realised that I had not taken any supper and worked up an extraordinary hunger by telling myself that I was not at home and therefore could not get anything to eat. I must have said something about this because one of the 'old sweats' said 'come on' and we walked past the guardroom.

'Any buckshee cha, lads?' he asked.

We were rewarded with a cup and a wad. Usually, if I had not been visiting relations, on my way back at night I would stop at a milk shop and have a glass of milk and a bun.

On one such occasion I saw a slovenly looking girl taking a glass from someone who had not finished his milk and simply topping it up for me. She put her finger inside the glass, which still had the previous customer's stain on the rim. I nearly got sick. The horror of creating a scene outweighed any possible satisfaction, so I just walked out, noting some dust on shelves as evidence of how right I was.

On the following summer the camp was in Youghal. At the end

of the two weeks' camp, as we marched behind the pipe band to the train for home, a friend, nick-name 'Tatneen', whispered to me.

'Hey, how about doin' another week, the sun is shinin'?'

'Good idea,' I replied, 'we're so far back no one can see us. Let's fall out.'

We simply headed back to camp with our rifles slung on our shoulders, rested on the beach, weapons stacked against a rock, admired the view, or views as several girls passed on occasions, and eventually returned to our billet in our sandy uniforms. People noticed us during the following week, but all assumed someone else had accepted responsibility and it was not until pay-day that it was discovered that no pay had been requisitioned for us.

Now learning and toughening, (becoming an 'old sweat'?), when one day my book went missing, I announced that I intended to take official action. I left the billet and in view of our windows approached a PA (Military Policeman) and told him of some rowdiness in a restaurant down town. He took a note and I returned to the billet. The book was on my bed.

I continued my attendance at the weekly FCA parades and eventually was appointed a Temporary Acting Corporal. This allowed me to dine in the NCO's Mess on my next camp, only to be back in the meal queue with my tin plate, when it was discovered that I had not yet been put through Routine Orders. This allowed me to demonstrate my unfortunate tendency to tell the truth when a diplomatic lie would save hassle. Comrades tried to cheer me up.

'Ah, sure there's more fun outside.'

I had to say, and hated having to say it:

'Well, to tell the truth, I prefer being served my meals.'

Yet it was my membership of the shooting team that gave me the most pleasure. On my first day on the open range to fire the Lee Enfield .303, I put the five grouping shots at 100 yards touching each other on the small white marking paper in the centre of the bull.

I eventually won the Battalion Shooting Competition at Ballymullen

Barracks with the highest possible score, 60 out of 60. Lieut. Burke (solicitor, later District Justice) joked afterwards about my shy acceptance 'speech'. I returned home happily displaying my trophy, a small silver cup (which I still treasure), even though it was somewhat overshadowed by thoughts of the approaching Leaving Certificate.

But it was my attendance at my first camp that created the greatest impact at home. From what they knew, or thought they knew, about me, nobody expected me to do the full fortnight in the camp. Most gave me to the end of the first week. So I came home after that fortnight to the humble gratitude of people, who had been given a surprise, a most unusual thing in the Dingle of the time. The men at the Corner *Dáil* waiting until it was time to go to the cinema or the pub, who had seen (and heard) me practising with my FCA boots around town, greeted me as a soldier.

One says: 'When Chou-en-Lai jumps off a boat down on the quay, boy, you'll be there with your rifle to defend the town, good man yourself.'

c. Career Decision

The phrase 'cusp of history' was probably true of those times of old privilege and new merit. My friend Bob had got in to the bank helped, no doubt, because his father was the manager of the Dingle branch of the Munster and Leinster Bank. Meritocracy was coming, but not all that quickly. I could get a 'nomination' for the Bank of Ireland because my uncle knew the necessary directors, whereas, sometime after that, the agent's own son failed. Bob (regrettably no longer with us) eventually became a manager himself and I am absolutely clear that if they were alive today, neither himself nor his father would ever have considered the so-called 'sub-prime' lending business.

At that time, strange as it may seem to the current generation with information overload, even in our final year in school we had very hazy ideas about what we wanted. It was Bob's sister, Pauline, who pulled me out of my daze, when I mentioned my call for interview for 'Junior Ex', in the Civil Service, saying something like: 'Oh, is that the kind of work you want to do?' Until then, I had never really thought about 'jobs'.

My focus sharpened further when my mother shot down a job in the *Kerryman* with my uncle (editor) as a likely disaster (i.e. working with a relation). I did the examination for 'Junior Ex' and got called for interview but did not attend, nor did I attend the ESB interview because by that time I was clear that the Army was what I wanted. We did not have career guidance in those days and to me then the idea of a clerkship of any kind seemed no better than factory work. Nobody pointed out any potentially satisfying possibilities on promotion in large organisations. Paddy Moriarty went to the ESB and eventually got to the top.

I felt considerably cheered when my FCA Platoon Commander, Lieutenant Burke, said: 'I think you're the right type for the Cadet School.'

I applied and was called for a medical examination and interview, one of 600 looking for one of the 40 places in the Cadet School of the Military College. In a recent competition there were 2,700 applications and in a recent cadet class of 36 there were 24 graduates, 4 with masters as well as some foreign cadets.

I was in Collins Barracks in Cork on FCA training when the call arrived. I asked a Cork City FCA man the time of the Dublin train and believed him. I eventually arrived in Dublin on the night mail for interview on the following day, my suit crumpled and myself pale with tiredness and hunger. I had run out of money.

I took a taxi to Bob's house: his father had sadly died and the family were now living in Rathfarnham. The taxi circled but the driver said that there did not seem to be any hope of finding the house where I said, when I explained that I had seen Bob's father's car outside one of the houses. He turned and stopped. Bob came out and paid him, but that car had been sold. I have no explanation. Perhaps my tired brain produced a solution to a problem that seemed insoluble at three in the morning: no money left, nowhere to go.

Bob's father had bought a black second-hand Anglia, which he treasured. Like all the rest of us, they had one radio and only the official telephone. This can be contrasted with the large family car, the second one for the wife, the two TVs, video recorder and mobile phone of a bank manager today.

We have made quantum leaps in material standards. While at school we were supposed to yearn for a return to a golden age of pre-Norman Ireland, but as Liam De Paor once asked:

'Who now denies progress when they see a child lift a hand and bring a large bus full of busy men to a halt? What would have been the fate of a lost child who tried to stop a galloping chariot coming from the local king's fort?'

After a medical examination and the Irish test, I was interviewed by a board of six army officers, mostly grey hair combed straight back, shining leather and polished buttons.

For the standard 'sports' question, I had felt a bit shaky, not having any sporting involvement, beyond shooting, to boast of. Shooting over the hills of Kerry would have been worth mentioning, but I assumed they wanted to talk about football so, when asked, I indicated an interest in the Kerry Team.

They sat back.

'All right, what are their prospects?' asked one.

'Where are they now?' another added hopefully.

'I'm not sure, but they always seem to get to the final.'

That seemed to satisfy their interest in my sporting knowledge. They sat forward again and asked me about my ideas on the military life. What did I think were the responsibilities of an officer? The nodding response to this indicated to me that at least my reply was satisfactory. Sitting on my chair out in the middle of this big room and doing my best to answer the officer on the left, who had just told me to continue to answer the one on the right, took all my concentration after my sleepless night.

On the subject of men I admired, I mentioned General de Gaulle. They sat back again (perhaps not as confidently as the first time) but encouraged me to 'go on', assuming this to be a prepared party piece.

'Where was he born, and how did he develop?'

I had to admit that I did not know but commented on his contribution during the Second World War, and added that I particularly admired his purging of the Civil Service. They all smiled at this, but had to lean forward again much sooner than they had expected.

On my reading, I felt that it would be safer to stick to P.G. Wodehouse. I felt that telling them that I had read all the books of military interest in the Carnegie Library could have sounded brash to professional soldiers. One, who turned out to be the Cadet-master, asked me about the FCA and if this was my first interview. At the end of what felt like hours I escaped to find that Bob, who had come in with me, had just avoided the medical examination.

On my return home I reviewed my interview with Captain Long, the local regular officer with the FCA. My heart sank when he confirmed my belief that it seemed to have been a washout.

'Next year won't be long coming,' he said, 'I still think you can do it'.

I sat that evening in Nancy Brown's Parlour, sited across a narrow inlet of deep water from her cave. The side near the water is open. Two other sides of the rectangular parlour are almost perpendicular, smooth, dark rock with a perfectly proportioned seat running the whole length for her guests to rest on.

All Dingle know Nancy Brown to be a golden-haired mermaid, who lives in a cave under the lighthouse headland and has saved many a fishing boat from the treacherous rocks that sucked and dribbled water from the waves. She handed over to Fungie, the friendly dolphin, some years afterwards but I cannot imagine her deserting the town forever. That evening, however, the piercing cry of a seagull seemed more in tune with my feelings, as it wheeled over a fishing boat passing around the headland in the gathering shadows.

The lights were going out in my world. Yet almost immediately, as I walked home past the little tower of Hudson's Folly where my friend Bob and I had sat so often allowing the 'long long' thoughts of boyhood take shape and help form our visions of the future, the first red-gold tinge appeared in the western sky. Clouds and hilltops soon added their share in a great fugue of colour turning the green sea into a wine dark Attic ocean. I began to feel that perhaps I might still escape the bank or the Civil Service. After all, Uncle Paddy wanted me to come into the *Kerryman* and my mother would like me to be an architect and redesign Dingle, or, at least, design houses that would avoid grandfather's predictability.

Some time afterwards, Bob came and stayed with us for a short break. I had only just returned from seeing him off on the bus when I was handed an official letter. It was from the Minister for Defence. He had instructed someone to write a letter from him to me. Someone called, I think, R6d, who would probably otherwise not have bothered. In it he expressed his happiness at my being awarded a Cadetship. He sounded happy sure enough, but was he also slightly surprised? I was.

3

The Cadet School

a. Arrival

What moves people along the rocky road of life? Hope of bringing order out of chaos in their own small space and time? Tunes of glory, or the ring of a till in the family shop? Or simple contingency, life just moving us along: 'as flies to wanton boys'. Apply for jobs and take the one you get; look after the farm; take over your father's business?

Whatever the reason, I found myself on a bus from Dublin, on a bright November day in 1950, moving between seas of pale wet grass, seeing the tall brick building with the flag, towering over the lines of trees that concealed the two-mile-long Curragh Camp.

The Curragh in Kildare was an ancient rallying ground of the Gael and burial ground for their kings. Where there were kings there had to be captains. So the wide, windswept plain was no stranger to the shouted orders at the Militia Camp set up to prepare for the Napoleonic invasion. The camp was abandoned after the defeat of the French. But, as all armies have a severe inability to give back any land they consider to be theirs, try as they might to so oblige, small outposts defended the area from civil service incursions until it was needed again for the Crimean War, proving the military right.

A permanent camp was then constructed to house 10,000 troops. It eventually became one of the best training installations in the British Isles: the complete self-contained military town, red-brick barracks replacing the temporary structures. There were seven barracks with their barrack squares, officers' messes, married quarters, soldiers' billets and dining halls, stores and drill sheds, as well as other expected features of any small town, church, post office, shops, cinema, swimming baths and bus terminus.

On the bus I saw another tight haircut, white raincoat and pensive expression which I recognised as another pilgrim on the military road: Dennis Heuston, whose father was OC of the 1st Battalion.

'Are you?' he asked.

'I am,' I nodded.

Where there are captains there are corporals and as the bus arrived at the terminus we were met by Corporal Hartley, (for it was he), looking active even when standing still, who told us that we would get to know him. We did.

He took us to the Cadet School in a station wagon but did not even remotely treat us as soldiers. Totally unlike the silly reception recruits seem to get in the US Army as they arrive in camp: 'hup, two three' etc. We were beneath consideration until we were in uniform and on the square.

The expected Prussian austerity manifested itself in a soldier's billet: if we were to command men, we first had to learn how they lived. Our rooms as senior cadets in our second year would allow more serious study.

From the first day in this novitiate of the profession of arms, and for two years, we were daily made aware of our mission, of being men apart. Even when drawing our first issue of kit, the Company Quartermaster Sergeant would say to someone who had fumbled: 'You're supposed to be training to be officers'. Or an entertainingly cranky old soldier waiter in the Cadets' Mess, when his arrangement of cutlery was upset: 'Is it officers ye're going to be?'

With first parade at 07.30 hours, and from that brisk march, through the dark and over snow in winter, until late at night, with study and preparation for inspections, there was no time to spare. An abiding memory is the constant changing, no time allotted, from lecture hall dress, to drill order, to battle order: the expectation was of cadets, properly dressed and on parade at the programme time, for whatever the activity.

The objectives of the Cadet School are to develop the cadet's character, personality and leadership qualities, as well as equipping him with the level of military skills essential for his rank on commissioning, as a platoon commander. Future professional requirements would be taken care of by the other schools of the Military College, for battalion, brigade and more senior appointments. Some of the main developments since our time have been the acceptance of female cadets and the development of adventure training: canoeing, sailing, orienteering, etc. Is there a connection?

New cadets arrived in January bringing our number to forty. The class was divided into sections by height. I was in Section 2 with seven others. In the billet on one side were Mick Moriarty, Frank O'Donovan, Sean MacNiocal and Mick McGreal. On my side were Jack Spillane, myself, Barney Dobey and Gerry Kenny.

Our Section was as keen as any other but we seemed to develop an attitude that today would be described as 'cool'. We brought the quality of calmness, 'no sweat', to a high degree of polish, admirable in higher command but fraught with peril at our level. Slow to get started, lying on our beds chatting, we felt superior to the 'hacklers' (swots). Yet, buttons and leathers had to be polished and web equipment blancoed, especially for the Cadet-master's Saturday morning inspection. So, long after 'lights-out' on many a Friday night, in the pools of light coming in the windows, we would be hammering studs in boots. In those days soldiers wore hob-nailed boots and Cadets had to have the exact number of studs on kit inspection. This was to inculcate the concept of thoroughness and precision in all things, which the future officer would demand of others.

We did military history and drill, military geography and drill. We prepared papers and talks and drilled. We did the principles and practice of tactics and battle drill. I was delighted, but could not show it, ('cool') to be selected as platoon commander for an attack exercise.

A real platoon commander would have had a batman to carry his radio, which was not like a modern mobile. It was a heavy, square, primitive piece of equipment with a high aerial which kept knocking my helmet off as we attacked across a bog to take a small hill. On arrival on our objective, my camouflage of brown bog water was real. I might have surrendered to an enemy offering a dry bed.

Our principal task was the study and practice of the art of leadership of small groups, as a foundation for the central task of military command at higher levels. Every week one of us had responsibility for allotting the 'details' (chores) of the billet: cleaning, tidying and keeping the large open fires going. We did as much scrubbing as any sailor: lecture halls and bicycle sheds had to be scrubbed out once a week. We gradually learned, however, how to 'swill out': pouring buckets of water and brushing it out with large brooms. In due course we further polished our performance occasionally by simply wetting the floor with someone on a lookout, as it dawned on us that floors in the Military College were never really dirty anyway.

The principle of personal responsibility meant that instead of being lectured, for some aspects of our study, we had to do a lot of the work ourselves. I had to do Portugal for military geography (terrain, communications, etc.). I wrote to Portugal and the government of Salazar seemed to think that I was showing signs of being commendably right wing so they sent me on wads of stuff, and, long after I had forgotten about that talk, they kindly continued to send me information.

They may not have been terribly wrong, and examining all I can remember about myself. I think that both Herr Hitler, if he had held on to power or Mrs Thatcher if she had taken power by then would have nodded appreciation of some of my ideas. My contribution to a debate on trade unions and strikes would have gladdened their hard little hearts.

We covered a wide range of material. In my boyhood I had read about brave young subalterns on the Khyber Pass in the *Bumper Book For Boys*, pacifying troublesome areas in time to return on leave to admiring families, or dying gallantly for the honour of the Regiment. So I found real military history enjoyably serious.

I used some of the campaigns of the American Civil War and the operations of the Irish Guards in North Africa in the Second World

War in my chosen studies. I had already known of the exploits of the old Irish regiments of the British Army in the First World War, like the Munster Fusiliers, and was proud of the Irish Brigades in the service of France, Spain and Austria, but I was glad to discover the Irish Brigade in the American Civil War. This has been very well covered by Captain D.P. Conyngham in his book, *The Irish Brigade and Its Campaigns.*

I decided, on one occasion, to do a paper on General Robert E.Lee to analyse his leadership qualities and style. Leadership 'qualities' were all the vogue at that time, before it dawned on military colleges all over the world that all their lists were somewhat different and could have added up to an impossible paragon; apart from the fact that the terms had different meanings for different people. I remember 'judgement' and 'fortitude', defined by the Cadet-master as 'mental robustness'.

I was slow starting on this project. We usually had a few going simultaneously, but I had seen a large book in the library on Lee and I was always able to produce something quickly enough. I duly collected the book and got stuck in, only to discover shortly before the hand-in that the large tome was in fact only Volume One of six. I had to dash to the library and collect five more and had some very late nights.

During our 'public speaking' training phase members of the class would be detailed to give a critique of the effort of the previous student. A response was developed whereby the cadet would rise and look frowningly into the middle distance before saying: 'I thought it was a good talk, but', and then offer a few criticisms.

For occasional guest lecturers, like Professor T. Desmond Williams, Professor of Modern History at UCD, who gave us the benefit of his work on the German archives, a cadet would have been detailed to propose a vote of thanks. One such visitor was Sir Charles Petrie but Willie, who had been detailed to propose 'thanks', was sitting just inside a large window of the lecture hall and directly under a sunbeam. A cadet could snooze at anytime, anywhere. The Cadet-master's cough caused him to jump to his feet and caused the whole class to sweat as he started: 'I thought it was a good talk, but', to a startled Sir Charles.

With admirable aplomb he saved the day by following up with: 'I don't think we get half enough of these military history lectures.'

b. On the Range

I had enjoyed shooting with the Dingle Battalion FCA and was familiar with the .303 Short Magazine Lee Enfield keeping the 'action bright and lightly oiled' at all times, wood glowing richly from polishing. This beautiful weapon was replaced later by the FN FAL, afterwards ousted in turn by the Steyr Aug A1 with optical sights. Light, accurate and durable it may be but it will never dislodge the affection of old soldiers for the Lee Enfield.

The green of the grass, the blue and white of the sky were familiar backdrops and at the 300 yards firing point, the wind was a vital element, the subtlest variations of light significant. I found an intellectual as well as a physical satisfaction in a properly squeezed second pressure, a crack of sound, a thump on the shoulder and then, the mental journey with the bullet to that speck of white on the tip of the foresight, 300 yards away. Shooting was a practical, no mystery thing, to me. I knew what I could do and, from what I saw of the preliminary practices, I made a smiling remark about the possibility of me winning the class sweep.

I had no enemies and, never having boarded before with contemporaries, I had no idea of the precipice I had walked myself towards. Word of this got around fairly quickly and cadets came up to me and asked, 'Did you say you were expecting to win?'

I got a feeling of doom at that stage but I could not see in my innocence what was wrong with my statement. Luckily I won, because if I had not I would have suffered, perhaps for the rest of the two years. As it turned out it made me into something of a minor celebrity. Despite the real danger of the other possibility, the surprised congratulations in turn were genuine.

While there was no physical violence, there was a practice called 'riding': verbal harassment, mild but continuous ridicule that affected some more than others, of those who drew the wrong kind of attention.

This was close to the officially accepted 'hazing' as character training in foreign military schools.

One sufferer was the only cadet to voluntarily resign, apart from Ronnie Delaney, who left because of his training routine, that I had heard of. He sold me his Cadet School tie on leaving. I still have it. Wearing it at the funeral of Lieut. Gen. Sean McKeown our ex-Cadet-master, known to us as 'Johnny', many years afterwards, brought the 'light of other days around me'. Cadets were 'given their tickets' at the drop of a hat: no questions. One day I met a senior cadet, who being a brother of a classmate, actually spoke to me, 'I'm to see Johnny.' He returned in about half an hour saying, 'I'm a civvie.'

At that time I was a curious mixture of the blasé and the committed, depending on the subject, but when I was selected for the College Rifle Team to compete in the All Army, I entered fully into it. We were advised by the Cadet-master to practice wearing our respirators (gas masks) as often as we could in order to be prepared for firing one of the sections of the competition wearing one.

I insisted on wearing mine with my helmet in bed at night, applying anti-dim to the eyepieces and trying to read. This was too much for my Section 2 comrade, Gerry Kenny: 'Oh, for fuck-sake, I don't believe it.'

We practised most days hail, rain or snow, even on the occasional Saturday morning when the Cadet School paraded in battle order with the band on the square for the Cadet-master's weekly inspection. The Senior Class, next for commissioning, in front, followed by the 'Junior A', then the 'Junior B' and finally the 'Civvies' (us). Brass glittering, web freshly blancoed, uniforms immaculate, battle order packs showing one inch of groundsheet and rifles ready for the inspecting entourage who would note any speck of dust (which was denied existence in the College). Saturday morning at Inspection Parade time, was something that had to be experienced: even with the sun shining there was a kind of chill, and even with the band playing there was a kind of silence.

One Saturday the Cadet-master ordered shooting practice on the range for the team. We assembled looking, as usual, like a small group of mercenaries in the bush; worn fatigues, rifles slung rakishly from shoulders. The team officer would join us on the range. In a rare reversal of roles, I persuaded the NCO member of the team that, as we were under Cadet-master's orders, we could pass by the parade on our way out. As a member of the rifle team I felt I had a subtly different status for the moment from the rest of the class on the square.

'I don't think we have to go out of our way around the sheds,' I said, 'I believe that as we are under orders to go on the range we should go the direct route.'

It was a greyish area, but the team accepted the logic of my statement with a certain amount of private anxiety. So, to the consternation of everybody on the square, except, it would appear the Cadet-master, we appeared and passed like the vision of Mirzah. My explanation for it now would be that I must have been trying to exercise my potential leadership muscle.

Our chief coach was Company Sergeant Peter O'Connor, an All-Army individual winner, who had us doing regular 'dry practice' bolt-action, ejecting the empty and loading the fresh round up the breech in one smooth seamless movement.

It all paid off when we beat 27 other teams, as reported by *The Irish Times*:

'Marksmen of the Military College gave a grand display of shooting when winning the rifle team championship in the All-Army. Although they scored well in the early practices the college team struck top form in the finals, the difficult rapid and snap shooting tests. Here they established clear superiority, each member of the six-man team shooting with brilliant accuracy.'

I cut it out.

c. Departure

I sometimes look back on that stranger. I now wonder how did I reconcile my total commitment to the military ideal, to shooting, the study of leadership and tactics and yet be so blind as not to realise the importance of subjects like Signals and 'Q' Administration? Maybe I did not realise that all marks from all subjects would be added up to decide our final place on the commissioning list, until it was too late to do a lot about it.

Also I think that I might have developed a fear that I might find myself eventually posted to a quartermaster's office or some other corps besides the Infantry if I did well in certain subjects. On one occasion we were asked if any of us had science as a subject in our leaving certificates and I pretended to forget that I had honours in that subject in case I would end up in a technical corps.

The class officer, Captain Sean Gallagher ('Jildy') pointed out that he was surprised at my position in the class at the end of the second phase. I had not really thought about it up to then. I think I assumed that, like school, I would somehow ease my way up, without much study. However, I improved my position considerably in time for commissioning.

I also adopted a rather superior attitude to sport, largely due to my ignoring that aspect of life up to then. Shooting was my only sport. Despite enjoying the time walking on river banks, my Uncle Joe failed to interest me in fishing. I walked the dogs several miles a day in all weathers and loved the hills but never felt the urge to enter what I looked upon as the artificial arena of organised games. A rare appearance on a team list at school caused some wag to write *'non est'* under my name. With my pal Bob I was very much a member of a Kiplingesque 'Stalkey and Co.' group who escaped from the sports-field at the earliest opportunity, having spent most of the time there wearing down the last of the brother's shredded patience.

I gathered that I had gained a certain notoriety in the Cadet School, when some Cadets were questioned as to why they joined 'Comrade Goggin's' cross-country group on the Wednesday afternoon 'recreational training', with the apparent implication of an absence of Brownie points. I enjoyed the run but was careful not to overdo it. We usually rested when we got around the back of the cemetery and only jumped up and continued on the run when a car would pass on the road below to the shouts of 'taxpayers'. On less clement days I had the non-swimmers parade to the baths: towards the end of the two years questions were asked about 'progress' but the danger passed.

I had a moment of glory when we were informed one day that it would be possible to organise 'seven-a-side' rugby on Sunday mornings. This would have been an unmitigated disaster for those of us who looked forward to the freedom of the weekend, because with 'sevens' all members of the class would be involved – not just the rugby team and enthusiasts. I stood up and reminded the meeting that the latest doctrine on training for sport was that the complete event should be practised, not the component activities, and that therefore, the best training for the College Team would be to play the game with a full side at all times. The shock of a suggestion coming from one of the non-enthusiasts perhaps allowed the idea to be accepted.

Nonetheless, I took genuine pleasure in watching the Military College winning the 'Golden Sword' in the 'Triangular' with Newbridge and Clongowes. I continued to enjoy rugby internationals and anybody who knew me then would be astonished if they were made aware of my later conversion by Jack Charlton. Soccer was not considered to be an officer's game in our day.

Apart from regular drill periods, writing paper mountains and attacking up real wet heathery ones, cadets were given intensive training in physical self-confidence on the Obstacle Course and rope climbing. Part of a recruiting film was to include Section 2 going over the Assault Obstacle Course and coming down the high cliff face at Harepark with ropes.

I imagine I must have been somewhat apprehensive, (very?), at the rope climb especially, but we repeated our rehearsal so often that in the end, on the day the film unit was due, we could do it in our sleep. However, on that day someone in higher authority decided that it was too dangerous so we never became film heroes.

Being the lowest form of military animal life, floating in a never-never land, not being allowed attend soldier's dances and not being yet 'officers and gentlemen' so that Officer's Mess functions were out, our social life, apart from weekend passes and the cinema, revolved around the Tennis

Dances. The problem was that all cadets had to be back in the College by 23.59 hours. The dances never finished by then, so, invariably, to the tune of 'Good-night Sweetheart' and accompanying laughter, sticking out in our College blazers, we had sheepishly to leave the dance and head back. To have the pleasure of looking into a beautiful face under the Curragh moon, precise timing was essential. To ask one of the young ladies to go 'out for a breath of air', it had to be before it was time to retreat and after the time that they would be helping with the tea.

Tea seemed to figure largely in those days: at Halverstown Cricket Club with Willie, I remember lying on the grass in the sun, until the girls arrived with the tea and buns. On a 'day pass' at the 'afternoon tea dances' in the Metropole we met others, like student nurses, also allowed out to live on the wild side for a few hours.

Rules were black and white, but the Cadet-master rejected the American 'Honour Code' where cadets were supposed to report themselves for every small irregularity, as being unsuitable for the Irish psyche with its inbuilt sense of balance. Newbridge, the nearest town was out-of-bounds. Cadets reported for breaking this rule lost whatever honorary appointments they had.

One of the principal expectations was loyalty to the College. We were all summoned into a lecture hall on one occasion to be addressed by the Cadet-master. He arrived at the podium and we all expected an important lecture. He simply looked up to where a particular cadet was sitting and said: 'You will never wear the College jersey again.' The cadet had played for his rugby club on a day when the College team was playing.

I was lucky to be able to stay in Rathfarnham in Bob's house on our full weekend passes (a privilege chopped very easily by a bad inspection on the square or in our rooms). I shared a room with Jack Spillane in our senior year and we had two pieces of cloth inside the door to step on and move around so as not to spoil the shine on the floor. We set up a poker game one day in our room because we felt that the seventeen and sixpence for the camera club outing was too much, but by the time the group returned that night we had little left of our cheques. Unfortunately, we lost Jack, the first member of the class to go, still in his twenties, as a result of a car accident.

We had run out of polish once before a room inspection but I accidentally spilled brasso on a small table and on wiping it off, it shone. As the inspecting group was not far away we decided to take a chance and applied brasso and polished the whole table. They arrived, inspected our room and bookshelves, but as they were going out the table began turning white. The door closed. We breathed a sigh of relief, until one returned, looked in the door and said:

'We did not look at your DFRs (Defence Force Regulations), make sure they are amended to date.'

The table, now snow white, fortunately was behind the door which he held open. We had another similar escape when a leg of a chair had been broken in a bit of horseplay and we did not have time to fix it. We simply stuck it together. It held just until the last of the inspecting staff banged the door on the way out, when it collapsed.

Our course in 'Military Courtesy and Etiquette' was intended, according to the précis issued, to help us to learn to become officers and gentlemen; officers in barracks and gentlemen in dealing with others. We must learn 'to meet a soldier as a soldier and a civilian as a gentleman of the Army'. The first paper issued indicated that Captain Watson and the Cadet School Staff had a clear view of their students:

'Many amusing situations might arise which will tempt cadets to ask questions rather to excite mirth than to dispel doubt. This must be guarded against.'

I do not imagine that Westpoint or Sandhurst would have given such an acknowledgement.

The course took a naval turn when we were invited aboard the aircraft carrier *Saipan*. Saluting the quarterdeck, being 'piped' aboard, etc. For days before Section 2 were going around shouting: 'Belay there, you lubbers', only to find ourselves lost on the huge ship because we had not listened properly to the instructions. We wandered into an enlisted men's dining area only to be barred because we were not soldiers or sailors by a very tall rating who would not listen to our explanations until an even bigger petty officer came striding along shouting, 'What's your problem?' That was my first time hearing that phrase. The sailor's problem vanished and we passed through, muttering about a hundred lashes.

We duly invited cadets from the Annapolis Naval Academy for a return visit. Convinced that everything in the USA would be described as huge, we felt that we had better measure up, so we scattered the word 'our' around like confetti: 'The Bloods' (the Third Infantry Battalion) was 'our' demonstration battalion, the Curragh Baths were 'our baths'. The strawberries and cream in the Mess was 'our standard menu'. We drew the line at the Water Tower. The objective of all this effort was, of course, the commission, that would make us 'gentlemen by act of parliament'. The quantum leap from cadet to commissioned officer was the biggest move we would make in our careers.

Rules died on 23.59 hours on the night before the commissioning ceremony and the College usually turns a Nelsonian blind eye to the madness that possesses disciplined cadet classes. We held a parade on the sacred square in 'long john' underwear with the cadet bands tied around our heads, whereas up to that date carrying bottles from the milk shop through the camp, in uniform, was considered unacceptable.

There was always a pre-commissioning dinner and dance but we were informed at a mess meeting that it looked as if the Mess funds were very low and the festivities would have to be curtailed. I suggested that a significant flow of money from the Cadet School was for milk and biscuits and that it would be a good idea if we set up our own milk shop. On the following morning I was surprised to hear, 'Cadet Goggin, Cadet-master's Office, now.'

I tried to figure out what it was I had been found out on. As I entered, came to attention and saluted, he just looked up from his writing, and said, 'That was a good idea Cadet Goggin, go ahead.' Initially pleased at the comment on my idea, but somewhat numbed: a shop, this was the last thing a soldier would want to get involved with. Laying down of lives for Ireland was one thing, but a shop, this was strictly quartermaster or civil servant stuff. Yet it never occurred to me to do other than make the best job I could, just another 'detail'. I eventually managed to 'go ahead' with some help from my friends.

One night working on the accounts, I became aware of another presence, Colonel Feeley, the College Commandant, at the back of the hall. On the following morning the Adjutant offered me an assistant. The mess fund improved: we had a very enjoyable pre-commissioning dinner and dance to which I invited my friend Elma, Bob's sister.

My father and others came up for the commissioning. My mother was not well. A man at the chemist's corner said, 'I hear that Paddy Goggin is being ordained or something.'

The Dingle Battalion notes in the *Kerryman*, kindly offered congratulations and reminded their readers that they had 'expressed their confidence' in 1950 that I would 'survive the exacting training and tests with ease'. Some people never got over the surprise that I had stayed in my first FCA camp for the full fortnight.

At the reception in the Military College Officers' Mess, my father proudly commented to the Minister, who had very little detailed knowledge of the Dingle Cumann of Fianna Fáil, that nobody could say it was political pull. The commissioning ceremony had an impressive simplicity in the crowded gymnasium where relations and guests were seated. The Colours and Escort were marched on parade to a general salute from an officer sword guard and the bugles and drums of the band.

The class paraded in tunic, Sam Browne belt, breeches, knee high leggings and boots, with the junior class providing a Guard of Honour. On an order, the platoon marches forward, the front rank continuing to a line of tables while the others come to a halt and stand at ease. Lifting bibles, they swear allegiance to the Constitution, and, with 2nd Lieutenant rank markings fitted on epaulettes and swords hung from Sam Browne belts by the officiating officers, they turn right and approach the Minister for Defence who presents their commissions, signed by the President. The final act in the drama is the first salute from the College Senior NCO, no doubt wearily remembering the performance of each on the drill-square.

The sword as the symbol of military authority is recognised by all armies: the righteous instrument of justice, wielded by the silver knight, who rides against Saladin. By the time the class is exercising in sword drill, the flashing blades signify the light at the end of a two-year tunnel.

The Cadet School years end with a feeling of satisfaction in the award of the commission, but the officer goes through life with a set of friends that lasts through the vicissitudes of career and private lives. Class reunions continue down the years, to the situation where all are retired from military or civilian careers, with a parade strength reduced by the casualties in the war of attrition that is life. I think of us as a platoon of forty soldiers leaving the trench, going 'over the top' in November 1952, facing into the machine guns of life. The first to fall was my room-mate Jack Spillane, followed by the others over the years, as they fought the good fight.

While the Cadet School covers only about half of the total full-time military education it can be a personally enriching experience that provides a solid foundation for further education or the lessons of practical experience. To end on a positive note, we were glad to hear that the Golden Sword (the 'Triangular' trophy competed for by Newbridge, Clongowes and the Cadet School) has since been back in the Cadet School.

PART TWO

OPERATIONS

4

Infantry Officer

a. Embarrassments

At home, to anyone enquiring for me, when out with the FCA, my mother would answer, 'He's gone to fight for Ireland.'

Now, having completed my two years in the Military College, as a 2nd Lieutenant, with the President's signature not quite dry on my commission, I was posted to the 2nd Infantry Battalion at Portobello Barracks, Rathmines, Dublin. I was finally available to fight and die for my country or the honour of the Battalion, if only I could find it.

I had arrived with 2nd Lieut. Des Ringrose, another newly commissioned Cadet School class-mate, that morning, but in the evening, on returning from a visit to Bob, I got lost in the sprawling barracks. A soldier, as young as myself, courteously showed me the way to the Officers' Mess and did not attempt a joke. I learned sometime afterwards that soldiers never take a chance with young officers, even soldiers of the dug-in variety, who say what they like to the officers they work with.

I had got the posting I wanted (Infantry) but the class had been detailed for a 'Q' Administration Course immediately after commissioning. I did my best to fail in order to remove the danger of a 'Q' (quartermaster's) appointment. I failed to fail because the College ethos of 'trying' prevented me from a total abandonment of effort. The 'Q' glorious mysteries of the 'part-worn clothing store' and ration indents magically producing 'eggs in lieu of fish', had, in any case, already been unveiled in front of our wide open but glazed-over eyes.

The senior subaltern in the Kildare Artillery Barracks, where we did the course, Lieut. Tadgh O'Neil, had felt obliged to tell us that in the Officers' Mess we could eat as much butter as we wanted. In the Cadets' Mess butter was rationed in that each extra pat added a penny to the mess bill. Unsurprisingly, he was later Chief of Staff.

Having come directly from the Military College and being still all together made the transition from cadet to officer a much slower process of modification of behaviour than is normal, like an extended adolescence. We played poker during intervals of lectures and would queue to open doors of Trodden Hall, the lecture hall, rather than coming in together, which meant ages of door opening and closing to the annoyance of lecturers, who never suspected us of such childish nonsense. This hall was named after Captain Charlie Trodden who had brought his Royal Artillery expertise to the new founding Irish Army.

I remember getting my first salute outside that barracks, slightly embarrassed to be at the receiving end of the military courtesy, after two years saluting anything that moved and scrubbing anything that didn't. However, another incident, as I was finding my balance in the new situation, caused me real embarrassment. One evening, in Dublin, when walking past the Metropole in uniform, a soldier in uniform ignored me. I wished the ground would swallow me up because here I was being seen by a crowd of civilians (taxpayers!) allowing the President's commission to be insulted. Despite my almost paralysing shyness, the College demand for the moral courage of self-assertion became paramount. I stopped and called to the soldier, who must have instinctively weighed up the situation, (embarrassed young officer) and saluted, 'Good evening sir.' Returning his salute, I could cheerfully have given him my cheque.

A somewhat happier memory, though not without a certain amount of embarrassment also, was of queuing for the Theatre Royal in uniform in the days when the queue would stretch for what appeared to be miles. The tall, stately, plump and brilliantly uniformed commissionaire approached at an appropriately stately pace, halted, saluted and escorted me to the door, announcing that officers in uniform should not have to queue. He had perhaps, given the state some service during the Emergency, having the bearing, presence and personal authority of the Military Police Corps.

As the Battalion had a successful Rifle Team I was not needed, to my private disappointment, but I gradually settled into the life of a junior infantry officer with the 2nd Infantry Battalion. Morning inspection of my platoon: uniforms, rifles, haircuts; my Platoon Sergeant noting defaulters. Handing it over to the Company Commander, Captain Andy Cunningham, and marching as 'B' Company to the square for the 2nd Battalion OC's inspection.

Return to the Company Office and prepare for a training exercise, attend to any regimental duties, but ensuring that I did not miss coffee at eleven in the Officers' Mess. I liked the comfort of the Mess anteroom: Jim, the waiter, bustling about with slightly dented silver; sun on leather chairs; the gentle rustle of papers, and the pleasant aroma of coffee. The Mess President took it upon himself to ensure that the coffee was good and the bar well stocked (i.e. with his favourite Powers Gold Label).

I also got some egg on my face during a Brigade Inspection when, as one of the three Platoon Commanders in front of 'B' Company, one of the Brigade Staff approached and said something about getting the Company 'standing easy'. I responded like a clockwork soldier only to realise too late that the Company Commander was still on parade. Andy considered having me shot but the Company Clerk, an old soldier, a man of infinite jest, reminded him of my value to the Company in terms of how much my education and training cost them all in tax.

My first experience of where the Army met the outside world was during the flooding in December 1954, when gale-force winds and torrents of rain swept Ireland. The Tolka River burst its banks. Fairview Park and Ballybough were flooded. A bridge on the Dublin-Belfast railway line was swept away. Parts of the north inner city were flooded up to four feet. Some 250 people were evacuated. One person died. The Army set up field kitchens and the Red Cross supplied rations for hundreds of hot meals. Hundreds of people were transported to safety, some had to be rescued by boat. The Army, the Garda, the Fire

Brigade with the help of other services like the St John's Ambulance all did what they were there to do.

I was launched into this to do what I could with my gung-ho warriors. I arrived with my platoon on trucks with blankets and other items. A scene of desolation met us as we de-trucked: small terraced houses drenched up to the windows; walls and furniture green with slime; people wandering looking for help. All I could do was stand looking calm and officer-like but not really knowing how to get started with the disorganised crowd, all talking and milling around.

This was solved when an old man shouted, 'Here's the man in khaki with the belt.' The crowd fell silent and looked at me. At that, I turned to the Platoon Sergeant, making a Michael Collins type move, tightening my gloves. 'OK Sarge, we'd better get started,' not really knowing what exactly.

The Sergeant got the warriors generally bustling around, which is how armies bring a calmness to panicking people by appearing to know what to do and to be taking charge of the situation. The soldiers loved just handing things around, no signing or procedures. One intelligent, concerned soldier looked at the Sergeant and asked: 'Sarge, is there much point in putting blankets into the wet rooms?'

He was frozen out by the looks from the rest, as well, I must confess, as the Sergeant and myself. By late afternoon, by which time we had as it were, got a grip on the situation and what we could do to help, I was proud of the way that the three section corporals were moving their men, when a lady member of some committee complained that I was not actively engaged lifting and carrying. A man I discovered afterwards to be Lord Killanin, said: 'That's an officer's job, remaining calm and in control.'

Later that afternoon, a message from Battalion HQ, 'Where are you, what are you doing and why have you not returned for food?' In my boy-scout enthusiasm, I assumed that, in an emergency, we simply soldiered on until released. It was, in fact, an emergency, with Fairview Park and Ballybough under water and 250 people being evacuated from places around St Brigid's Avenue and James St North.

An astounded Battalion Adjutant ordered us to return to barracks immediately, but, seeing the misery of the people, not one of the men had availed of the soldier's privilege of 'cribbing'.

A sense of duty is as much a good soldier's virtue as an officer's, I learned that day.

b. The Officer Corps

Where did I and the Army in which I was proud to serve fit in to the history of our country? What kind of an Army was this post-war Army in the early 1950s?

The founding army was the Free State Army, that defended the fledgling Irish Democracy and from which, in my time, we had most of our senior officers. Baptised by the blood of brothers, the strength rose to 55,000. Some 10,000 were IRA from the commands that accepted the Treaty. Others were civilians and others, who laid the foundation of the military knowledge essential for a modern professional army, had gained their expertise in the British Army. The Emergency Army that defended our neutrality, in my day, gave us most of our junior officers. Both of these armies had reached strengths of over 50,000. The post-war Army I found myself in was more of an echo of the Army in the doldrums between the Civil War and the Second World War, with a strength of less than 9,000. We were only the 25th cadet class and the numbers in each class were limited, so that the total of Cadet School graduates, up to then, was small.

Shortly after the foundation of the Irish Free State, in 1923, a Defence Forces Act provided for the establishment of a Military College. However, it was not until a Military Mission to the USA, with Major General Hugo MacNeill in charge, returned, and all aspects of training for the military profession were considered, that the Military College was set up in 1930. Contributions to the pool of knowledge have since been provided by officers trained in the UK, the USA, Germany, France and India. The setting up of the Military College was vital to the new professional Army.

But the real defining moment in the history of the country and the

Army in the metamorphosis from armed civilians to regular soldiers had come with the decision of Michael Collins and the founding fathers that military force could be used only on the orders of the elected representatives of the people and not at the nod of a conspiratorial elite. However noble and self-sacrificing were the volunteers previously, on that day those of them, who had transferred to the National Army, became the inheritors of Ireland's proud military tradition of centuries of professional soldiering in the British, French, Austrian, American and other armies.

They continued in the same straight line of advance under Mr de Valera, after that other critical and steadying day in our political history, when power was handed over peacefully between old enemies. The Army that accepted our cadet class in the 1950s was professional and loyal to the people's representatives regardless of political colour.

The ex-Free State Army officers that I remember were men of colour and vitality. One white-haired Commandant, who would respond to a mock innocent remark about his hero with an emotional, 'Let me tell you about Michael', was the subject of Donal Crowley's party piece. I met him with another recently commissioned classmate, Ray Buckley, in the bar one evening and we were treated to a most entertaining dissertation until Ray said, 'If you'll excuse us, sir, we're going down town.' He looked at us as if we were heading for a red-light district, 'Down town, down town, what the hell would you be doing down town?'

The Army had lived a very self-sufficient life with its mess functions, billiards and bar, like an echo of the British Army in India. As with our parliamentary system and the administration of the Civil Service, the Army fitted easily into the model that soldiers in this country had known for centuries. Yet the first regular uniformed unit in the new National Army was the ex-IRA 'Dublin Guards'. They had had a 'mixed' war, taking part in the unfortunate destruction of the Custom House and leaving even more unfortunate memories in Kerry, which, including the notorious Ballyseedy outrage, seem to be still determining factors in that special brand of Kerry republicanism.

As a cadet at a funeral in Ballyferriter, an old man asked my father,

'An mar sin ata siad gleasta anois?' ('Is that how they are dressed now?'). I smiled to myself thinking that he was referring to the Auxiliaries, with my breeches and boots. He was actually referring to the unwelcome Free State Army.

Yet there are balancing memories also of men like Con Brosnan, a Free State officer who was credited with saving the lives of republicans. He was a Kerry football hero: the GAA were a powerful force for reconciliation in those bitter days. Welcoming what used to be called 'foreign games' in Croke Park today allows them to continue in this healing role.

At least one of the founding officers came from the American Fighting 69th, Major-General John T. Prout. He was a relation by marriage of my late father-in-law, Commandant Charles Byrne, who served at the time, but unfortunately, left only his 'Game Book' record of his shooting as his only written legacy to historians. Like so many others he did not talk about his involvement in the early struggle for democracy in this country.

Another member of the new National Army, a charismatic and popular officer, Colonel Tony Lawlor, ex-Royal Flying Corps, addressed our class, as we were about to leave the College. I still remember his advice, 'Always make the best use of whatever equipment the Irish people can afford. Don't be looking for miracles', and 'now that you are leaving here, you can start really learning'.

At his retirement party he announced that he was going to 'A high position in civvy life, the summit of Howth'. That night he was looking somewhat down until the realisation dawned: he had come along in his second best uniform and was patiently waiting to be thrown out the window of the Cavalry Mess.

c. Stand by my Men

I met another of the 'old-school' officers on a temporary posting as Assistant Adjutant on the Camp Staff in McKee Barracks.

The Department of Defence Company was about 400 strong. The

Lieut.-Colonel, Camp Commandant, was another who had served his country well and deserved a rest by the time he was given me. He was the only Barrack OC to have a key for his square, which was surrounded by a chain, and this information should have alerted me to be careful. Barrack squares are holy ground in all armies. I remembered the Sergeant Major in Portobello shouting at an unfortunate recruit crossing the square, 'Hey you, are you an officer or a dog? Get off the fucking square.'

I surmised that even for officers or dogs, a chained square could be fraught with peril. But my three dashes down the Monastery steps would no doubt stand to me here. Fate, as in battle, however, struck from a different angle catching me unaware, despite my boy-scout motto: '*Bi Ullumh*'. On one Saturday morning inspection the CO commented unfavourably on the haircuts of some of the assembled warriors. He was entitled to his opinion, I graciously accepted, but I felt that it was my duty to stand by my men. What followed has not been revealed before now, but the scene was his office. I offered a friendly, 'Sir, if I may say so in fairness to the men, I inspected them yesterday and thought that they looked neat and well groomed. So I told them that they seemed OK. It's really my fault.'

That might have been half-accepted, if I had not added for emphasis, and to indicate that it was not a casual decision, (than which, of course, there is nothing as bad), 'I would not like them to look like convicts, sir'. He sat even straighter in his chair, unbelieving eyes boring into mine, which still tried to retain a respectful but friendly glow. The morning sun shone on his tightly grizzled head.

'Do I look like a convict, Lieutenant?'

A soldier has to take life or death decisions in split seconds. The thought of a witty, urbane reply flashed and was dropped, while I bumbled on about the Irish Brigades being Royalist troops, not really in the Prussian tradition.

Gathering that there was no immediate contrition, he commented: 'This will have to be discussed with the Command OC', with the air of a difficult decision on his part but, something that was his unpleasant duty, part of the loneliness of command.

My twin guardian angels of genuine commitment and innocence, had me saying, 'Well, actually, sir, I would be most interested in the Command OC's views on the matter, I consider it important for morale.'

He looked genuinely shocked at first, and then as if some realisation dawned he looked closely at me again before slightly slumping in his chair, putting his hands flat on the desk, and saying with the voice of a man in uncharted waters, 'We'll say no more about this. The Company turned out well in every other respect. You can talk to me about things like this anytime, I'm busy now.'

On his retirement he called me in and pointing to a press full of his collected copies of *An Cosantóir*, the Defence Forces Journal, said, 'Here, you had better take those, you're the sort that would make some use of them.'

I was not very keen on leaving the 2nd Battalion for this posting but it had turned out to be a satisfying mixture of being responsible for men as well as reports. The men in those days lived in huge Victorian billets and I submitted an idea of cutting off one end as a kind of rest room with arm chairs, writing table, etc., so that they did not have to go to the canteen for a break. I never knew how that was received but nothing happened in my time there.

I was more successful with another move. Supper for the living-in men finished at the time most would be going out to town; there was no late supper at the time most would want it so that they had either to go out or to the canteen if they could afford it. Nobody objected when I asked could I be allowed do something about it, beyond telling me that the Cook Sergeant was operating in his own republic and it might require special staff. I simply asked the Cook Sergeant if it would be possible to re-arrange his roster with no extra staff and he promised to have a word with the others. Supper was available at normal supper-time after that.

McKee Barracks was alive with history, even though it was a late Victorian building. With its steeply sloped roofs, turrets and tall windows, the story was that it had been planned for India. Old drills and memories survive in armies. I heard that one of the sentries, in the 1930s, was in what some observant Barrack Orderly Officer thought was a peculiar location. He discovered, on checking the archives, that this particular warrior's job was to ensure that a tree planted by the Queen was not interfered with by being watered by soldiers or dogs.

One of the Cadet School gods was logic. I always aimed at clarity in everything I did. In that appointment I wore the Army HQ flash of a sword hilt on my sleeve, so I therefore believed that I should follow through and put the red backings under my bars in accordance with the regulation in Army HQ. In those days my rank markings were not 'pips' but bars, one for a 2nd lieutenant, two for a lieutenant and three for a captain. Red backings under one bar must have caused some surprise socially, but such reactions were never conveyed to me. In a macho disciplined organisation there is often also a kindness to its young.

d. One of the Best

Shortly after that I returned to the 2nd Infantry Battalion, Portobello Barracks, (by then re-named Cathal Brugha Barracks) at the request of the Barrack CO, as I was still carried on his strength. I would have been happy to have been left with the battalion in the first place but I had since got to like soldiering in McKee Barracks and was glad to return some time later to another posting. Nonetheless, Portobello Officers' Mess was my first military home and it was good to return to the familiar surroundings.

Messes may not be 'centres of excellence', but they can have a certain university character in the sense of people contributing to ante-room and dinner-table conversation from different backgrounds of expertise, medicine, engineering, science or architecture, as well as the usual military mix of cavalry, infantry, artillery, transport, etc.

I remember Colonel Bill Kelly, of Dublin Grand Opera fame, who used to orchestrate the lunchtime conversation of the young officers, encouraging the quiet ones to contribute. This would contrast with

Osbert Sitwell's experience in a British Cavalry Mess where young officers were allowed to comment only on horses or subjects connected with equitation in their early months.

For me one significant influence was Colonel John Brennock of the Army School of Music. John opened my eyes to the enjoyment of the theatre: a heightened awareness of the spoken word in exploring concepts in human and political relationships. Some of us saw every new play that came to Dublin. We would spend meal hours in entertaining argument: *Look Back in Anger, The Quare Fella, Sive*.

Arguments that I still remember were over Othello as a leader, the death penalty in civil and military law, after *The Quare Fella*, and our national maturity in accepting peasant caricatures after *Sive*. I also remember irate advice some mornings from officers in the rooms down from the Mess to 'Jacko' Phelan and myself to finish our discussion in the Mess and not to be continuing it in front of their windows late at night.

To further encourage my interest in the world of art, Lieut. Fred O'Callaghan, also of the School of Music (later Colonel and OC) encouraged me to enrol in the College of Art for an evening course. Sadly, despite Sr Kevin's praise for my crayon art in Senior Infants, I did not seem to work up sufficient interest in the world of art to finish.

One other memory of that Mess was of someone who, in later life, lived in political media attention. Walking from the Mess we would occasionally ask a lovely little girl, 'And who are you, little lady?'

Just to hear again, 'Bawbwa Bwoune.'

Barbara Browne was the daughter of our comrade, the popular Captain Jack Browne, who had a house in married quarters.

The Commanding Officer was another who had started his military career with the State and understandably, expected that he would personally also advance in parallel. To emphasise a return to peacetime, walking sticks for officers were issued in 1923. I do not know when he started carrying his, but he had it when I saw him for the first time, on my return and I never saw him in public without it. Perhaps he took the 1923 wish on the part of Army HQ as their command, because he sincerely believed in the sacredness of orders. As indeed, so did I. Over his head in his office was a simple soldierly notice: 'A SOLDIER'S FIRST DUTY IS TO OBEY'.

He had been through the Tan War, the Civil War and the Emergency and no doubt was puzzled as to why he was waiting so long for the recognition he deserved. A stocky figure, grey hair brushed back. He was most impressive at his Monday morning Battalion Officers Conferences behind the 'table, mahogany, dining-room, officers' mess' that he had got the Barrack Services staff to acquire for his office. During the conference, he would usually ring Brigade HQ: 'But, what can I do, all my best officers are away.' I was told, perhaps jokingly, by one of those in attendance, that I was included in that distinguished list.

I had retained my 2nd Battalion collar badges: Infantry, Crossed Rifles with a '2' on a small shield underneath. I was wearing them on my first meeting with the CO and, on seeing them, he almost beamed, perhaps because one of his best officers was back. Later in the ante-room of the Mess I saw again the portrait of Cathal Brugha, an extreme republican who opposed the Treaty and was shot by, I suppose, us, after whom the Barracks was now named. The Board of Works man who had put it up had already voiced my puzzlement, 'A gas Army, first they shoot him, now they're hanging him.'

I lasted for several weeks as 'one of his best officers'. My appointment in the Battalion was as assistant to the Lieutenant Quartermaster, who had been retained after the Emergency. The Defence Forces Act had been amended to allow recruitment for the duration of the Emergency and in the expanded army there was an urgent need for more officers. Those with obvious potential for officer rank were selected for Officer Training and awarded Temporary Commissions. Enlistment had come from all sectors: the old enemies of the Civil War were prepared to fight shoulder to shoulder. Among the latter must have been the senior officer who said that on the arrival of the Fianna Fáil ministers, 'I didn't know whether to salute them or shoot them.'

Some Emergency Officers, who had left good jobs or worthwhile prospects, returned after the war to their civilian lives. Some, who had remained in the Army, were not so lucky at a time of stagnant promotion and had not gained much advancement. These officers were anxious to make up for lost ground: an extremely difficult task in the shrunken post-war Army.

One Sunday morning I was late arriving at Government Buildings with a new Infantry Guard, to take over from the officer who had completed his tour of duty. I did not see any real problem in the short time involved and said, 'You'll have no trouble getting twelve o'clock Mass in Rathmines.'

On the following day I was sent for by the CO. 'Did yesterday go all right?' he asked.

'As it happens, no sir, unfortunately, my guard was held up and I was late relieving the old guard.'

'I'm glad you admitted it, because I already knew. But did you know that the officer is a Protestant?'

I do not know who told him about the late hand-over but nothing happened in the barracks that was not brought to his notice by many sources, including the barrack police sergeant. There were, of course, Church of Ireland members in the Army and I did not attach any great importance to the fact. I felt foolish about the Mass advice, but, seemingly, I was still one of the best.

There were several ex-Temporary Officers in the Battalion, many in their green whipcord as worn during the war. Many more, who had made excellent contributions to the Army, had returned to their civilian appointments, like Lionel Booth, Liam Cosgrave, Douglas Gageby and Seamus Kelly (Quidnunc in *The Irish Times*).

Some of the ex-TOs (Temporary Officers) remaining told about how well they could have done outside in 'civvy life' and how foolish they had been for staying on, and appeared to harbour some resentment for the Cadet School graduates that they seemed to think had life too soft. I arrived back in the Mess one night and found a few having a 'crib session' in the bar. One looked up and said: 'The last thing we need is you waving your Cadet School scarf in our faces'. The others stared at him, one winking a hint at me.

I had heard, however, that during the Emergency some Regular Officers went out of their way to demonstrate their difference. One officer told me, that he continued to wear the high-necked pre-war style tunic which marked him out as a Regular Officer.

Laughing at his own outrageousness, he said that when acting on regimental duty as Barrack Orderly Officer, he would ride on his horse through the huge open hangers used as dining-halls at meal times and tap a soldier on the shoulder with his crop. 'Any complaints?'

The officers commissioned during the Emergency gave excellent service. But we had heard their stories about the 1942 Blackwater Manoeuvres so often that eventually we developed a code. If one started a story we would pick up the ends of our tunics and squeeze imaginary water until he got the message. Nonetheless, those exercises were very impressive and produced many lessons.

The area chosen was a likely German landing area, which B.I. Gudmundson in the *US Military History Quarterly*, states was between Dungarvan and Waterford for the five infantry divisions of 'Enterprise Green' (to follow 'Operation Sea Lion'). These ports were outside the mine belt laid by the Royal Navy across the southern entrance to the Irish Sea. The concept of the exercise included the assistance of British reinforcements. I'm sure that they all would have slept more soundly had they known that no less a soldier than Captain Evelyn Waugh and his Royal Marines had already spent some time in an ancient cross-channel steamer, ready to forestall any German invasion of 'Eire'. He records in his diary for 17 July 1940 of them being 'busy doing appreciations of the Irish coast'.

According to Col. J.P. Duggan's *History of the Irish Army*, under no circumstances would it be contemplated that the supreme command of the combined force be given to a British general. A naval or air force commander would be 'marginally less unacceptable'. There were four drownings, but two divisions were exercised and administered in the field, carrying out complicated operations of war with a high degree of efficiency. British observers were present and the operation generally engendered confidence in the Irish Army's capability to play its part in any likely scenario.

The message also was that an aggressive attempt by any side could be costly. Taking this island would be possible, but at a price. As well as the over 50,000 in the Army, there were also about 100,000 in the LDF (Local Defence Force) and about 50,000 in the LSF (Local Security Force).

If one adds the 50,000 (including 5,000 deserters from the Irish Army) from the South in the British Forces (with another estimated 20,000 Southerners enlisted through Northern Ireland) plus about 40,000 citizens of NI, the total approximates the figures for the First World War.

The 'Emergency Officers' really had something to boast about, even if some at the time were not prepared to give them their due credit.

e. The Fall

I was stoically balancing myself on my unaccustomed pedestal as 'best officer' and really just hoping for the grace of a soft landing.

It was not to be granted.

One of our 'Q' tasks was to accompany the CO on his monthly inspection of soldiers married quarters. We would wind along from door to door, the CO swinging his stick. Stopping at a door, he would put the stick by his side. After greeting, he would ask the lady of the house if she had any problems. The Barrack Foreman would take note and we would look around, walk out and continue, the CO once again swinging his stick.

The Quartermaster was on leave for one of these and, therefore, as usual, I was to be the representative of the 'Q' side, except that I had a tooth extracted on the previous day and as I kept picking at it with my tongue, it continued bleeding for a sleepless night. The following morning I took a day's 'Uncle Charlie' (uncertified sick leave). I recovered during the day as my orderly brought meals to my room, got up, showered and shaved to face the evening, wondering if there was to be a poker game.

As I was coming out the door the CO was driving home. I saluted. He ignored me. I was no longer on the pedestal. I thought, what the hell, forgive and forget. He did not.

I was relieved to think that the waiting for this inevitability was over as, on the following morning, he said, 'I paraded myself at 10.00 hours. No sign of you.'

I had the feeling that I would no longer feature in chats with Brigade HQ. The only consolation here, as the Quartermaster told me, was that I was now welcomed aboard as one of the lads and indistinguishable from all the other officers in the unit.

One of the entourage on the married quarters inspection that I had missed, told me that on that day one of the ladies thanked the CO for something that had been done for her.

'Oh, was it something that the Quartermaster or myself had agreed to do for you,' he asked.

'No,' she replied, 'it was the gentlemanly young officer who occasionally comes around with you.'

I do not know if this story, as was told to me, is true but I had always been careful on this round, remembering my uncle's story of his inspection of police married quarters in the Malaya States.

On one occasion, he was idly waiting for the lady of the house and toying with an ornament on a table when a small child came into the room shouting, 'Leave that alone, there's an old bastard coming to catch her out and Mammy was all morning getting ready.'

As a bachelor with everything taken care of, he had not realised the trauma he caused. He never entered the houses again except to greet the residents at the doors and make himself available if needed.

On our round, I had admired the photographs on the mantle-piece of soldiers and sailors in British uniforms, as well as our own, and I think perhaps that might have gone down well.

Sometimes it seems that an officer's strengths can very easily merge into weaknesses. As Col. Tom Feeley, College Commandant (who had come in to the room as I was finishing my accounts for the Cadet School shop late one night) when reporting on a student on the Command and Staff Course, under the heading of 'A Mixer?' wrote 'To a fault'.

I believed in granting NCOs their due respect, and never referred to one as, for instance, 'Murphy' without the rank, always Cpl Murphy or Sgt Murphy. I had an eighteenth-century ideal of service but I was forced to re-examine some of my ideas by the CO when he called me in one day to discuss one of what I thought to be my minor responsibilities, the administration of the Sergeants' Mess.

From his background knowledge of barrack activities, he questioned me about my approach to the job.

'How are you getting on with the Sergeants' Mess?'

'Well, I trust the Sergeant administrator, sir. It seems to be working out all right,' I replied in the self-confident voice of youth.

'What does that mean in specific terms?'

'Well, I look at the lodgements and accounts and sign them when necessary. I am too busy to spend much time checking.'

Looking back I hope that I did not say anything about having to trust him with my life in battle, but I probably did. The CO's reply is another one of those pieces of advice that I fully absorbed and retained.

'Your job is not to trust the NCO but to keep him out of trouble, and not to be putting temptation before him. Do you know how many children he has or what his living expenses are?'

The idea of talking like that about a respected NCO horrified me but I could not deny the value of the advice. Once again it must have been the unhesitating honesty of my reply that allowed me to escape the 'bollicking' I deserved. This was another learning experience and it reminded of Col. Tony Lawlor's advice on leaving the Cadet School: 'Now you can start learning.'

The Army of today acknowledges the status of NCOS who are really, as the cliché has it, the backbone of any army. In my Army, an officer always had to be present, in command and carrying the responsibility, regardless of the activity. On the firing range, there always had to be an officer in charge of the firing point and an officer in charge of the butts (target gallery) where the shots are recorded from the targets. No range practices could proceed without them. When soldiers left barracks for any official duty, they had to be accompanied by an officer.

I saw many a rugby international at Lansdowne Road because the Pipe Band had to be accompanied by an officer, even if he had nothing whatever to do with their performance. On one occasion the band was performing superlatively to the delight of the crowd (all the tunes of glory), the Pipe Corporal throwing his staff over a small cloud, catching it unerringly and swinging along, saffron kilts and green tunics highlighted in the sunbeams.

The problem was that the Garda Band, in a corner of the pitch, playing its more civilised music, but not making itself heard above the wind, finally had to sound the Presidential Salute as His Excellency arrived. To my horror and the entertainment of the crowd the 2nd Battalion Pipe Band did not seem to notice and blazed away. I had to write a report, which I spent some time trying to forget.

f. Postings

Apart from the Lansdowne Road disaster, bands and martial music form a colourful and pleasant part of my military memories. They play an important part in training and the cultivation of the *esprit de corps*. On long route marches the arrival of the Pipe Band for the last mile smartened up flagging steps. Barrack and public ceremonial are given life and colour by the bands.

For Brigade Inspections all brigade units in barracks would parade on the square for inspection by the colourful and charismatic Brigade Commander, Col. J.D. McGrath. He would step out the door of the Officers' Mess, on to the square, at the first stroke of 10.00 hours on the barrack clock, to the general salute by the brass band. After the inspection there would be a march past, which the Colonel would take on a stand with the COs of the units.

On one such occasion I found myself as part of the Battalion Staff, in front of the parade beside the Adjutant, a Captain, who always referred to me as 'mister', (in his view the old and correct way to address a 2nd Lieutenant), and wore yellow gloves as befitting ex-Artillery. I marched alongside his large moustache until we noticed that the band and the marching warriors had taken a different turn, in accordance with their orders. We were alone, but marching in a brisk and soldier-like manner.

'Do not panic, Mr Goggin,' he said, out of the corner of his mouth. At least I guessed that was where the sound was coming from.

'Right or wrong remain steady. Keep swinging up your arms. We'll do a good about-turn on my order. We'll meet the parade on the way back.'

We did and nobody even noticed anything odd.

Some time before another such inspection I had called in to see the new Captain Adjutant.

'I'd like to apply for that Russian course being offered by GHQ, Intelligence Section.'

'You'll have to apply to Brigade.'

The Adjutant, a busy man, thought that that would put me off, indicating that the unit was not in favour.

'May I have a sheet of paper, please? I asked.

He put down his pen with the startled look of someone being approached by a particularly disreputable beggar. But I was still full of the old Cadet School thing of doing what I thought right, so I sent in a formal application.

On the morning of the inspection, as the CO handed over the parade, the Brigade Commander shouted, 'Where's the Russian officer?'

To his astonishment the CO had to point to me.

I thought: 'This is it, I've overdone it again.'

I was called in after the parade and told that the Brigade Commander had ordered that I be given every facility to go ahead.

All military orders are obeyed equally: some however, more equally than others. For some time I enjoyed my twice-weekly trips to Army HQ for the Russian lessons with Comdt Brunicardi, but, in one of the few phrases I remember, '*nichto ne vechno*' (nothing lasts forever). In time, different 'genuine' reasons were found to send me on temporary duties to various outposts so that keeping up with the study was not possible without constant revision and being brought up to date at the cost of lesson time for the others. Failing the College spirit, I gave up.

It is somewhat difficult to explain the old military ideal of discipline and obedience in an age when even military 'representative associations' are flexing their muscles. It was not just a matter of being prepared to 'go over the top' on a lawful command. It was a wholehearted acceptance of the overarching importance of the needs of the unit and the comparative insignificance of the wishes of the individual.

It was obvious that the unit did not want me to be spending two afternoons a week in Army HQ. The complexity of my thinking on this included an awareness that this might be what the Brigade wanted or even what the Army wanted. If the unit did not want it, then I would accede to its wishes. I would, of course, reserve the right to 'crib' in the bar, and in that soldier's sense of balance, they owed me one.

Being a single officer I was posted to the Camp Staff at Gormanstown for the duration of the FCA summer training period. The Quartermaster of the Camp was a Captain who boasted that we fed a thousand men in seven minutes due to the efficient system he had in place of hotplates and groups of dining-hall orderlies working under the supervision of corporals. I felt that the lunch-break was a time for relaxation for the FCA men and that the rush was overdoing it. It was, nonetheless, a vast improvement on my own FCA days in the meal queues with our tin plates. I took a particular interest in the fatigue-men wondering if there were still flyers on brushes or buckets.

My only memory of it now is of the Captain Quartermaster bustling about with his shirtsleeves rolled up. I thought this to be totally unnecessary because the sergeant in charge of the operation was completely on top of the job and controlled the supervising corporals with an iron hand, or voice to be more accurate. Perhaps he believed that we should be making an impression on visiting staff officers, but I felt that he was letting himself down. I could only make oblique comment so I decided on the non-verbal statement of being gloved and fully dressed at all times on my visits to the dining area and standing still while the bustle went on around me.

I used to carry a shooting stick in the camp and was thus equipped when a visiting press reporter interviewed me. On the following day an evening paper made a reference to something like 'a very regimental young officer with a shooting stick'. I saw the Quartermaster carrying one some time after that.

We lived in the Air Corps Officers' Mess but an addition to our social life was the proximity of Butlins, which we all pretended to look down on. Yet we were glad to avail of the free passes we received from the ex-British Major, who was in charge. I took pride in the fact that regardless of how late we got home, I never missed, or was late for, morning parade.

Some of us were persuaded to visit Belfast: none of my group had ever been North of the border. As we drove around that city we were given a running commentary by a man with local knowledge, which we found in parts repetitious and boring, but detected a peculiar note of aggression on that sunny summer's day that sounded like something out of our history books. Today every word of his story would be familiar to all.

We saw a parade passing ahead of us at one stage and I could just make out what I mistook to be the orange end of our national flag. So, afraid that we were not responding to the drama of our new friend's stories I said, 'Could that ever be our flag being paraded through this so-called "foreign" city?'

We nearly crashed as our driver/commentator turned around to look at me.

'This is useless,' he said, 'someday you'll all learn.'

We did.

On my return to the 2nd Battalion, one afternoon, I watched a sunbeam exploding a shining bugle in a blaze of burnished gold, as I listened to the store-man intoning, in the time honoured chant of the Quartermaster's store, 'Bugles, one, complete with tassel, sir.'

He was waiting impassively for me to tick my list as part of a stock check but quite happy if all I was going to do was nod, and moved on to, 'Sir, brushes, long handled, soldier's, for the use of, six'.

As I stood there nodding, he perhaps thought to himself, 'a late night in the bar'. He was a happy soldier of the 'roll on half-four, inta bed or outa barracks' variety. He was happy to be 'dug-in', had no other ambitions and all armies need men like him.

'Randles, pairs, a half', for one randle, pushed my acceptance to the limit.

I took pride and pleasure in avoiding discovering what a randle was, like a British officer who joined a party of us on a holiday tour of England, whose social boast was that he had never been to Blackpool and sat in a pub outside that town until we returned.

In fact, my problem was something much more fundamental. The bugle symbolised the side of soldiering that I had really wanted. I mentioned my feelings to the Assistant Adjutant, Lieut. Leo Walsh, who was ready when my application for a platoon arrived in Battalion HQ.

He published me in the Barrack Routine Orders as:

'Lieut. Goggin, P.D., from Asst QM, 2 Inf Bn, to OC No 15 Platoon, 'A' Company, at own request.'

Leo added those most unusual last three words on the grounds that, if he did not, then someone might say that I had to be let go because I was not able to do the job.

The Quartermaster was genuinely puzzled. I had only just handed him a paper making recommendations for soldier's dress involving larger flashes, lanyards, white web belts and other items that afterwards became standard. But it indicated to him that I was happy where I was. So what was the problem? He stood with the look that adults reserve for awkward children.

'You're a gas man. Here you are in a cushy job, and there you'll be tomorrow, out in the rain. If there was anything I learned during the fucking Emergency was get in out of the rain. What's this all about? I'm quite happy with you. You're learning; the only crib I'd have with you is that you are always talking about other things; you don't seem to focus on "Q". The CO tells me that he did not suggest it. Who put this into your mind?'

'I'd like to get experience in all areas,' I said.

'Oh, I know, you want to be fucking Montgomery.'

I simply could not tell him who put it in my mind, those ideas seemed to be always part of me, I just did not question them. At the time I would not have thought about it, but now I wonder was it a committee of officers of the British, German and American Armies on a wall in a bedroom? Like football stars for others? Perhaps I wondered if my destiny were to die for Ireland on a battlefield, what was I doing as a 'box-wallah'? As I left the office the Quartermaster advised, 'One thing, if you want to be a cowboy, you're as thin as a whip, you'd better start eating more or start drinking pints, and you wouldn't want to be taking those great soldiers out there too seriously.'

g. Platoon Commander

Having completed my two years of a probationary period as a Second Lieutenant, I was promoted Lieutenant, thereby adding another bar on my epaulette. My name as one of the Platoon Commanders was now on one of three prongs down from Captain R.A. Hinchy, Company Commander, on the organisation chart of 'A' Company, the recruit company. I enjoyed the time with my platoon. I had three experienced corporals, one for each of the sections, but I was particularly fortunate in my Platoon Sergeant. One of the old school NCOS, who considered it his responsibility to continue my training where the College had left off and, like a good civil servant with a minister, to keep me 'on line' with advice that kept me out of trouble. Handing him the week's training programme for the platoon, he would comment that it was well balanced and very well laid out. But, for instance, would I mind if the period shown as 'stacking and unstacking of arms' (an old drill to keep the rifles off the wet grass during long delays in camp) could be used for the 'close order foot drill' that would be necessary for the passing out parade?

I was wise enough to agree.

When I would outline a plan for a change in an exercise in which he saw hidden pitfalls, he would be lavish in his praise for my imagination and originality, but like Sir Humphrey, would add something like, 'A very courageous break from the way the CO always wanted, sir.'

Like all soldiers, I enjoyed getting out of barracks. A battalion exercise was planned shortly after I was given my platoon, and, again in keeping with my age and enthusiasm, I asked to be allowed to take my warriors. That phase does not last long. There is some truth in the cinematic clichés: the enthusiastic young lieutenant with dreams of glory at one end, the decent old colonel who has seen it all at the other. And in between, the cynical, 'please don't disturb me' captain, feeling unfairly burdened by his lieutenant's eagerness and his colonel's expectations. The Captain, Company Commander, did his best to discourage me on the reasonable grounds that if things went wrong, he would share the blame.

I was granted permission to accompany the Battalion on the understanding that I was to keep the recruits out of people's way, as they would not be part of the exercise. I succeeded in keeping out of the way by setting up a 'cowboys and Indians' type 'bang-bang I got you' stalking operation on the other side of the hill to the genuine entertainment of the platoon. They fired sackfuls of blanks at each other, and carried equally large sackfuls of camouflage on their helmets. It was not long before the Sergeant's feared snags began to emerge. We had to issue special instructions about firing. One had nearly blinded another by firing too close. However, it was, I felt, a very valuable help in their training and morale to be, however loosely, operating with the Battalion.

What eventually hit us, however, was a typical military snag, not anticipated even by the Sergeant or any other of the worried people, like the Captain, who had already probably regretted his trust. Horace warned about it in one of his Odes. The soldier, who fears the Pyrrhic arrows, can be killed by falling branches in his own garden. A visiting group of Army HQ and Brigade Staff, who had come to observe the battalion exercise, wound their way in a convoy of staff cars around the hill. They stopped, to my astonishment, on the road below my platoon cowboys, who were blazing away happily at the last of the Mohicans on the high ground in a confusion of rocks, bushes and smoke grenades.

Luckily, as the leading members of the visiting observers were consulting map-boards and starting up the hill, battle intelligence saved the embarrassment of a confrontation, as a despatch rider arrived from the Battalion, and all returned to cars and drove around our hill somewhat late to the exercise area.

As we came marching back to camp, that evening, we got odd glares from all, from the most junior NCOS to the Battalion Staff.

Marching at ease, and having enjoyed their mornings campaigning, the platoon NCOs failed to discourage the recruits' disastrous, salt in the Battalion's wounds, singing. It seemed to have been agreed that nothing more would be said, but this agreement must have come close to breaking when my warriors began boasting at lunch that the visitors came to see us first.

After returning to barracks and continuing the training programme, the strength of the Platoon was gradually reduced from its original 45 down to the 35, who would finally pass out as 'one-star' trained soldiers. I had eliminated those, who did not seem to have the will or the potential to reach the required standard.

I remember one with a semi-permanent expression of 'dumb insolence', who seemed to make very little attempt to improve in response to corrections of drill faults, the Sergeant commenting with distaste. Finally one day, from inside the window of the company office, I had heard his name being bawled amid all the friendly advice being roared by the Corporals.

'Don't be looking down, if there was anything on the ground the Board of Works men would have picked it up hours ago', and on handling the bayonet, 'Feel for it, like you do in the dark.'

They were doing the 'fix bayonets' drill movement that has been admired by other armies. The Sergeant was enjoying himself, getting in the classic, 'On the command "fix", ye don't fix.'

What happens on that part of the command is that a soldier marches out from the end of the front rank, turns to be seen by all and then leads the movements. He takes the bayonet from its scabbard, holds it at the ready on the rifle and then, when he 'fixes' with a satisfying click, all the platoon fix their bayonets on the rifles, ready for action.

The sullen-faced soldier rattled with his fixing long after everyone else. His section corporal came snapping at his heels again, but he just stood there with the bayonet held loosely. I had observed him before and noted in the Platoon Diary that he was a doubtful starter. I had spoken to him but could find nothing to explain his performance. He did not seem to have any family or other troubles. On kit inspections he always seemed to be one degree under in his layout. I did not know what was wrong with him. Perhaps he was having a rethink about being a soldier, in which case my decision would be of benefit for both himself and the Army.

But what was happening now was not merely dumb but open insolence. I went on the square.

'Stand the platoon at ease, Sergeant.'

He did.

'March that soldier off the square, Corporal.'

He did and I said loud enough to be heard by all, 'He'll be a civvy this evening.'

I do not know if this would be acceptable in the trade unionised modern army. The power of officers in those days included ordering men to be confined in the guardroom on occasions, which must have clashed with their constitutional right not to be deprived of freedom without due process of law.

On regimental duty one night, as Barrack Orderly Officer, I was made aware on our round of the barracks, checking sentries and general security, that there was a fight in a billet. I went in and saw two soldiers with knives confronting and taunting two others. A very worried BOS (Barrack Orderly Sergeant), who accompanied me, made a move to caution me, 'They're troublemakers, sir, and dangerous.'

I walked between the groups and said something like, 'Are you soldiers or corner-boys? Stop this nonsense.'

They did and I ordered a corporal to fall in an escort and march the two ringleaders to the guardroom until it was sorted.

I was within my rights on this in military law because they were a danger to themselves and others and there was no requirement for any immediate due process. I did not think about being in any personal danger. I was lucky, but it was the trained response of abstracting myself from the situation and taking necessary action. Officers' training develops in them a tendency to emulate Balubas on the magic drug that makes them believe themselves impervious to bullets.

I had another lucky day on the range with the platoon on grenade throwing practice. In previous centuries, when the current anti-armour bullet trap rifle grenades were a twinkle in the eye of Mars, specially selected soldiers were appointed as grenadiers, with distinctive uniforms and higher pay. In the seventeenth century they formed special companies within battalions, the tall mitre shaped shako being associated with them as the flat topped Polish cap for Lancers or the Hungarian tunic tied over one shoulder for Hussars. Now all soldiers are trained in the use of the grenade, as one of the basic infantry weapons.

We were familiar with the 'No. 36, Mills, High Explosive, hand or rifle, grenade', with a 'Noble Buff seven second safety fuse'. As the name implies, 'it does exactly what it says on the tin'. A pin holds a lever on the side of the grenade. When the pin is pulled the soldier keeps a firm grip on the lever, which then flies off when the grenade is thrown. This releases the striker, which starts the fuse burning causing the grenade to explode after seven seconds.

The men shelter in a trench for throwing practice and come up one by one to throw under instruction by the NCO. On rare occasions, something prevents the grenade exploding. So where it lands must be noted, and the officer waits to see if it has properly settled. He then fits a detonator and fuse into a piece of explosive, climbs out of the exercise trench, walks to the grenade, places the explosive beside it, lights the fuse and walks back to the trench. He walks because to run could risk a fall, which could expose him to lethal shrapnel. The risk inherent in the operation is that it might be just a little spot of dust that prevents the striker from descending and exploding the detonator and movement of any kind, like the grenade rolling over, could dislodge the obstruction. I am aware of only one being wounded over the years but most will have had to take this action at least once in their careers.

This was my first time having this responsibility and as, every so often, grenades failed to explode I went through the drill, my nervousness decreasing as the fear became more remote with every repeat. When we returned to barracks the Sergeant handed in to the Battalion Quartermaster Sergeant the red detonator box with the rope handles. The BQMS looked in amazement at the empty box.

'Where are the bucking detonators, we had an almost full box?'

I arrived in and said, 'I used them up, BQ.'

'You were an unusual type of an Assistant QM, here sir, but this is the best ever. The whole Battalion wouldn't use a full box in years.'

He held the empty box sadly in his hands like a dead pet's basket. I'm sure that he added me to his list of stories going back to the South Irish Horse. The explanation I heard afterwards was that it was a bad consignment of grenades that should not have been issued. I should have ceased after the first few failures.

I was surprised and sad sometime later, when this senior NCO, who had added so much to our store of colour and history of change into the new Irish Army, had no formal retirement parade. On departing the barracks he gave me an officer's valise he had 'acquired'. This is a canvas carrier in which clothes and bedding can be rolled for camping. He was remembered for years for his sayings, as, for instance, about people acting very busy: 'Jasus, you'd think they were working on the fodder account for the South Irish Horse.'

h. Warriors

In my first platoon, leaving and intermediate certificate holders happily soldiered side by side with 'no interest in certificates' men. They seemed to be excellent material but one was, early on, identified by the corporal I/C his section as potential trouble.

The Company Commander formed the same opinion, when he saw him in a 'slashed peak' cap, in the manner of the Irish Guards. I defended him because I knew that, whereas this was contrary to our dress regulations, it was a sign that he wanted to be a good soldier. He had been acting a bit 'bolshy', according to reports to me by the NCOs, even though nobody could say that he offended in any specific way. It could have been due to his undoubtedly self-confident air so I decided to give him a chance and appointed him as 'football captain' for the platoon.

He took it seriously to the extent that when he was selecting the team for the company game, his first act at the meeting was to salute me and to address the platoon. I was amused and impressed and jokingly asked if he would mind if the Sergeant and myself left. He did not mind. On the way out the Sergeant said:

'He'll make a good corporal.'

'I think he'll make a good Company Sergeant someday.'

'Don't say that to the CO, sir, for Chrissake.'

He had the platoon subscribe to the purchase of a football, so as not to depend on the welfare store, and controlled its lending himself. This arrangement suited me also because I was never very much involved with football. He, like some other excellent top class soldiers in my platoon, came from Fatima Mansions.

I had one puzzling soldier because, while his immediate problem was petty theft I judged that it was related to a deeper set of worries. The men in his billet used to give him money to buy things to show that they trusted him, but it never worked. I believed that he really wanted to do the right thing but seemed to be trapped in some psychological mess. I tried talking to him and advising as best I could but even with the help of the chaplain I got nowhere. One of the saddest conversations I had at the time was with his father, who said:

'Thank you very much, Lieutenant, for your interest in my son, but we have failed to get any results and sadly have given up. He is too much of a strain on the family. I suggest that you do the same.'

Dick, the Company Commander, said:

'You'll have to let him go, he's taking up too much of your time and there's no hope of a miracle.'

My idea of always trying to see the good in people, did not work on this occasion. He got me reading my first books on psychology, which I studied afterwards in UCD.

I also had the son of a serving officer in the platoon, who was perhaps hoping for a cadetship. He was a bit finicky over the tea when we were out on the range. I advised him to take the tea that the platoon was brewing in the big tea vat or he would be considered odd. As in the Cadet School, being considered 'odd' in a recruit platoon would do him no good. I told him that the sight of the wooden mallet sometimes put floating on the tea to gather the bits was equally off-putting to me. But I always made sure that I took what I was offered even though I could have got a flask from the Mess with my packed lunch.

He was obviously in competition for 'Best Soldier' on the passing out parade. My regret about him centred on the way I dealt with him on account of who he was. I knew his father. I thought that I would save him becoming the subject of talk, so I said, 'Look, I consider you to be one of the best soldiers in the platoon. But would you mind very much if I didn't nominate you for "Best Soldier" on the passing out parade because the others would think that it was because of your father.'

I was wrong on two counts: apart from the obvious one, I am quite sure now that the others would not have seen anything wrong with it. Being a good soldier he fully accepted my word, but I regretted it afterwards thinking about Nelson's son who was ignored by his father on the ground that Nelson's son should not have any special privileges. He allowed him to be bullied aboard ship and refused to intervene because he was his son, until the realisation dawned that whereas he should not have been given privileges, neither should he be penalised for who he was and Nelson sorted out the bullying bosun.

I was pleased, however, with my handling of the case of a soldier of whom the 7th Battalion wanted to be rid. It was suggested that we might take him on his last chance. The Company Commander told me he was being posted to my platoon to see if we could improve him. His problem was AWOL ('absent without official leave') and he had gone down all the punishments in fines and confinement to barracks but did not show any sign of reform. He had not offended in any other way nor indeed been absent for more than a day at a time, always Saturdays, but he had reached an unacceptable nuisance level that was disturbing the discipline climate of his unit.

On his first day, I spent some time with him. His story was that his parents had moved to England and he had very young sisters at home in the flat. They were normally OK except on the occasional Saturday that his older sister had to work and there was a worry that they would not be safe in that location, 'too many peculiar characters around'. I had heard so many sob-stories that I asked to see his sister to verify the situation. She duly came in to see me and explained what he meant. I told him that any time he needed a pass for a Saturday to come and see me and I would fix it for him. He never went absent again and became a very useful soldier.

Normally a drill presentation would be expected as the centrepiece of the passing out parade. As my platoon's day approached, the CO called me into his office and said, 'As the battalion is so busy and particularly your recruits being involved in so many other activities, as we are so short of men, you need not bother with the usual drill display.'

'Right Sir, does this mean that we're not having a passing out parade?'

'No, just that I do not see how you will have time for rehearsals for a special drill display.'

He assumed that that was the end of the matter but the thought that we would be having a passing out parade when all the recruits' families and girlfriends would be present and that it would fall flat without some action worried me. The Captain, Dick Hinchy, the Company Commander, said, 'It's up to you. You'd be taking a chance, but I won't stop you. If it's a disaster there will be considerable egg on face.' He added in his serious voice, 'For all of us.'

The Sergeant was frankly horrified, it strained all his diplomacy and tried and tested turns of phrase: 'I respectfully suggest sir that we think about it.'

He looked defeated when he had to fall back on: 'A chance to take it easy, sir. The lads deserve it.'

I firmly believed that the same lads would like to show off in front of their families and girl friends who would be invited in to watch them being handed over to the Brigade Commander as trained soldiers. But did I also want to show off to the Brigade Staff? On putting the matter directly to the men, my belief was confirmed. They agreed to parade in the evenings for a number of days to rehearse the drill display I had designed. Other officers found it hard to believe that the lads would voluntarily parade for an hour of their otherwise free time, but they did. My boy-scout enthusiasm probably did it, coupled with their pride. I could never see myself again putting an idea like that to any others. Nor, indeed gambling on a series of complicated drill movements that could easily have gone wrong to my severe embarrassment, in front of the Brigade and Barrack Staffs, as well as all the other units and invited guests.

Youth has its way of handling things. I would have had no safety net: the CO had told me not to; the Company Commander had told me it was up to me; my Platoon Sergeant grew ten years older, but backed me. The glory day made up for everything. I knew that I handed 35 good soldiers over to the Brigade Commander and their performance of the drill showed that they believed it too. The CO half beamed. Dick looked relieved.

Soldiering is a young man's game, as indeed is chasing the 'Silver Tassie' of glory in war. Anyone observing the sons of Ulster, Munster, Leinster or Connaught marching towards the Somme would have seen it. I had my triumphs and my defeats, all of them equally low-level. I was one time detailed for a minor duty in Arbour Hill for a ceremony at which the President was to be present. Trying to banish my memory of the 'Lansdowne Incident', I resolved to be perfect: as I always did only this time even more so. Something happened which delayed the car to take me there and we arrived late. Lateness is a crime the gravity of which depends on the level of VIP for whom one is late.

When we arrived and saw that the President was already on parade (if indeed such personages can be so described) and everybody, including the Guard of Honour had assembled, my heart sank. The driver must have panicked because instead of driving around the back of the crowd, he bombed into a wheeling stop in a shower of gravel in front. His panic must have been pretty severe because he started behaving impeccably, springing out, opening the door and saluting.

'Will I wait, sir.'

'Will you fuck off at the high port as fast as you can,' I whispered.

As often at moments of great drama: the *deus ex machina* – a plane droned low overhead and everybody was distracted. The band started to play and I made a flanking movement to my position, under cover of the Guard of Honour.

i. Sport

As well as shooting competitions, sport was of serious importance in those pre-UN days. The CO demonstrated his commitment to the ideal by calling for weekly barracks sports meetings in his office. I happened to attend one such meeting by accident. Someone was out sick. I remember hearing all the enthusiastic reporting of sporting events. Even failure had to be a triumph of effort by the battalion team: 'We held them to a scoreless draw, sir.'

I became aware at an early stage, however, that there was a disturbing element present at this particular orgy of self-congratulation. A soldier, who had come to represent the gym instead of the corporal in charge, like myself there by accident, kept trying to interject something and was talked down every time. He spoke with an accent that made him pronounce jerseys as if it had a 'g' in the middle. The officer representatives were being very friendly and polite to him, but not really allowing him to enter the discussion. I heard him trying to get a word in with, 'What about the jegseys, sug?'

I instinctively felt that there was something interesting here, so I turned to him and drew attention to his attempts. I could have been turned to stone by the looks I got, which convinced me all the more. The CO finally inclined his head and came nearer to beaming than I had ever seen him. Sport was in a democratic field.

'You have a problem?'

'Yes sug,' came the relieved reply, 'we did not have enough jegseys for the last fortnight.'

Heads dropped towards files full of good reports. The temperature fell palpably. That was my last attendance at a sports meeting.

I enjoyed some tennis, but also the occasional pint of cold lager sitting in the sun watching pleated white on tan. Single officer's quarters were in blocks of four in line with the tennis court. I did not have a shower in the bathroom so, to get a shower, I had to walk out our door and get in the next one. I did this in an old red silk dressing gown. As the shower was of the old fashioned, fixed on ceiling variety, I wore a helmet if I did not want my hair wet during a quick freshener. Some wag put it out that they had an eccentric officer living in the Mess, who walked around wearing helmet and dressing gown, so that when I emerged people temporarily lost interest in the tennis.

The only sport I ever really enjoyed taking part in was shooting. It was my Uncle Joe who had got me started. He had the honour of starting a race in the Dingle Regatta by firing a shot in the air. After his death Charlie Haughey took over this task.

My uncle was an all-round sportsman. He wrote to Lord Harrington complaining about the condition of a river and got a letter back giving him permission to fish wherever he wished. This letter, I'm sure, was waved in front of his fishing companions. He tried but failed to get me bitten by the fishing bug. I still remember the names of flies; the Coachman, Purple Grouse, Orange Grouse, the Coch-y-Bondhu, etc., but I did not have the patience to stand and stroll for hours by a river bank.

Shooting was different. I just loved watching a dog quartering the hillside, waiting for the 'point'. I still remember the glorious, scarlet and gold, sunsets as I headed home in the evenings. I invited Terry McNulty, an officer of the Battalion, who had a charming girlfriend, Ann, from Dingle, now his lady wife, to come out with me one day on a visit home.

I rashly predicted what birds I expected we would rise in various places and, to my relief, we did find more or less as my Uncle Joe had advised. We found snipe on the bog, woodcock in a bushy area beside a stream and even one pheasant. This was the centre-piece of a very pleasant dinner, to which Ann kindly invited me.

The only problem was that the ancient spare hammer-gun that I was able to lend to Terry was damaged as he was getting down off a wet bank. I took it to Tralee for repairs and as I needed money I went into the Bank of Ireland to cash a cheque. I had removed the barrels and wrapped the action in paper, carrying it under my arm. Even in those innocent days it produced incipient indications of shock on the staff.

I have never hunted in my life, despite having a daughter and grand-daughters who are keen, but I am a member of the Hunting Association of Ireland, as a means of protecting field sports against those trying to kill them.

Sport is an important component of fitness training. It is also intended to provide character formation, how to deal with victory or defeat with honour. As Kipling put it, be able to look 'both these impostors in the eye'. This seems to have been lost sight of today when anybody, who scores in a football match, seems to look immediately for a clap from the crowd and when opponents are treated as enemies. Taking part no longer seems to be enough, contrary to the hope of Baron de Coubertin, founder of the modern Olympics. Football now seems to have become show-biz entertainment, echoing Juvenal's 'bread and circuses' for the masses. The circus now consists of millionaire players on the field for multi-millionaire clubs entertaining the ordinary citizens. Whatever about young footballers, however, the most annoying sight, even for someone who does not follow the game, is to see large, mature, male, cricketers hugging and dancing around after a score.

The GAA has fulfilled a very worthwhile social function, especially as a healing agent after the Civil War, despite its exclusive nationalism and attitude to 'foreign games'. Rugby and 'God Save the Queen' in Croke Park has banished lots of old ghosts. Interest in soccer seems to be booming and it allows for a more inclusive form of nationalism, more in line with Tone's hope for 'the common name of Irishman'. We continue to hope for an all-Ireland team in this sport as we have in rugby.

But the Army, however, is not simply a boy-scout organisation, offering a healthy outdoor life and the prospect of learning useful trades. All the drilling and training in physical and military skills is focused on a day that civilians prefer not to have to think about, but that recurs in this country in cycles.

For this the people have the Defence Forces as the first line of defence, the Gardai as the second and the, usually overlooked, Prison Service as the third. These organisations provide the vital national service of defence of lives and property of the Irish people, against threats from any source, external or internal. The principal threat today, to our security and democracy, even in a Europe under the *jihadi* war cloud, as in the days of which I am writing, comes from internal sources, Green and Orange.

A serious source of this political virus is the officially inspired confusion in the teaching on our 'glorious' past – the Yeatsian 'mystery play of devils and angels we call our national history'. In this we glorify militant republicanism, even when it does not seek the mandate of the people. In the 1950s it was still in its high noon. We were given doses of it from school, political platform and even from the pulpit. As a result, it is understandable how some moved to action in that direction. Even into the twenty-first century, the Irish language TV (TG4) carries on the cult in for example, its '*Seachtar na Casca*' programmes.

In contrast, our other strand of political striving, constitutional nationalism, from O'Connell, through Parnell to Redmond, was air-brushed out of the national picture for all of the twentieth century. Those honourable constitutional nationalists, who answered their elected political leader's call and volunteered for the 16th (Irish) Division to lay their lives on the line in the First World War, beside their Northern Protestant fellow Irishmen, were written off for years as traitors. The State has since made amends to their memory, with President Mary McAleese and afterwards President Michael D. Higgins, taking a high-profile lead.

Grandfather, David Goggin – the return of the Riasc Stone

My father in uniforms – 'British Indian Line' during the First World War

My father in front of Dingle Post Office –
Uncle Brendan (SECOND FROM RIGHT), *brother Colman* (SECOND FROM LEFT)

Maurice and Elizabeth Goggin – London 1929

Chief Inspector Tom Goggin, ISM, OCPD
(officer in Charge of Police District),
Kuantan, Federated Malay States, 1930s

Tim the Tiger

Tom Goggin (RIGHT)

Chief Inspector Tom Goggin, ISM, OCPD and his men in Kuantan

With my mother – the Wine Strand, west of Dingle, 1933

(BACK ROW, RIGHT) *Dingle FCA, 1949*

With my Mother, Father and cousin – c.1952

With Uncle Joe's dog – Dingle 1937

Uncle Joe fishing

Wedding – 14 September 1961

Guests (FROM LEFT) *– Lieutenants Colman Coggin, Noel Clancy, Sean McNiocal, Gerry Kenny, Brendan Smyth, Mick Gillespie, Jack Spillane and Mick Tallon*

5
Stormy Weather

a. The 1950s

In a world when Korea, Suez and Hungary made headlines, one of the big events in the 1950s at home, apart from Mr de Valera's elevation to the Presidency, was the Tostal annual festival, which we hoped would attract visitors to see the 'real Ireland'. Captain Jack Dowling, a witty source of intellectual energy, on loan from the Army, organised a St Patrick's pageant in Drogheda. The national flag was hoisted in front of the Taoiseach, Mr de Valera, and up to 10,000 people.

In the year 1956 the Irish tricolour was also raised for the first time in twenty-four years at the Olympic Games, for Ronnie Delaney's brilliant victory in the 1,500 metres. It was also the year in which we took in over 500 Hungarian refugees, who probably did not know that as a schoolboy I was on the side of the Emperor against their forefathers 'fight for freedom'.

But, in that year also, coffee time chat in the Mess took a serious turn, by then the seeds sown by politicians in their 'Anti-Partition Campaign', had sprouted in fields tilled by Christian Brothers, as yet another recrudescence of Pearsism.

It was a time of grave political ambiguity, of 'sneaking-regarders'. We had looked into the abyss, and the abyss had looked back. A TD had actually suggested that the Government should give the 'republicans fighting the common enemy' the full support of our army and police. However, the Army had a duty to make themselves absolutely clear-minded, as a prerequisite to arriving at sound 'estimates of the situation' and, as a result, taking correct decisions and issuing orders with clarity and conviction.

But nobody seemed to see anything schizoid in duty as Officer I/C the Infantry Guard on the Internment Camp one week, ensuring the incarceration of the internees, and marching down O'Connell Street on the Easter Parade on the next to honour their exemplars. Although we were nearly all constitutional nationalists then, as had been O'Connell, Parnell and Redmond, yet in our public ceremonials we genuflected at the name of Pearse, who had not sought the mandate of the people.

In the year after Ireland had been admitted to the United Nations Organisation, most had expected that our interests were at last going to be focused on the world stage, leaving behind the memories of the dramas of our history. But in 1956, for another minority, the national clock reversed, once again, to 1916. They had not gone away, their 'Easter Message' in 1957 was:

'We base our claim for the support of the Irish people throughout the world on the proclamation of 1916.'

As I saw it, the IRB conspirators in 1916 had brought a reluctant Ireland to a crossroads: 'constitutionalism' or 'physical force'? They judged constitutional nationalists, including those, who answered the call of their political leader to put their lives on the line in the hell of the First World War, as 'traitors'. I had no doubt that the current 'volunteers' saw themselves once again as the patriotic 'advanced' minority wearing their rejection by the majority as a badge of honour like Jean Genet's 'outsiders'. It seemed that Pearse's philosophy had come down through various stages to become the motivation of the newly re-awakened militant republicanism. But there appeared to be a national mental blockage, a refusal to accept that they were, in fact, the inheritors of 1916, deciding that they did not need a mandate from the people.

I have to confess to the moral cowardice of saying very little to anyone of my worries, clinging to the raft of the professional soldier and waiting for orders. My rationalisation was that there was very little I could do about it other than be considered eccentric.

For the Shia the martyrdom of Hussein at Kerbala, on the day of Ashura in 680 AD provides the ideological basis of their contemporary politics. Our Kerbala was the GPO and our day of Ashura was Easter Monday 1916. For the Shia every day is a day of Ashura and every place is Kerbala. In the 1950s for some politicians, teachers, priests and journalists, in their public voices, every day was Easter Monday and every place was the GPO.

The Shia however, have a way of disposing of my problem: of not giving voice to something that will produce no good but will cause pointless hassle. They call it '*taqiyya*' (precautionary dissimulation).

I had another reason also, which may not be understood by the younger generation ('*eheu fugaces, o tempora, o mores*') in that I had a respect for my seniors and I would have considered it very bad form to sound totally rejecting of what I took to be their dearly held views. However, I learned some years later from my father-in-law, Commandant Charles Byrne, who had served in the Free State Army, that their thinking was in no way blinkered.

As to how we came to be at this point, my hypothesis was that for the vast majority of my parent's generation, not in favour of 'physical force', some mechanism had to be found to readjust the resulting cognitive dissonance when peace returned.

With very few exceptions, the 1916-21 generation of bystanders put all doubts behind them and by unspoken mutual agreement never offended each other by any unkind reminders. It seemed that those referred to as 'the gunmen' had won and jobs and business were going to their supporters. The most popular re-alignment mechanism was, of course, the executions as shock-horror.

'Oh, I was all against them but the executions changed my mind,' they told each other, nodding.

'They were given no chance to produce evidence.'

Evidence?

'It was the long drawn out series of executions.'

Long drawn out? Fourteen men in fourteen days. In fact, the execution of conspirators, who planned with the German enemy, ('our gallant allies'), had surprised nobody. But British political short-sighted bumbling eased the slide into violence with their ill-timed negotiation immediately after the rebellion. As was said:'violence pays'.

The country remained peaceful until the 1919 provocation by Dan Breen at Soloheadbeg, getting the response as planned. Eventually the British 'police solution' bringing the undisciplined and murderous 'Black and Tans', brought international revulsion. The prolonging of the futile conscription debate in 1918 resulted in the hierarchy and the Irish Parliamentary Party taking sides with Sinn Fein, thereby legitimising them in the eyes of the ordinary people.

I have always bought any books on offer on Pearse. Agree or disagree with his decision at the time, what can never be taken from him was his honourable public stand. Pearse and his fellow poets dressed themselves in uniform and stood up to fight for what they believed. Whether or not he actually fired a weapon or personally commanded any action does not change that.

It seems that in the GPO he was getting in some people's way and Clarke suggested that someone should get him paper and a pen and let him write. He wrote some colourful, morale boosting, if somewhat fanciful, 'situation reports'. He had never considered the possibility of a 'dirty war'. In the years since, questions have been asked. Sean McDermott's name for him was 'P.O.P.'. 'Poor Old Pearse' was a truly strange man. But these stories and references to the naïve sexual innocence of some of his poetry can not detract from his essentially noble sense of self-sacrifice.

Yet he was a man who had run out of hope of borrowing any more money from institutions, friends or supporters. He saw no way of avoiding the collapse of his school and financial ruin. He told Desmond Ryan that he was not prepared to walk around Dublin 'with people pointing at him as a failure'. His hagiographer, Le Roux, quoted him also, 'By God, rather than go on living as we are, I would prefer to see Dublin in ruins.'

Inspired by Robert Emmet, whose death he said was Christ-like in its simplicity, he had nowhere to go to salvage his pride, except on the national stage with his own production in the GPO, even if

100

the script was written by Clarke and McDermott. He must be given credit however, for standing up in uniform, raising his flag and taking part in an honourable fight for his ideals. He had written himself into history and the popular imagination, overshadowing Clarke and McDermott, who gave the Rising its practical planning and Connolly who gave it its practical military expression.

In the 1950s we had another fluttering of the eyelashes of the 'terrible beauty'. The intellectual soup producing the pre-conditions for the re-creation of subversive life had contributions from many sources. The newspapers, especially the *Irish Press*, were full of the exploits of the old heroes. We saw huge arrows, worthy of divisional movements, flashing across maps in the centre pages, tracing the advance of a man on a bicycle to ambush a local policeman.

Whatever about Pearse the man, or his motives, as I saw it in the 1950s, his legacy of Pearsism was still alive. Although in a changed form, it was still essentially the Pearsist right to act.

The Pearse cult lived on. The minds of its public spokesmen placid lakes of certainty. Pearse was, and is, still being used to provide exculpatory words and a noble façade. What was offered as a noble dream in 1916 was put in chilling black and white in *An Phoblacht* in 1967, where independence won by 'parliamentary agitation' would 'do no good; for freedom to do good it must be gained with heroic sacrifice'.

Even though de Valera came into power, in my childhood, on an 'all singing, all dancing' Gaelic Romantic version of Irish history, yet, as a decent, intelligent man, he finally opened his eyes to the world of reality. He also showed how to move down the slower constitutional road in the 1930s, with his new constitution. The other road from that 1916 crossroads, we had hoped had ended. Yet dissident voices continue to be heard, despite the good work of Sinn Fein, especially Martin McGuinness in the North.

In the 1950s, once again, Eamon de Valera had no hesitation in using the Army as an instrument of the constitution. Soldiers have not got the luxury of the moral and political grey areas that academics seem to value. For journalists and historians, some doubts can be entertaining and even productive, but for soldiers it was essential to have clear minds and think the matter through to a workable conclusion. This was the cultural and intellectual background for the Army in the service of the nation in political or military contexts, for those who had to take decisions, high or ground-level, for the security of the State.

At the McGill Summer School in 2004, Dr Garret Fitzgerald said that among Northern Nationalists in the 1970s there were those 'still gripped by memories and myths of a violent past, who were prepared to throw away the gains being made by their new constitutional leaders by futile armed action designed to secure by force what was already in the process of being achieved through a combination of skilful nationalist politics and futile Unionist reaction.'

Even in the twenty-first century we get a programme from TG4, '*O Pheann an Phiarsaigh*', produced as if by someone on a hallucinogenic drugs trip, with shadowy figures, flashing lights, clashing colours and crashing sounds. Pearse described the Irish people, including presumably, between 200,000 men at home and 300,000 abroad, who volunteered to lay their lives on the line in the First World War, as being in manacles and chains, under the lash of the tyrannical oppressor. Pearse himself came across, in the programme, as someone in a severe state of manic-depression. He said of himself, that there was 'a light Pearse', who was cheerful, and 'a dark Pearse' who turned people away. James Connolly said that anyone who believed what Pearse said, about the First World War, that 'the old heart of Europe was warmed by the blood of martyrs' was 'a blithering idiot'.

Looking back over the twentieth century, is there any hope in the fact that the much derided, co-operative , democratic ideals of John Redmond have finally flowered in the Good Friday Agreement? As Dermott Meleady writes in *Redmond the Parnellite* he represents 'a more inclusive concept of the nation', 'a reconciliation of the British and Irish components of the Irish psyche'. He adapts Seamus Mallon's words and describes the Belfast Agreement as 'Redmondism for slow learners'.

There seems to be hope also in what Brian Cowan as Taoiseach told the *Journal of Cross Border Studies*, that 'we would be working the agreements we have, recognising the legitimacy of our respective traditions – one loyal to Britain, the other looking to Irish unity as a legitimate objective, but one that will be pursued peacefully by common consent.'

Are we foolish to hope that we have seen the end of the strangest revolution the world has ever seen – the 'Revolution because the People were too Content'? In Pearse's final oration in the GPO before moving to Moore Street he praised the volunteers saying: 'No man asked why.' An *Irish Times* picture of flowers left as an expression of national grief after one of the tragic acts that stained the closing years of the twentieth century, featured a card with one word:'Why?'

b. Field Exercises

With my platoon of young Dublin soldiers, for whom, up to this, Phoenix Park was 'the country', I found myself marching, and even sometimes singing in the rain, up hills and down valleys in 'Exercise Youghal'. This, I believe, was part of the State's attempt to 'show the flag' in response to the threat to national security in 1957.

It was a brigade exercise, with reinforced infantry battalions from the Eastern, Western and Southern Commands marching to a 'Brigade Concentration Area' in Youghal.

As the first large-scale exercise for the post-war Army, it was an opportunity to test the performance of soldiers, whose most extensive physical tests up to then had been short route marches or practising for the Easter Parade. On the Easter Parades, through the sheltering Dublin streets, the main hazard was the weight of the old pattern helmets pressing on foreheads. On Exercise Youghal they were faced with marching long hours in the rain over bare hills and arriving in camp soaked because they had not taken the precaution of using their waterproof groundsheets properly. These were primitive ponchos, to be worn over the shoulders during the march and under the mattress in camp.

On a recent class-reunion day we had a demonstration of the modern soldiers camouflage battledress: waterproof, bulletproof vest and radio. I was proud of the way that the men gradually learned to cope and measure up to the strain. On one night march I tried to take a Bren Light Machine Gun off the shoulder of a small, pale young soldier, who refused to part with it. I was learning myself also. The platoon was marching in ack-ack (anti-air defence) formation: the lead section on the right of the road, the next on the left after an interval and the third behind on the right again. With ack-ack intervals between the sections and the men, they stretched quite a distance. I had been walking from the front to the rear and back again, when the Sergeant, an Emergency veteran, said, 'Sir, you'll end up in the truck with the men with the gibby heels.'

'Why?'

'You've already covered the distance. You're now on your second lap.'

By the time we reached our objective I had considerably modified my performance, nonetheless I was secretly pleased that as a non-athlete I did not have to fall out for heel or feet trouble. The years of shooting over the hills West of Dingle must have paid off. Our tented homes had been taken ahead of the march by trucks and the camp was set up before we arrived at each new halt. One such camp was in the grounds of a lovely Queen Anne house in the Clonmel area, owned by an ex-Royal Navy officer, who invited the battalion officers for drinks. My problem was that I had not, at that stage, had any experience of 'drinks' beyond a glass of wine at special dinners. The CO and my Company Commander had gin so I decided to follow their example. The *bean-a-tighe* approached me and poured a large gin into my glass and came back with a carafe of lime. I decided that I had better be careful and just have a small drink so, just as the lady had poured a tiny drop of lime, I indicated, with a man-of-world gesture, that I had enough. 'Oh,' she said, with a smile: 'Here's someone who knows what he wants.'

The others registered due astonishment on hearing their young officer thus described as the makings of a hard man. The lady must have been equally surprised because after an hour of lively debate on the theatre, during which she put Joan Denise Moriarty's ballet forward as proof that not everything happened in Dublin, I was still sipping the same strong drink, finding it hard going.

Many years afterwards, I enjoyed reading David Marcus describe a similar incident in his early life on a visit to interview Edith Somerville and being entertained by Sir Neville Coghill, who offered him a drink of whiskey of which he, like myself, had had no experience. As the whiskey chugged into the glass, he eventually said 'when' as advised, but by then had more than half a tumbler. Casually refusing water, as he was not quite sure, he must have impressed Sir Neville as 'someone who knew what he wanted'.

This marked an advance (backward?) in my social life however, because even on one of our preparatory exercises for Exercise Youghal, when we camped on the grounds of Colonel Palmer's magnificent house in Rush, on his invitation for drinks I usually took tea. Both himself, ex-Irish Guards, and a retired Captain he had as a guest, both Great War veterans, came down to visit the camp every day and were very interested in the weapons and the camp layout, which was my particular pride and joy. I was saddened to see, on a visit some years afterwards that all that remained of this architectural treasure was a line of pillars. I remember one of the grounds-staff saying quietly to me, 'I never expected I'd see green uniforms playing croquet on this lawn'.

I had been sent in command of the Advance Party whose responsibility was to set up the camp and have security organised before the arrival of the main body of the Battalion. I had an adequate squad of men with an ideal NCO in charge of them. He was a corporal of about six and a half feet tall and at least a yard wide who was known as the 'Lion Tamer' because his civilian job had been with a circus. His summing up of a town would be something like, 'I never saw a good crowd at the circus there.'

We were delayed waiting for the transport and arrived later than planned at the campsite. I could see only disaster in front of us of a more serious kind than my usual. How could we possibly have the camp organised in time? The normal drill took ages of dressing the tent poles into line, then setting up the tents square with this line and hammering down all the tent pegs so that the ropes were taut. The 'Lion Tamer' had an inspiration: 'We'd never have time for that now, sir, I suggest ack-ack formation.'

The logic was inescapable so I ordered accordingly. In a short time I had selected sites for the tents in a wide circle under the trees bordering the field. I waited the arrival of the Battalion wondering how was I going to sell this idea to my CO, who had already looked on me as at least one of the nails on his personal cross for Ireland. I could only hope that my Company Commander, an experienced Captain, would sort things for me.

In fact, worse was to come for my already shaky morale. With a shower of gravel and mud flying from under the wheels of his staff car, none other than the 'War Lord' himself, the Brigade Commander, drove in the gate of the field. Worse again, while he returned my salute, and nodded at my 'air defence formation' explanation, he did not respond, but, in another whirl of mud, rocketed out the gate again.

Eventually the pipes and drums heralded the approach of the Battalion as they came marching in. I would have preferred the saints. The fact that the CO thought as little of most other officers of the battalion as he thought of me was no consolation.

I expected the worst but was taken totally by surprise when he came straight up to me and returning my salute, tried to beam, putting his stick at the 'stand easy' position. 'Excellent job,' he said, 'well done, the Second Battalion scores again.'

I was mystified until the Adjutant and my Company Commander, Captain Dick Hinchy, came over to join in the celebration.

'The War Lord has been singing your praises,' said Dick, 'you are once again one of the best officers in the Battalion,'

'For a while anyhow,' said the Adjutant.

It seems that the 5th Battalion were setting up their tents in the proper drill manner when the Brigade Commander visited them on his way out to us. On his return, he asked if they were setting up a summer holiday camp and suggested that they go and look at the 2nd Battalion's tactical layout.

One of our stops on Exercise Youghal was outside Ballyporeen. We visited a pub in the village and the officers were invited into a parlour with a green cloth over a table. The bar outside was full of soldiers. At eleven o'clock came the dramatic appearance of the local Garda Sergeant at the door. The soldiers stopped singing in the bar and the officers stopped arguing in the back room. I was now on my first bottles of Guinness having discovered it to be a pleasant beverage worthy of our national pride. For a battalion in the middle of an extensive exercise to end up in court as being 'found on' after closing time, would be disastrous.

For a few frozen moments, as the Sergeant filled the doorway, I could not help thinking of him as 'the civil power' to whose aid we were to be called in this national emergency. He smiled and took off his cap, a gesture understood by all soldiers, so, as he came to join us in 'the room', the singing resumed.

The following morning, at the 06.30 hours reveille, I was introduced to Mr Morning After for the first time, but luckily in a reasonable form. The few bottles of Guinness I had would not have too much effect on anybody, even the uninitiated. Leaving my tent in the morning mist, I went to the platoon lines to find the Platoon Sergeant roaring about getting on parade. My warriors were looking even worse than myself which restored me somewhat, but I think that they all, and indeed, their somewhat fragile Platoon Commander wished that the Sergeant was not so Roman Legionary rock-like healthy and loud.

The Battalion set off at a quick marching pace under a dark and sullen sky, over the bleak Knockmealdowns. We passed the pub but the hospitality of the ladies of the house and our snug comfort of the night before was now only a memory in the cutting wind-borne rain. The weather cleared somewhat eventually. The retreating rain front darkened the hills in its path, though, as we passed, a whitewashed cottage stood in a pale green field in the centre of a brilliantly lit patch of ground as a sunbeam broke through a gap in the clouds. A little girl came to the door and then went back in. I thought I knew what she was thinking: 'It's only a sun-shower.' But the moving cloud quickly swallowed up the vision and like *Tir-na-nOg* it vanished into the dirty grey landscape.

The sun finally settled for the final stages of the exercise but the most tiring section of the whole march was the last lap through Youghal to our final canvas home in the Brigade Concentration Area. We picked ourselves up as usual with the arrival of the pipe band and swung into the camp with something approaching élan. Swimming parades brightened the programme for the following week.

I had come a long way from my first exercise in the grounds of Russborough House, the eighteenth-century Palladian mansion, bought by Sir Alfred and Lady Beit some years earlier to house their famous art collection. One day, as I lay in my bulls-wool battledress in the sun with my platoon, Captain Hugh O'Donnell-Keenan called to me, thinking that I was a recruit: 'Hey, young lad, could you bring up a bucket of water'.

At lunch in the mess tent in Youghal, one sunny day, a dispatch rider arrived from Battalion HQ. The DR pulled up with an impressive flourish and handed his despatch to the Adjutant. It was an order appointing me as Company Commander, B Company, 2 Inf Bn. I was thrilled skinny, to be taking over a company as a lieutenant, as companies were commanded by captains in those days (later commandants), until one of the mess staff said, 'You'll be taking over mainly floorboards, sir.'

He was right. As I found on return to barracks, it was an empty company with a Company Quartermaster Sergeant, a small staff and almost empty stores.

I do not know what effect our exercise had on the people of the towns and villages through which we marched. As was asked of the Volunteers two centuries earlier, 'Were our drums more sleep-disturbing than spirit-stirring?'

But I think it had a very good effect on the morale of the Army to be taking to the field again. Singing only happens on close order marching and there was not a lot of that but, when there was, the usual medley of tunes surfaced: 'On the long road, maybe the wrong road, on the road to God knows where', interspersed with ragged whistled 'Tipperary' and 'Lily Marlene'.

This was the biggest exercise since the Emergency. Some veterans of the 1942 manoeuvres, who had not been on this one repaid our joke of wringing the Blackwater out of our tunics by regular enquiries as to whether we had all the sand out of our pockets, referring to the swimming parades. I found that beetles and similar denizens of the open country seemed very natural in that setting and were not at all objectionable around our tents.

When I unrolled my canvas valise (presented to me by our ex-BQMS) back in my room in the Mess, a familiar black scuttling shape came marching from its folds. I carefully lifted him up on a sheet of paper and brought him out to the lawn. I felt he deserved that respect. Like Hannibal's mule he had come through the campaign.

Before going on the exercise I had been given an extra responsibility as a Recruiting Officer for the barracks. I had formed some ideas on the march from casual chats with my young soldiers as to how or why they had joined the Army. On our return I put them in a memo to someone that I described as the 'Chief Recruiting Officer, AHQ', not knowing then that he was none other than the Adjutant General. We were anxious to build up the strength of the Army at that time and my idea was to have a recruiting office in O'Connell Street rather than behind the barrack gates, which many would find off-putting. It would have a 'jildy' staff, flags, photographs, etc. I was amused to hear some years later that my hand-written letter of suggestions was produced to a class on an 'A' Administration Course by the Deputy AG.

On one occasion I received letters from a superintendent of the Garda, a parish priest and a TD, to request me to re-consider a boy I had refused enlistment. He had been involved in minor housebreaking and given the benefit of the Probation Act. My reasoning initially was that one bad apple in a billet could influence others and when an enquiry came from the Minister's Office I replied accordingly. But after some further communications I decided to give him a chance. If he was so keen to be a soldier that he went to all that trouble and if so many people seemed to believe in him, he deserved it. I hope he eventually did well in his army career.

c. Internment

One of the more serious responses to the threat to security was the opening of the Internment Camp at Hare Park in the Curragh in 1957, when de Valera had come back in power. On dark and damp winter nights, on occasional duty as Officer I/C the Infantry Guard, I did the rounds checking sentries at the Internment Camp, carrying a revolver in a webbing belt outside my greatcoat. About 120 internees were snug in their huts. As the lights came on around the camp at night, highlighting the four elevated sentry posts at the corners, rising out of the wispy mists, it symbolised for me the ongoing vigilance of society for its security. I felt that the scene could have been anywhere in Europe. Outside the first two wire fences, in order to prevent tunnelling, there was a deep trench, in which were trip wires and flares. There were three other wire obstacles between that and freedom, making a total of five.

This was not the first time such camps were in use. During the Emergency, while the State prepared to face external threats, internal security posed an immediate problem. Even before the Magazine Fort Raid in December 1939, there was a bombing campaign in England and even a small explosion in Tralee near where the son of the British Prime Minister was staying. De Valera expressed sincere regrets. The *Dáil* passed the 'Offences Against the State Act', which provided for the setting up of the Special Criminal Court of five army officers, and, under parts V and V1, internment. The known wish of the IRA for a German link-up tied any threat to one of the major external ones. There were about 600 interned.

Mr Deasun Brethnach, writing in *The Irish Times* fifty years afterwards, informed us that 'the IRA offered to defend Irish neutrality', but added that 'their offer was rejected and their volunteers interned'. The internees were a lot more comfortable in the late fifties than their predecessors of the forties, but we were just as cold and uncomfortable as our comrades had ever been.

Nonetheless, as much as we would wish to have been somewhere else, we understood that it was a response to the assessed threat to the security of the State. Yet we could find ourselves marching down O'Connell Street on the Easter Parade on the following week as part of the same State's doffing its cap to the men in whose name the internees would claim that they were acting.

We all knew that any internee could walk out by simply signing a paper to the effect that he would not endanger the State. As expected, the usual people argued that this would be 'unacceptable to innocent men'. I read that Mr Labhras O'Murchu, who had set up *Cumann an Phiarsaigh* 'dedicated to the ideals of Patrick Pearse', was one of our guests at the time. He told an interviewer that this was for 'his refusal to account for his whereabouts as a matter of principle'.

There was a family story that I liked that – an uncle of mine had been arrested for drilling in the early years of the century, I assumed he was one of those who had emigrated to America. This was, I thought, to balance my father and Uncle Tom, but, however, there was never any corroborating evidence. It was a different time, but what would it have been like if he were now on the other side of the wire?

On my first duty there, I think I may have had some rather naïve idea that I might get the opportunity to listen to their views and put the other side to them but the Infantry Guard had no contact with the internees. The duty at the camp was mind-numbingly boring for the Officer I/C the Infantry Guard, so I wrote reports about the security of the camp as seen by me.

I remember a hedge that came close to the wire on one side being the subject of one but, when I met one of the Military Police officers, he did not mention it.

'Fuck this for a game of soldiers.'

'What a bore.'

We comforted each other, yet each happy in our own way: I was going off duty, back to town, in the morning, and he was in receipt of the special '*per diem*'.

Nobody seemed to expect any serious attempt at escape and it was believed that senior internees, who were in command, were sensibly against it. Yet it should have been anticipated that within the camp there was a strong escape lobby. We now know that some of the senior internees had the same ideas as ourselves in that they did not want to do anything that meant a pointless risk to lives in that situation. Yet the escape lobby prevailed.

The Military Police Corps ran the camp and there was a strict rule about having no weapons within the central hutted area, as the normal method of obtaining arms for a breakout is by overpowering or holding a guard as hostage. Military Police, under the control of a Provost Marshal, like the poor, have always been with us. The office of Provost Marshal was created by Charles I.

'*The Provost must have a horse allowed him and all the rest commanded to obey him, for he is one man and must correct many and therefore he cannot be beloved.*'

Charles was shrewd enough about the failure to be 'beloved' but all armies accept the unavoidable necessity for the enforcement of discipline, the regulation of refugees and POWs and the insistence on standards of dress and deportment. They have served in most of our UN overseas missions and in 1997 a company was detailed for duty under NATO command in Bosnia. They shared the boring duty with us in the Internment Camp in the 1950s as well as the frustration of our sense of order, (perhaps like the senior internees?) when the 'breakaway' group of prisoners literally broke away. They cut through the wire with home-made wire cutters and called the bluff of the sentries who did not fire on them. A Military Police guard fired some revolver shots. It must have been mostly over their heads as there were no wounds other than some cuts by the wire and the tin of some gas grenades as they got away.

We now know, from the archives, that they had the same problem in the North even in the late 1970s. The prison authorities believed that the 'presence of armed soldiers in the watchtowers' was 'the decisive psychological factor in deterring a mass escape' but the army disagreed, saying that the law demanded 'reasonable force' which could be argued in court. However, this was at a time of the incompetent, one-sided use of internment in the North in the 1970s, based on extremely thin intelligence, when innocent men were arrested and forced to contemplate 'other means'. Eventually Ruairi O Bradaigh, Chief of Staff of the IRA, in the early 1960s, took the good decision to end the Border campaign and ordered that the arms be dumped.

With the imminent ending of the campaign in the North the camp was closed to the relief of those inside and outside. As I was escaping from the camp duty back to town in the morning, I, as usual, looked back at the wire and wondered, why has there always to be a line in Ireland, ever since the days of old, of the 'kings in opposition'? Irishmen looking across a line at each other, as in the madness of the Civil War, both sides convinced that they were right. I wondered if it was that all Irishmen feel vastly superior to all other Irishmen? However, as Kevin O'Higgins once commented: '*Salus populi suprema lex.*'

d. A Career Asset

At coffee one morning in the Mess, I was sitting beside Alan, a Protestant officer. We laughed again over the day that I had arrived somewhat late with the new guard at Government Buildings and advised him, 'No problem, you'll have no difficulty in getting Mass in Rathmines.'

'You know,' he said now, looking serious, 'you're a gas man, you could use your ability with Gaelic to score, like some others. It's currently a career asset.'

He was right. Some had already displayed the necessary enthusiasm. It paid. He was reminding me that I had indicated some doubts at a recent briefing about this new development, on the use of Irish in the Army. As well as internment and the military exercises to show the flag territorially, in 1958 Kevin Boland, Minister for Defence, seems to have decided that it would be an equally good idea to show the flag in its cultural mode, presumably to reclaim the 'green' high ground from militant 'patriots'.

The instrument for this was to be us, the Army, which was to be re-created as a totally Irish-speaking organisation. The Military College was identified as 'vital ground' and a team was detailed to re-cast it as the driving engine of the operation. Captain Padraig O'Siochru recollects how he was sent to 'translate, teach and help Gaelicise the Military College'. This was carried out despite the fact that tests had demonstrated that a lesson period that was intended to carry ten learning points could only succeed in getting eight of those points across in the same time through the medium of Irish.

I did not feel comfortable with the idea of the Gaelicisation of the Army. I had a feeling of disquiet about the way the Army was being used. What about the fact that the bulk of our outside training was in the UK or the USA, through the medium of English?

On the broad national front, I worried about how compulsory Irish made the idea of a United Ireland seem a somewhat cold house for our English-speaking Northern fellow-Irish. Specifically, if that day ever comes, will the Northern Protestant/Unionists be happy to join an Army that was an Irish-speaking subculture?

I had always believed that the Irish language was used by career *gaelgoiri* as a professional and political point-scorer, backed by the strong Irish language lobby organisations: *Connradh na Gaeilge*, *Comhdhail Naisiunta na Gaeilge* and *Foras na Gaeilge*.

I have never believed that it would return as the every-day language of the people. In a poll, in the Republic (Ipsos MRBI, 2012), 79% said that they can 'speak very little' or 'cannot speak Irish at all'. When asked if they 'would like to see it revived as the main language', 61% said 'no'.

We have two languages, a national and an international one. I speak and love the Irish language and treasure it as a gateway to the land of our forefathers. However, the sovereign people have voted with their tongues to retain the international language that now allows them to listen to, for instance, the Presidents of Afghanistan, Pakistan and the USA on TV, or read reports in the papers, of their discussions on matters of importance to our security. The most widely spoken second language in the world, it also allows them to visit or emigrate and fit in to a variety of countries from the USA to Australia. After the national tragedy of the famine opened our eyes to the big world outside our shores, the Irish people took the democratic decision, as individuals, to learn and speak English. Contrary to some *gaelgoir* lecturers they were not beaten or forced into this by some Brit bogeymen. By 1850 the change had started.

None of the national plans for 'the restoration of the language' as 'a principal national aim' have worked. Tons of paper have been printed with translations of official documents in Irish to be read by a person or persons unknown. All this at great expense with money badly needed elsewhere. One large national training organisation (FAS), when asked about its annual report for 2009 being four months late, gave one reason as the necessity for translation into Irish. The only answer to this in a State where everybody understands English, and almost everybody speaks it, seems to be a constitutional referendum to amend *Acht na d'Teangacha Oifigiula,* changing the status of the two languages to one of equality.

The other idea floated by *gaelgoiri* is that the best hope for an Irish-speaking State is education through the medium of Irish. But as I wrote of my school-days, despite doing all our subjects through Irish, for six years, I never heard any students exchange even a few words in Irish, in jest or in earnest, once we stepped outside the school gate. Moderate *gaelgoiri* talk of bilingualism as an achievable objective. The problem with that is that that is a stage to be gone through when people are either moving into a new language or moving away from an old one. We are long past the moving away stage and there is no sign of many people wanting to move on to Irish as their everyday language.

My first serious encounter with this new idea was when I had to return to the Military College, this time to the Infantry School, for my six months 'Standard Infantry Course', for lieutenants hoping for promotion to captain. It was enjoyable to be working and living with some of the cadet class again after seven years experience in our units. We faced tests on the ground, company and battalion tactics, but, this time, on occasions, after a late night party, not as fit as our cadet selves, isolated from families and civilian friends, back again in our little rooms.

We all did our best to learn and get past this latest hurdle which was a stepping-stone to promotion to the rank of captain, command of an infantry company and appointments as battalion staff officers. It was also a means of the general broadening of our professional knowledge. As well as tests and exercises of attack and defence on the ground, by day and by night, we also had to prepare papers and talks on operations of war and once again I returned to the regimental histories of the Irish soldiers in other armies (the French, American and British) who had earned us a reputation as an honourable fighting race.

This was also my chance to use my 'career asset' as advised by Alan, even though my Irish was of the school, '*Cuirt an Mhean Oiche*' type. I never felt that it suited the military subject matter, which wore it as an ill-fitting hand-me-down. Military science needs a terminology to convey its meaning, with clarity, brevity and vigour, in unambiguous terms that are understood by all. However, soldiers learn to speak in acronyms very early in their careers, and, perhaps it probably did not matter whether we referred to 'TICs' (*Tull Ionaid Cosanta*) rather than the familiar 'FDLs' (Forward Defended Locality).

Yet we were then at a more advanced stage of our military education and the real difficulty arose in the discussion periods. People stuttered over a combination of *Cead Cath* Irish ('*chuadhas ar wheekend ar mo bhicycle*') and our newly acquired terminology.

Two years before I was born, the question of teaching through Irish in University College Galway was discussed in the *Dáil*. Professor Michael Tierney of UCD described it as 'little short of humbug', saying that, 'I have grave doubts whether any man is capable of delivering a full course of university lectures in Irish. I do not care how fluently he may speak the language.'

My competence, such as it was, meant that I was one of a minority in the class. Most had attended schools where Irish did not have a central position. Some of my classmates had to go in their maturity to the *Gaeltacht* with school-children, to acquire the necessary language skill for the course.

Our public speaking exercises then were, of course, in Irish. I was detailed to give a talk in Irish on 'Self-respect as a Determinant of Morale'. My main message was the difficulty of maintaining self-respect while stumbling along in a language unsuited to our professional requirements. I quoted College doctrine:*'The principal characteristic of a properly formulated objective is that it be within the capability of the unit'*.

I claimed that as a class we were given the objective of conducting our work and discussions through the medium of Irish but were obviously not capable of doing that, unless we confined the subject matter to our *laeannta saoire* or the weather. I explained that I found it particularly discouraging to see grown men attempting to make pseudo-conversation in Irish with the College Staff. I believed that what was bad enough as schoolboys under the Christian Brothers' ethos was intolerable as soldiers. I wondered if my ideas would be badly received but, in fact, I was given extra time to elaborate by the Lieut.-Colonel in charge of the exercise.

The Minister gilded the lily of the Gaelicisation by the introduction of a 'G' Badge for those with a certain level of competence in the language, mainly officers because they could only locate seven NCOs with a competence to instruct through 'the medium'. The 'G 'was an Irish G in Gaelic script (i.e. a 'Ge') and it was to be worn along with the 'Fainne', the Irish speakers' badge. I loathed the idea of civilian 'badges' on a military uniform so I did what the vast majority of recipients did: I lost my 'G' and found myself too busy to apply for a new one. It could be a distortion of perception but I was under the impression that the only officers, who retained their 'G'badges also had the *Fainne* and the pioneer pin in line. The story goes that a visiting French officer was told that the *Fainne* was for not speaking English and the pioneer pin for not drinking alcohol. On offering a cigarette and, being told that the officer did not smoke, the visitor is reported to have asked if the '*G*' Badges were for that.

Today, when we seem at last to have a glimmer of hope that John Hume's 'Agreed Ireland' might one day come about, we must move on from the egregious use of the Irish language as a political point scorer. Like those who used to address the Assembly in the North in Irish knowing that it was not understood by the majority of those present, presumably conveying the message: 'I am Irish, you are foreigners'. We always liked to remember that the Normans became '*hibernior hiberniores ipsos*', but now we have native Irish trying to pretend that they are 'more Irish than the Irish themselves'.

An Coimisineir Teanga threatened to bring an adverse report before both Houses of the Oireachtas on the crime by the HSE of publishing swine flu warnings in hospitals and ports in English.

I see pretence and bullying as the main enemies of the language. The pretence that it is necessary to publish documents in both languages and the bullying like Mr O'Cuiv trying to bully the people of the old town of Dingle into accepting the non-name of *an Daingean.* It is not possible to cycle for any great distance in Ireland and not have to go through a few Daingeans.

Dingle, an old walled town in the Middle Ages, with a wine trade with Spain and Portugal, still has crests over the doors of some of the older houses to remind us. The people of the town like the Irish form of the name – *Daingean Ui Chuis* – but want it to be referred to as the old name of Dingle. The researchers for the Kerry Placenames Archive discovered the name 'Dingell de Couche' in documents of a local merchant dated 1500. Politely, as is their wont, the people of Dingle woke him up, by voting over 90% against his plan. The name Dingle had been painted over in 2005 in accordance with the Place-names Order of the Official Languages Act, but it now has to be restored at a cost of €10,000.00 to the Kerry County Council.

e. God's Army

We had the Chaplain to talk to us once a week for the duration of the course and he did his best to answer questions that were starting to disturb the complacent *status quo* of the Catholic *magisterium*. He obviously had worked very hard to produce a talk for us on the question of birth control, and we appreciated his effort. On sitting back with obvious relief when he was finished, he asked, 'Any questions?'

'Yes, Father,' came one either sleepy or mischievous response, 'is it a sin not to pay your income tax?'

We tried to obey the laws of the Church, but there were new doubts floating in the air that perhaps produced that silly question as a cover. Whereas we generally saw the Ten Commandments as an excellent life plan, nonetheless, we were members of a Church that preached charity as the greatest of its commandments, yet all around us it seemed to offer merely unyielding judgementalism. The clergy were the Church and owned the Church. The rest of us were just about tolerated. Every man in black was a walking infallible little Pope, who one dared not question. Yet, when it came to the impenetrable mystery of God, the priest with his years of theology reminded us of the story of two men looking at the moon, one standing on an orange box.

I believe in God on the evidence of creation. I do not accept the explanation of accident. I find it impossible to believe that the forces that seeded the universe, gravity, magnetism and nuclear, simply popped into existence out of empty space by accident. Mr Accident has made many godlike decisions. How come that, by accident, as well as man, strong animals like horses, oxen and elephants were created to do the heavy work without which man could not have progressed? How come, of course, by sheer accident, plants as food for man and animals came also, and equally accidental, trees that gave shelter, fire and tools to primitive man? How come by accident four million years ago, a member of the ape family had an accidental change and then so many other accidental changes that he ended up writing the plays of Shakespeare and painting

119

the ceiling of the Sistine Chapel. All this while the rest of the ape family went on down the millennia with no more accidents?

I also consider as further evidence, the existence of 'conscience', the clear awareness of right and wrong, which everybody has, that is a quantum leap above the Dawkins' concept of altruistic behaviour, which is merely intended to ensure that the individual seen to be helpful is helped in return. All organisms are supposed to do things that improve them but conscience tells us that a certain act, like stealing something, which could be helpful to us, is simply wrong. A team of psychologists at the infant cognition centre at Yale University have established that this is not merely a faculty that is simply shaped by the accident of the individual social environment. The research suggests that they may be born with the ability to tell good from bad hard-wired into their brains.

When the crimes then secretly being committed in the Industrial Schools, eventually came to light, we were all shocked. This was very sad as we remember the good priests, wise and witty men we all knew, like Fr Fergal O'Connor and Father Des Connell, two of the most interesting, open-minded and helpful lecturers in UCD. Yet we were all part of the system. We all collaborated. We all knew. I had been informed in the 1940s by a boy who had experienced the beatings in one of those God forsaken hell-holes of Industrial Schools. I just took it as 'the sort of thing that happened in those places' and told nobody. Punishment and humiliation were part of our theology of atonement. The savage women (nuns!), who would call young girls 'out to the landing' for midnight beatings, probably felt that they were doing God's work. They seem so utterly different to the kind nuns of my early youth.

Also, as a child, I was sent by a Brother up to the house of a boy to get him to come down to the school, from where he was to be taken to some other school in Tralee. I thought that this was a great chance for him and he came willingly only to be met by a garda in a car and taken off. I often wondered had I been partly responsible for any misery he might have endured.

In later years the powerful ideas of Pearsism, religion and their bridge of 'Irish Culture' meshed in the person of Cardinal O'Fiach who, in an earlier life, led the breaking up of a meeting of the Language Freedom Movement. His contributions to the public debate, especially during the hunger strikes in the North, caused me to think deeply. Apart from a one-time rant from Dr Paisley, how come so many of the senior Protestant clergy were saying all the right things that I as a Christian expected and some of ours were so wide of the mark, so often? My comment would be 'a plague on both their houses' for not being able to sort the Christian family between them ecumenically. I do not know which side is more to blame, in their apparently never-ending competition for 'best Christian'.

One of the puzzles of contemporary Ireland is the extraordinary amount of coverage in our media of priests who err in the area of human sexual relations in comparison with the almost casual reference to some priests who seem to be actively breaking the law. Apart from the 'fellow travellers', who simply offer verbal support, we have read of one who tried to smuggle parts for bomb timers into the country. All disposed of in a few casual paragraphs of simple factual reportage: no outraged comment, no 'shock horror'.

Other questions also swim in and out of our minds, rarely asked, afraid that they sound like 'what is the stars, Joxer?' like 'what is Heaven?' Is it a place with gravity or do all pure spirits float around like a swarm of bees? Or, in an eighty billion light years long universe could it be a planet in another galaxy?

Are these some of the reasons that dark-haired twenty to forty year old men seem so scarce at Mass, in a sea of grey-haired men and women? Perhaps as an ex-Adjutant, I seem to find myself checking the 'parade state' every Sunday. We are now told that only 2% of people in certain areas attend Mass on Sundays and nationally less than one in five. The Church seems to need now more men like Bishop Willie Walsh who are prepared to talk in normal tones and words about these mysteries, admitting the occasional difficulties in belief and re-affirming the primacy of conscience.

The church must speak to us as adults.

f. Border Patrol

On my first tour of duty as Officer I/C the Infantry Guard at Government Buildings, I wanted to see the *Dáil* in action. That place of infinite drama, my father seemed to think, as he read snippets from the *Irish Press* to a family that barely paused in its unending consideration of 'what is the stars'? In those days regimental duty was performed in breeches, knee-high leggings and boots, armed with a service revolver in a holster on the Sam Browne belt. Thus attired, I was halfway up the back stairs to the *Dáil* Visitor's Gallery when the Garda Sergeant came pounding after me.

'Oh jaysus sir, you'll scatter them. You can't go in to the House armed. Give me that and I'll keep it 'til you come down.'

'Sorry, Sergeant', I said, 'I did not think it important,' handing him my revolver.

'Oh its important all right, people have been afraid of that for the last half-century.'

The nightmare of armed subversion of our democracy was never totally out of the nation's mind, but, in fact, people need not have been afraid of an Army that had widespread democratic support in this State in the Civil War and during the Second World War.

The Army has been acknowledged in international studies on the survival of democracies, as being one of the principal 'intermediate groups' that sustain the health of the Irish democracy. The key decision here was taken when the Free State Army, as they said, decided to 'salute them rather than shoot them' on the hand-over to Fianna Fáil ministers in the early 1930s. I'm sure that my father must have been delighted, but nobody asked me for my views on the matter in my pram.

However, in the depressed 1950s, with a thousand a week heading for places like Cricklewood, the forces of discontent were gathering strength. An IRA Army Convention decided that, as presumably, they were just as entitled as the men of 1916 to act without a mandate from the people, now was, once again, a time for action. A 'General Directive for a Guerilla Campaign', was issued, hence 'Operation Harvest' was to commence in November 1956. However, a rival group had attacked some border posts so action was postponed until 12 December.

At a Government meeting with the Army and Garda, decisions were taken as to what I (and, of course, others) would have to do to deal with the threat to national security. Showing the flag on large-scale exercises, demonstrating the commendable tone of our 'greenness' on the language question, even interning some to keep them and us out of trouble, did not seem to be enough. We had to be seen on the ground and that was principally on the Border.

Detailed for Border Patrol I reported for duty to Dundalk Military Barracks from where we would cover our assigned stretch of the operational area. We were there in 'aid of the civil power' and military and constitutional law came to life for me with the forms signed by the local Garda requesting patrols that would not otherwise leave Barracks. It was a rare experience in peacetime to be part of an Infantry Company in our own little republic: a captain, company commander, three lieutenants, platoon commanders, and over one hundred NCOs and men. The Officers' Mess in this border barracks had fallen into decay because nobody seemed to think that it would be ever used again after the Emergency, so we had to live in a makeshift Mess.

The men also lived in a confined space. I became aware of their feeling of confinement behind the high perimeter wall. As cut off from the outside world during their duty hours as any French Foreign Legionnaires in a desert fort. Soldiers on sentry duty seemed to move like zombies knowing that nobody would see them. There were not even the usual comings and goings, as in the barracks in Dublin, to keep them interested. Also, as our belief about the men was 'leave them alone, life is miserable enough as it is', they were not checked on as often as they would normally be.

I came to the conclusion, however, that the opposite should be the case i.e. visiting sentries reasonably often, as Barrack Orderly Officer, and even drawing attention to the performance of drill, could break the mind-numbing monotony and give them a focus for their unhappiness, even if it was only me. I considered this to be a constructive use of 'bull', and I had reason to believe that my approach broke the spell of the blank wall syndrome. I thought that after a while they looked more alert and alive and that hands snapped on the rifle butts in a much sharper fashion.

At the start of any exercise in the Military College there was always the 'foreword' on the 'General Situation' in which the attack or defence exercise was to take place. It was, of course, an imaginary situation with perhaps a para-landing by 'Red-land Forces' on one of our airfields, listing the available intelligence indications. The exercise took shape in that context.

On the Border we all knew the 'General Situation'. These were not invented 'Red-land' invaders from some hostile external source. They were from our own internal ideological Green and Orange wastelands: a no-go area neglected by the forces of democracy but cultivated by 'patriotic' writers on both sides, some biased historians and politicians.

But how much blame could we apply to the Green side if they were a product of the ambivalent political, media and educational, Ireland of the time and if they were responding to the perceived repression in the North? It was a depressing time, and, very much in the foreground of the reports and stories were dust-covered bodies, like that of an RUC Sergeant, father of three, at Coalisland. Even though it seems that the RUC had been used from time to time as an instrument of political, sectarian aggression, the horror of those scenes remained.

On patrol with the moon 'looking down on the nothing new' on long winding grey ribbons of dark-hedged roads, I often used to wonder. Why was the 'Orb'd Maiden with white fire laden' so associated in this country with death, 'at the rising of the moon', rather than being the gentle scene setter for romance?

Night patrols went out at 20.00 hours and returned at 03.00 hours, in our case up the Monaghan salient, passing through moonlit towns and sleeping villages, in a very different mode from Exercise Youghal.

Having inspected men and weapons on the square before boarding the Rovers, I would issue patrol orders, telling where we were going and why, warning them to be alert for any potentially dangerous situation. I would remind them of the various drills in response. And yet, on one occasion as we were getting underway on a night patrol I heard a young soldier ask the sergeant:

'Sarge, if these hoors fire at us I suppose we can fire back?'

'You'd better have no bucken doubt about it, boy, if you don't want to hear the Bugler Walsh blowing a tune over you.'

Despite my warning, that soldier was not asking a foolish question. He was simply echoing the perceived ambiguity of the time. We were aware of IRA 'Army Order No 8' not to shoot at Irish soldiers or Gardai. Yet it has happened. Some will react in different ways to situations, regardless of policy.

I led a patrol once as part of our operations in the Greenore area and was surprised that our activities were reported, I do not know how or why. *The Irish Times*, reported: 'Military unit visits Carlingford area.'

'A fully armed mobile military unit, accompanied by Civic Guards, visited Greenore, Co Louth, and other areas of Carlingford Lough. Reports say that the unit seems to be reconnoitring the area rather than patrolling it.

It was the first time in recent years that a military unit has been seen in daylight in the area, although units are known to have been in the district patrolling the area after dark.'

On what I took to be yet another routine patrol, the seriousness of our national responsibility was illustrated for me when the road ran out and open country lay ahead. The senior officer of the garda group accompanying us handed over to the military (me) by signing a paper on the bonnet of the land-rover.

I hoped that this *Irish Times* report, a small light on our activities, would go some little way to counteract a widespread view that the Army was really doing nothing. This view was cultivated by the unholy coincidence of requirements by two opposing positions: the prejudiced British/ Unionist and the remaining 'sneaking-regarders' in the Irish political and media establishments. Nicky Curtis, a British Liaison Intelligence NCO, refers in *Faith and Duty* to the 'blind eye' on the Southern side.

Eunan O'Halpin, in his excellent book, *Defending Ireland,* refers to the other British 'canard' about the untrustworthiness of the soldiers on border duty, on the ground that they were locally recruited and therefore were in danger of being undermined by republicans. In my experience the 2nd Eastern Battalion from Dublin took over duties from the 4th Southern Battalion from Cork. Units from Limerick and Galway also completed tours of duty.

The disastrous attack on Brookeborough RUC Barracks, on New Year's Day, 1957, where an RUC man was killed as well as two young IRA men, 20 year old Fergal O'Hanlon and Sean South, added to the emotional swell around the country as the funerals passed through.

However, after his return, de Valera made it clear that there was no longer any doubt about the national policy, when Part 2 of the Offences against the State Act was invoked, bringing internment.

Yet, even then, hope was still alive that the first step to a solution, to an 'Agreed Ireland', could be taken, as it was eventually in the Good Friday Agreement. There were high hopes then that if this campaign ended we could move forward on to solid ground from the bog of history. We were not to know that it would take the rest of the century, for a Martin McGuinness to emerge and get the right response.

Over a reflective pint in the Imperial Hotel the following night with the Captain, he reminded me that, in times like then, things can turn nasty for no great reason. Having got used to the routine at that stage, it was a sobering thought, that all that was ever necessary was for just one, who could be in any organisation or none, who could look on us in our green uniforms, of which we were proud, as 'the enemy'? The Imperial was our main escape from the monotony of the barracks except for one occasion when the good lady of the Ballymacscanlon Hotel sent an invitation for an officer of the garrison to a party. It was decided that I would be a reasonable representative, but the problem was that I still had to do my full share of patrols. There were too few of us to allow me off. This meant doing my day patrols and also a night patrol in between so that by the night of the party I was sleepwalking, as the soldier driver carefully deposited me at the door.

It was a very pleasant welcome and I expressed my appreciation to the lady of the house over a few beakers. She introduced me to some of the guests and I had a most enjoyable time being thanked for maintaining law and order. Singing started after some time and I joined various groups but gradually began to notice that my uniform was now attracting a different comment, like:'We'll be over the border with you whenever we get the word'.

I had moved in a matter of a few yards and a few hours to a different Ireland. I decided that it was time to retreat before the situation became even more entertaining.

I did tours of border duty also in an old Militia Barracks in Cavan where I got a brace of woodcock sent from home. The caretaker remarked that he had heard his father talking about birds like that arriving in the barracks 'in the old days', so he offered to prepare them for us and we had them cooked in wine to cheer us up by adding an extra little taste at dinner. Our quarters in Cavan were pretty grim. I remember being in bed after a night patrol on more than one occasion when I became aware that visiting officers from GHQ were looking around to 'see what they could do'. I assumed, from the lack of follow-up action that the answer was 'nothing'. Our entertainment as usual was in the local hotel bar, which we could visit in twos at a time. Was it there that I repeated my dreadful joke for a barmaid called Rosie, based on a then current radio ad: 'Eat Galtee cheese and feel rosy all over'?

I had enjoyed the occasional chat in the Mess with Captain Seamus Kelly, who had served during the Emergency. On re-reading his piece, writing as Quidnunc, in 'An Irishman's Diary' in *The Irish Times*, giving his review of the 1950s decade, he mentioned Mr de Valera's elevation to the presidency and Mr Lemass's succession as Taoiseach. I noted his comment on Operation Harvest and the Army's response was simply to ignore it.

6
Military Lowlife

a. Military Theatre

Back in barracks, from our position on the square on morning parade we saw that we had a new CO. We saw Lieut.-Col. Tom Gunne sitting in his office reading the paper. We knew that we had a new CO. We soon discovered that he was the kind of CO, who would be told all he needed to know, even if it was a personal embarrassment for the officer concerned. I always remember him with affection and respect. Until his unfortunate blindness before he died at a late age he would walk to the Club (the United Arts Club to which he introduced me) and stand ram-rod straight at the bar, tall, clipped moustache, impressive appearance, easily commanding the attention of the company. We had colonels and generals among those who served the full term in my own cadet class, who were on first name terms with the 'civilian' members. But even twenty years afterwards, I never addressed Tom Gunne as anything other than 'Colonel' regardless of the lateness of the hour or the heat of the argument.

One aspect of his history sums him up. He was the Irish officer who took over Dublin Castle from the British and remained friendly ever afterwards with the British Captain, with whom he exchanged visits. They were at a first night at an opera when the Captain complained of a 'cold shoulder'. Tom gave him his dress uniform cloak as a memento of their combined contribution to history.

My own contribution remained fairly low level as I put on a show for the men in the canteen, which included a pair of young 'starter' dancing girls as one of the acts. Soldiers attended Barrack Shows more hoping to be surprised than in the expectation of great entertainment. At least it would pass the time until the sun was sufficiently under the yardarm for a few jars. The usual very earnest singers were politely listened to and a dinner-jacketed, middle-aged, 'soft shoe' man was allowed to perform before the closed eyes of the warriors. A comedian told them jokes they had heard as recruits.

Eventually my two youthful smiling hopefuls (who did well in variety shows afterwards) came on and woke up the somnolent audience. The comparatively harmless reason was that they had not got round to equipping themselves with stage clothes so the display that had the men sitting straight up in their seats and craning necks was of ordinary 'unders' beneath very short skirts.

I was sitting between the Chaplain and the CO and got hooded looks.

'Did you check all the acts for this show, Lieutenant Goggin?' asked the CO, (no Pat, or Paddy) I thought for the benefit of the embarrassed Chaplain.

'Oh, I take help from the local theatrical clubs, sir,' said I, taking evasive action, by mentioning that tea would be available in the interval.

The old soldier and his wife, who looked after the tea, had a son in the British Army. I was on regimental duty as Barrack Orderly Officer one day when the Adjutant of the Irish Guards rang about that lady's son who had been in an accident.

'Adjutant Irish Guards here, bad news I'm afraid. One of our men has had an accident. His father lives in your married quarters.'

'Oh I'm sorry to hear that,' I replied, 'of course I'll inform his parents right away but I'm afraid that we can't ring you through because we do not have phones in soldiers' married quarters.'

He laughed and said, 'In these islands we must look with envy at our American allies and hope that someday we will catch up.'

We had a brief but pleasant chat. I had used operations of the Irish Guards on projects in the College.

'Well,' I concluded, 'fraternal greetings anyway from the rightful wearers of the green,' referring to their green cap-band.

He laughed again as if he had been expecting some remark like that and said he would pass it on. I felt, however, that I was not quite right. Soldiers in Irish regiments in any other army have the right to express their Irish pride.

b. Military 'Characters'

Another temporary posting from the Battalion found me on attachment to the Garrison Ordnance Company as Adjutant. The Company Commander was a technical officer of high academic qualifications and a reputation for bravery in his field of operations, dealing with dangerous explosives. He was commended for dealing bravely with a mine. He seemed to happily accept what he must have considered to be the bothersome frills of the military way. I, presumably, was expected to make up for that minor deficiency in the administration of the Company, which otherwise had an excellent record in the field of explosives and weapons care.

The Ordnance Corps has a very wide field of responsibilities: weapons evaluation, maintenance of items as varied as Laser Range finders, Surface to Air Missiles, Computerised Fire Control Equipment and Artillery Simulators. Almost all of the soldiers are technicians and even the NCOS have their stripes for technical excellence as well as square bashing skills. The Ordnance Corps has been given the task of Bomb Disposal and has developed specialist skills and expertise in dealing with this complex threat, as well as designing the HOBO Remote Controlled Robot. This has now been used successfully world-wide against a range of terrorist devices. We are now recognised as having special experts in dealing with the IED threat. We had an interesting talk at a class reunion from an Ordnance Officer, who is an advisor and UN expert in this area.

Armies live on stories, some of gallantry and pride and others of an entertaining and boredom breaking purpose. COs, who make a personal impact, usually have stories floating after them.

When word of my new posting spread in the Mess I was offered a variety of stories about the eccentricities of a particular Ordnance CO, in the early days of the Army, some too good to be true. Among others, Austin Crowe, unhappily no longer with us, passed on some stories he had gathered in postings with the Ordnance Corps. Austin, an entertaining raconteur, enjoyed acting them out over a few beakers in the bar, speaking the lines as if on the Abbey stage. I have no evidence as to their total truth, but will offer them as living history, resisting, I hope, any attempt at 'polishing' them.

One story was about this character, during an inspection parade, remembering a current advice about consideration for the men: not to subject them to unnecessary delays and bullshit. He was inspecting the rifles and the company was at the 'for inspection, port arms' position. That is, with the rifle held out in front of the body, the bolt drawn back and the thumb inserted to allow light to be reflected, facilitating the examination of the barrel. Admittedly a tiring position, but unfortunately he did not remember the comfort of the warriors until he was half-way down the front rank, so he beetled up to the end of the rank, peered around at the rest of the company and said, 'Excuse me, rear rank, order arms'.

Another memorable performance, again too good not to be true, was a trial of a soldier who was charged with being AWOL. The Adjutant had coached the CO on the finer points of the operation, as the accused was heard banging down the corridor, the Company Sergeant roaring, 'Left, right, left, right, halt, salute'.

'Sir, O556789 Private (), is hereby charged under Section 68 of the Defence Forces Temporary Provisions Act, 1954, with being absent without leave, in that he, on the 10th day of July, was absent without due authority.'

The Military Police Corporal then gave evidence: 'Sir, on the day and date in question, an absentee report had been placed against him at the main gate, sir.'

The normal demeanour of a soldier in this kind of case would be of total disciplined attention but, wearing on his face a suggestion that he was totally puzzled by all this as he replied to the charge. The Commandant listened impassively as the soldier's story unfolded, involving his mother-in-law, his wife and a borrowed bicycle in a series of bewildering combinations, without comment.

He then asked, glancing at the Adjutant, who had warned him about this aspect of the case, 'Any extenuating circumstances?'

As the soldier's story had been all of this and more, the puzzled warrior (with a nickname of 'Cribber') was struck dumb.

'OK, just as well,' said the Commandant, 'I find you guilty and fine you a pound,' and with another sideways look for reassurance:

'Do you accept my punishment?'

This, as the Adjutant had warned, was a requirement in military law, in that the soldier, if dissatisfied with the summary conduct of the case, could opt instead for a court-martial.

Some inspiration seemed to strike 'Cribber'.

'No, sir.'

A puzzled Company Commander, then fumbling mentally for a way out, responded, 'OK then, fifteen shillings.'

'Right, sir', entering into the spirit of this strange performance, wondering if this was a new rule or something he had overlooked up to now.

'March him out CS.'

'Right turn, quick march, left right, left right.'

It was too late to do anything about the surreal situation at that stage, but the Adjutant commented, 'He forfeits two days' pay as well as the fine.'

'Does he begod?', asked the Commandant, feeling that maybe the game had not gone completely against him. He went to look out the window as the soldier was heading towards the cook-house for a reflective cup of char.

He opened the window and shouted over at him, 'Cribber, you forfeit two bucken days pay as well', and slammed down the window.

These stories have lived so long in military folklore that there must be at least a grain of truth in them. At the very least they have provided hours of entertainment down the years. I felt that it was not my 'cup of tea', when I received the order for the posting, but it turned out to be a most pleasant, educational and entertaining tour of duty. I liked the Commandant and wished that the Army had more like him, he added colour and humanity. My belief now is that, to a large extent he 'played up' (down?) to his 'character' image.

In my short stints with the Ordnance Corps, contrary to my pre-conceived ideas about the supremacy of the Infantry (the 'Queen of Battles') I found the officers to be gentlemen in the best sense of the word. They came in from the universities rather than the Military College and were therefore, as 'technical officers' looked upon as 'somewhat civvy' by the more priggish young officers, of which I'm ashamed to say I probably was one, despite my happy social disposition.

In my world at that stage, the 'real officer' was the one who would draw his sword and call on his warriors to face enemy bullets for the honour of the fatherland, ready for *pro patria mori*. All others were simply auxiliary corps whose job was to lay bridges over which soldiers advanced or set up signals communication networks, which allowed soldiers to issue orders. I seemed to be able to keep myself wilfully ignorant of their well-recorded bravery under fire.

c. Military Weddings

I was invited for a pre-lunch beaker with the Commandant but I felt that he had something he wanted to say to me. Eventually: 'About the wedding, Pat,' he said, smiling, with the air of one who knows.

I was amazed because I did not know how he could have heard.

I had met Muriel at a party given by Leo and Una. I had already been out on that day to Skerries with Michael, where we had enjoyed several beakers before arriving happily back to the Mess to eat, only to get a message about a party from a waiter.

I felt that I had done my social duty for that day and was feeling like an early night, but the party 'battle drill' moved me along, without any great decision making. Shave, shower, change, order taxi, put a bag of bottles aboard and head off.

As a result of my previous patrol that day I was happy to sit and watch rather than stand and perform so I had more time than usual to notice a very attractive, brown-eyed girl in a suede jacket looking after the gramophone records. She seemed to be a smiling, gentle centre of calm amid the bustle of the party and yet had an arty air with her hair swept up and held with a copper shield with a pin through it. I eventually worked up the energy to ask her to dance, which she did charmingly despite my lack of social effervescence. I discovered that her name was Muriel and that she was an officer's daughter, who knew my ex-classmates in Athlone, where her father, Commandant Charles Byrne, had been stationed. Muriel was a fellow student at the College of Art with one of Una's friends. We sampled Una's elderberry wine and enjoyed the remaining beer. After the party, we remained with the rear-guard. As it was too late to go home, we sat around until morning, still talking but threatening to snooze.

The following morning was Sunday so we all made our weary and bleary way to Mass and as I stood beside this new girl in my life I knew that this was something different. As we sat and stood, shoulder to shoulder, I had the physical and mental conviction that this was 'it'. Being with her felt good. I wondered was this 'love at first sight' but was convinced that it was more solid and real.

She stayed in my mind until I had a good excuse to ring. I needed a partner for the American Ambassador's garden party. She agreed to come to my delight even as I did my best to sound casual. This was a pleasant affair enlivened by the American Third Air-force Band. I had one slight shock when Terry O'Sullivan, the then *Evening Press* columnist, stopped me with, 'Are you here to decorate the occasion?'

He was joking about the fact that I was in dress uniform but for a moment I wondered had the Battalion been expected to provide a fatigue party. After the party, we retired to the Shelbourne for a steak and Blue Nun. Downgraded by the wine snobs since, this wine still has a meaning for us.

The rest is my history. She was the last in a short line, beginning with Maura in Senior Infants and Eileen in my pre-teen years. They were only vaguely aware that they were the object of my romantic imagination in day-dreams, saving them from pirates and school bullies, neither category readily visible in the Dingle of the time. Our courting, for such word was still in use, was conducted largely in the Old Stand, encouraged by the barmen Noel and Louie. I had been a 'never miss a new play' student of the theatre up to that and a regular cinema goer, but we seemed to avoid any other stimulation in that period that was not live and in company.

My surprise at the Commandant's question was that, by then, we had arrived at the 'big decision', which our friends had already expected. On a late night in the 55 Club, I had asked on bended knee. We were going to get married, but how did the Commandant know?

'You know that song, Pat, about the sewer?' He asked. 'There's no question of that being sung at Austin's wedding?'

The penny dropped. I discovered that my 'brother officers' had been winding him up by suggesting that I had been heard practising a soldier's song for Austin Crowe's wedding.

In fact I knew only a few lines:

> 'Down in the sewer, shovelling up manure,
> I love to hear the shovels go clickety-clack, clickety-clack,
> It fills me with delight, shovelling up the shite.'

Austin's wedding went unsullied: the Commandant making a speech about it being the time of year for 'Crowes' to be making their nests. With the other members of his Sword Guard, we were photographed standing in front of a van advertising a well-known brand of beans, with the word 'BATCHELORS' over our heads.

Our wedding plans eventually moved to the action phase. On the evening before I was told by the chaplain in confession that I did not have to confess that I was getting married. At the wedding, Colonel Keenan's speech described as a 'canard' the old saying:

'A soldier married is a soldier lost.'

My own contributions included making the verbal error of thanking the barmaids instead of the bridesmaids in my speech.

The day (and the night before) went well with the help of my Sword Guard officers, mainly ex-Cadet School classmates. They were not to blame for the fact that I was in the bar with my father-in-law, Commandant Charles Byrne, and Brian Lenihan, when Muriel started to sing 'This is my lovely day'. I had no idea that she had such a beautiful voice.

I got married in our ceremonial uniform (green tunic, breeches, boots, Sam Browne belt and sword) even though I had the new black dress uniform. I'm glad I did because that ceremonial uniform is now history. Usually the battledress of one war becomes the dress uniform of the next and this type of uniform was officer's battledress in the First World War. My brother-in-law, Ken, recorded it on film.

That day was not simply my day of 'wine and roses', it was not just 'my lovely day', it was the day that gave me my life, for which I have been thanking God every day since. I was thinking about it at a recent family gathering for a birthday party when I looked at my three daughters with their husbands and six grandchildren around the table.

When the Colonel heard that my honeymoon was to be spent driving around the country, he had me agree to visit various barracks to collect bandoleers for the 1966 commemoration of 1916. This was presumably to ensure that this soldier was not 'lost'.

d. Military Staff-work

I was posted from the Garrison Ordnance Company to the Directorate of Ordnance, in McKee Barracks, where I was the only one with a Southern accent. The Colonel, the Lieut.-Colonel and the Commandant all had distinctly Northern tones.

So much so that for a while people who rang us would say, if I answered, 'Oh, probably wrong number.'

The Colonel, Director, had his office across the corridor from mine and always left his door open.

If I left mine open as well, he always joined in my telephone conversations, 'What did he want, Pat?'

When I would try to continue: 'Tell him we can't.'

As I tried to explain: 'What did he say to that?'

Colonel James Keenan was a stocky, white-haired, kind-looking man, who, in fact, was always very concerned about all members of his military family. He had a wonderfully cute Northern way of keeping tabs on us. At lunchtime some days he would say, 'Pat, I might not be back after lunch,' pause, 'but, then again (long drawn out 'again'), I might.'

To the day I left, I could not tell if the Lieut.-Colonel, another staff officer, a pleasant and jovial man, was saying 'artillery sights' or 'auxiliary sights' in his rich Northern accent; but perhaps, even then, I could have been hard of hearing in one ear after my shooting years.

When I had been serving with the Garrison Ordnance Company, I invariably excused myself if I heard his voice on the phone: 'Sarge, will you take the Lieut.-Colonel's call?'

It was after one of these that the Sergeant told me, 'It wasn't artillery sights he was talking about, sir, it was auxiliary sights.'

I had my first experience of staff work in that Directorate.

The first file that landed on my desk as a uniformed civil servant, which I opened with some apprehension, posed a question: 'Do we need more map measures?'

I scribbled happily: 'Yes, as many as we can get.'

Having just returned from a course in the College, where there was a scarcity of these essentials, I reported my action with confidence to the Colonel. His face registered the facts being run past his computer mind – amazement that this should have happened; awareness that this was my first morning; relief that the situation was retrievable because the file was still here.

As if talking to a well-meaning five year old, he practically patted me on the shoulder and said in a slow patient voice, 'What we do Pat is to request observations and recommendations from the Director of Training, the Director of Plans and Ops and the Director of

Intelligence, then discuss the matter with the Quartermaster General's office and then draft a suitable reply.'

I made one attempt to hold on to the outside world: 'But, sir, everybody knows we need them.'

He looked at me, a non-verbal statement that told me I had a game to play and that it would have to be by their rules. I accepted defeat and joined in with gusto.

e. Military Dancing Years

On returning from the honeymoon, celebrating in the Old Stand one evening, an ex-Cadet School class-mate of mine, Mick O'Farrell, (sadly no longer with us) approached smilingly and asked, 'Can I continue to call you Paddy?'

I did not know what he was talking about until he explained that while I was exploring the darkest West with gun and dog (as well as new wife) I had been published as promoted to Captain. The Old Stand, not far from the old Wicklow Hotel was where journeys and honeymoons were planned and where travellers returned to report; where the rugby internationals were celebrated because the Irish team won or were very good but unlucky. Like in bayonet drill, 'on the command "fix" you don't fix', the dancing years were really the drinking years.

A story from Edwardian Dublin tells of a haughty hostess approaching a group of drinking Hussars with a view to getting them on the dance floor.

Their senior officer replied, 'The 10th don't dance.'

She fixed him with a freezing glance and replied, 'Well, gentlemen, if the 10th don't dance, the 10th can march', pointing to the door.

I suspect that some at least of the indefatigable ladies who organised parties to which we were invited must have felt like giving us that kind of an operation order from time to time, but that they happily lacked the Lady Macbeth quality of the hostess in the story.

I remember once seeing the sun come up over Luttrelstown House, having champagne on the veranda, enjoying the beauty of the grounds, perhaps the last surviving eighteenth-century landscape close to the city. I had been lucky enough to have been asked to make up a party that had been invited during Horse Show week. Someone had fallen out at the last minute. Getting into dress uniform was as normal to me in my single dancing years as getting into 'service dress' greens, so I happily obliged.

Afterwards I invited some guests to breakfast in the Mess. We stopped in the cattle-market pub on the way and were graciously received by the sober cattlemen, before arriving in the Mess dining-room; some of us in dress uniform, some in white tie and tails, as mess members sat in green service dress at breakfast.

I showed the guests around the portraits of the Chiefs of Staff while we waited for our orange juice, bacon and egg. John served us with a fanfare of good mornings. I got a note from the Mess President on the following day to the effect that they would be obliged for a two hours notice for guests at meals.

We always had 'a few' before going to the Leinster Cricket Club dance, at which the leather-coated doorman would say, as we approached the queue, 'Ah lads, how much longer did you expect me to hold the tickets?'

What tickets?

To an address announced in the Old Stand in response to 'where's the party?' we took brown paper bags of bottles, which we hid around the location for security, often forgetting where and refuelling with someone else's hidden bottles. In the Old Stand under the canopy adorned with the rugby crests, I would know most of the regulars: Army; Aer Lingus (mostly ex-Air Corps); medical from the nearby hospital and some Trinity people. We were never short of company either in the Mess or the 'Golden Triangle' (The Old Stand, Neary's and the Bailey) where you entered another world, a kind of *Tir-na-nOg* that vanished at closing time. As evidence of the club atmosphere of the 'Stand' in all those years I remember only one night that could have gone wrong, when a civilian bumped into the corner of our table and spilled his glass. As can happen, he wanted to blame somebody and became loudly aggressive but was hauled away by his sensible girlfriend.

On one occasion, on overhearing that Sean Fenton had just been promoted First Lieutenant, a barman asked him in a somewhat smart alec tone, 'What do I call you so?'

'You may call me, sir,' said Sean, to much military laughter, echoing an army joke that had just been told.

This incident remains one of our memories of his happy approach to life, as he died tragically young, attempting to rescue his brother from drowning.

His response seemed to have provoked a resentful comment from a listening civilian: 'Who the hell do you think you are?'

He was ignored and soon left.

Officers in married quarters had orderlies, but we were on our own in Stillorgan and could not afford a maid. We had, however, a very helpful lady, who helped look after the children, as Muriel was teaching. Mrs 'T', was great with the children and fitted in, as in the country way, almost as a visiting relative.

She once took a very poor view of 'the Captain' going to a function aboard a visiting naval training ship in dress uniform in 'his little car' (my first, a small red Prinz). She scolded us as to why we did not tell her and her daughter would have driven us in her Cortina. That function was memorable also for the scene as we were being hospitably piped on board, with a guard of honour on deck, when her ladyship was nearly tripped by a cross bar on the gangway. However, she was restored by the arrival of a helpful, handsome Argentinian Naval Officer.

One of my memories of the motherly Mrs T, was her poor view of a lamp we had in the hall. She brought us one that her daughter had replaced, for a Christmas present.

I had to ask myself, 'What is it with me and lamps?'

I never worried about the first lamp given to me by my orderly in my single days, who told me that his wife was tired of it and it was better than the one I had in my room. But another within a few short years? We were duly grateful for the kindness but even now I hesitate before committing myself to a new lamp.

The postman occasionally arrived in our early married life holding his nose and handing in a brace of woodcock, held at the legs by a cord with a label saying: 'Shot by Uncle Joe, Mount Eagle, 3 o'cl Sunday. Best wishes, Daddy.' On one memorable learning occasion, as a young married man, still not broken-in, I was sitting by the fire reading, with Muriel doing what I took to be woman's work of some kind, when I noticed a brace of woodcock landing on the chair beside me.

A wife rightly felt that it was about time that I learned to play my part in running a home, especially plucking game-birds.

7
World War Three?

a. The Observer Corps

On my first morning back after the honeymoon, Colonel Keenan
came in to my office saying, 'Pat, you'll be going down the road.
I agreed to your going to the new Observer Corps on promotion. We're
sorry to lose you but I believe that you'll find the *per diem* handy, as a
young married man.'

My promotion to Captain had brought a permanent posting to the
newly forming Observer Corps. 'Down the road' meant Parkgate Street
across the road from Army HQ, where the HQ of the new Corps was being
set up: the *'per diem'* referred to the allowances, mileage and subsistence,
that went with certain posts. This unfortunately did not happen for me
because the only officers not on the allowances were the Commanding
Officer, the Second in Command and myself, as Adjutant. However, the
Department of Finance added the usual softener to the blow for the 'three
officers whom it is proposed to exclude' that the 'matter would be kept
under review' and indeed, how right they were. They were admirably
untiring in their review, which lasted for all of my service with the Corps.

Colonel Aidan O'Byrne, Officer Commanding the Observer Corps
was a colourful character with a certain charisma. One of the first officers
graduating from the Cadet School after it was established in 1930: a
stocky physical presence exuding supreme self-confidence, a bluff,
moustached, Colonel Blimpish personality about whom people happily
circulated stories whether they were true or not. He enriched my store of
army memories. I had enjoyed working with him. My last meeting with
him was on Dun Laoghaire pier in his eighties. I was walking reasonably

slowly concerned not to put too much strain on him.

He looked sideways and barked, 'Buck up, Pat old boy, I thought you were fitter.'

He did his senior training in the RAF. Earlier in his career, coming from the Air Corps to the Equitation School, on his first morning mounted on a horse, he is reported as shouting to the groom, 'Chocks away'.

I wondered if he measured up to Ward's definition of a colonel in his *Animadversions of Warre* (1639)? 'The office of colonel is very honourable, and a place of great confidence in the army, wherefore he ought to be a grave and experienced soldier, religious, wise, temperate, and valiant.'

I am sure that he would have agreed.

We had three commandants: two were technical officers from Signals and Ordnance, who had extra technical pay, referred to, by those who did not have it, as 'plumber's money'. One was from the Ordnance Corps, who had come in with a university degree, and a calm pleasant, personality, the other was from the Signal Corps where he had been commissioned from the ranks during the Emergency.

There were four captains but as the Company Sergeant used to tell afterwards, when someone was looking for 'the Captain' the staff always took it to mean me as Adjutant. Of the other captains, two, Ray Buckley (RIP) and Dave O'Regan, were from my cadet class. As it happened, this was the last posting for the three of us because we eventually took early retirement around the same time.

We had a Company Sergeant and a staff of NCOS and clerks in the Orderly Room. One NCO was familiar. I remembered him from my first platoon. I recalled marching up a long billet in Cathal Brugha Barracks to where a small figure was lying on a bed reading the *Beano* comic.

As the Company Sergeant and I banged closer he looked up, put down the comic, smiled and said, 'Oh, hello sir.'

We remained silent, until the CS said, 'He has just come in, sir.'

There are times when a dignified retreat is the most honourable way out, so with a half-hearted:

'Stand up when approached by an officer,' from the CS, we left.

Now I had him back as a Corporal with the same friendly self-confident smile of co-operation on his face. (He deservedly reached senior NCO rank before his retirement).

We had another young soldier who was never referred to by anything but his Christian name, Paschal. I never called 'other ranks' by anything except their ranks, but even those, who habitually referred to them by their surnames, called him Paschal.

He was the classic post-Emergency soldier. Once when asked to fetch bed-boards from the stores, he started to head in that direction and then came back: 'What are bed-boards, Sarge?'

While bed-boards were part of the memories of Emergency soldiers in makeshift camps, the Observer Corps was the visible sign that a new and terrible type of warfare threatened our future. We liked to think, that we were the only Corps preparing for World War Three, but we were also preparing for a non-war accident as in Chernobyl. Our task was to provide a nuclear radiation warning and monitoring service to the State, with a secondary role of general air and ground intelligence. To do this the concept was that we would recruit a Reserve Force commanded and trained by ourselves (a small cadre of Permanent Defence Force personnel). We would have about 300 underground monitoring posts around the country about 15 miles apart with the capability of detecting a nuclear explosion, estimating its size and plotting the likely path of the plume of radio-active fallout. Information would be channelled through three levels to a national control where the nation-wide picture would be plotted, analysed, a prediction arrived at and warning issued.

Officers went to the UK for training in the techniques and instruments: Scientific Advisers and Warning Officers Courses conducted by the United Kingdom Warning and Monitoring Organisation. The UK experts were extremely helpful to us in the setting up of the Corps and we benefited considerably from the lessons of their experience. When a problem arose about instruments or procedures, a letter would be sent requesting advice. I do not remember to whom it was addressed but it was invariably: 'Dear Dickie'.

If discussions got bogged down, someone would say, 'Dear Dickie?' 'It seems like the best trick.'

All who had completed courses in the UK, in turn trained other officers and the monitoring post crews. These crews were to include female members. We even had a 'Q' schedule of the clothing and equipment considered necessary, but the idea of men and women together in underground posts in those days must have been just too much to contemplate for some people so that aspect of the plan got binned. Also, although I had acquired 900 red berets, there were no reservists recruited in my time. FCA personnel were trained to man the posts. After I had retired, I never heard what happened afterwards to the red berets.

Dr Hayes McCoy and Lieut.-Col. P.D. Kavanagh suggested ideas for the shoulder flash and collar badge for the new Corps. Muriel used her art expertise to produce the final design for the flash.

The collar badge was a crane holding a stone in a raised claw: since medieval times the heraldic symbol of unceasing vigilance. If the bird was 'one degree under' and fell asleep, the stone would fall and the noise would wake him to full watchfulness again, if presumably, it did not land on his other claw, which might only make him cranky. Parachute-shaped, the shoulder flash was a new departure in Irish Army flashes, with an Irish round tower (of the tenth century Observer Corps) surrounded by stylised flames of the nuclear threat: pale grey tower and red flames on a black background. I thought that I might have to offer my resignation when I had to report home to the artist that I heard that the Clothing Committee wanted a yellow Corps name strip on top. It did not happen.

I was still in the glow of my idealised army, especially now that I had reached the rank of Captain at twenty-nine years of age. This was a big improvement on those in their forties and fifties in the rank, who, through no fault of their own, had hit a bad patch for promotion after the war. My ideas, however, were modified somewhat after my very good experience with the Ordnance Corps. I now had a mature acceptance of the essential contribution of the working Corps to the overall success of any military mission, but I was still, around that time, clinging to my belief that 'real officers' were those who led glorious charges and all others were simply auxiliaries.

My self-concept was one whose destiny was death or glory, ready to give my life for my country, choosing to ignore the obvious fact that ordnance or signals personnel were also heading in the same direction. It is quite likely that my early romantic military reading contributed to my general attitude, but, in one sense, it was a trained fault, in that armies like to inculcate a pride in oneself and one's unit (*esprit de corps*) to be expressed by aiming at excellence in performance. Is the Infantry Corps really still the 'Queen of Battle'?

It would be an understatement if I had to admit that, in contrast with the good impression made on me by the ex-Ordnance commandant, a friendly, unflappable, 'oil on troubled waters' type, I did not hit it off very well with the ex-Signals member of our HQ, who to me seemed to have an expression of permanent disapproval. There was also my perception that he, an ex-TO, seemed to be very vocal about 'coming up the hard way' during the Emergency and that I and other Cadet School products had got it too 'cushy'. At least that was the message I took from his many stories about the either lazy or stupid young officers that it was his misfortune to have to report. Without breaching military law, I must confess also that I perhaps did not give sufficient significance to his one pip seniority to me. The third factor in our relationship was his expressed pride in a connection with a 1916 man and presumably my failure to applaud enthusiastically enough.

I had a 'green field' start in this job in the sense of no SOPs (Standard Operating Procedures) already in place and empty filing cabinets. Bureaucracy produces paper so they did not take long to start filling. We had a corps submission once for the Chief of Staff's Branch, which came to over fifty pages. I had a feeling that nobody was going to read it at that weight. The Colonel agreed. As it happened, all the 'specialists' were away or going on leave so I suggested that I be allowed edit the whole paper, which consisted of our proposed plan, with individual contributions from our technical specialists. I started cutting, as I felt necessary, reducing it to fifteen pages, adding the technical material in appendices. The Colonel agreed with it but, by the time it was ready for consideration in GHQ, all had returned and asked to see it. They cheerfully fattened it up again. I had grave doubts that it was ever going to be perused page by page. My main worry was that the sheer weight of otherwise excellently presented technical information would bury our message.

b. PSO to ACS

Around this time I was posted, temporarily, as PSO (Personal Staff Officer) to the Assistant Chief of Staff, Colonel Shortall. He was, in turn, acting for the holder of this position, who was away. Working with him was an education. I was so used to passing things on, requesting 'observations and recommendations', that to be told, 'Ah, you'll be well able to deal with that yourself, Pat', was a very welcome change.

Once he was pondering on service medals. From when should they be dated? I suggested that a service medal should be from the first day someone puts on a green soldier's uniform, including the FCA. I was remembering some of the excellent men who gave their nights and week-ends free for the defence of the State.

Dealing with the military attachés was one of the areas of responsibility of the office of the Assistant Chief of Staff.

One day a request from the German Military Attaché, based in London, for a brief on the Irish Army, arrived with the morning post. I put it into Colonel Shortall's pile for attention.

Removing it deftly and dropping it on my lot, he said, 'No better man than yourself for something like that. I'll deal with this,' taking one of the files, 'you can deal with that and that and those two nuisance reminders.'

I particularly enjoyed dealing with the British Military Attaché, Brigadier Thicknesse. He had a great way of getting people to help him.

'Do you think we could get some clever chappie to sort this for us?' he would say, paying me the compliment of excluding me from the civil service 'clever chappies'.

His home in Eglinton Road was petrol bombed in 1966 as part of our joyous celebration of 1916.

Before I finished my time in that appointment we received a request to plan an itinerary for the visiting Canadian Military Attaché. I drafted a plan and had passed it to the Canadian Embassy when Colonel Shortall went back to his regular job and the permanent holder of the post of Assistant Chief returned. A new itinerary was drafted and forwarded. I was in the office two days afterwards when a call came through from the Canadian Embassy: 'Could we please have the first itinerary, the Attaché prefers it?'

I said to my Sergeant assistant in the office, 'Sarge, pass on that call, leave me out of it.'

One of my tasks was to arrange for the clearance of over-flights by the RAF, by contacting the OC Air Corps and checking with the Assistant Chief of Staff. On one occasion I had difficulty in contacting the OC Air Corps so I delayed my reply to External Affairs.

After a while an irate civil servant arrived in a state of angry anxiety: 'What's the meaning of this delay? Send back the paper.'

'I'm afraid that that is not a decision I have the authority to make,' I replied.

I seem to remember that I made a somewhat pompous joke about our job being to keep men in different coloured uniforms from entering or crossing our country without our agreement. In fact, it is now revealed in documents, released after the thirty year interval, that Mr Lynch, rightly agreed with Mrs Thatcher after the murder of Lord Mountbatten, in 1979, to provide an air corridor on the Southern side of the Border. Colonel Shortall returned, with, I have no doubt, the same relaxed self-confidence to his old appointment and I returned to my office across the road, professionally enriched by the experience. I had reached the 'thinking of applying for civvy jobs' stage of my career, hoping for a few extra bob on the cheque, facing increasing responsibilities as a young married man, but this had made me pause.

c. 'Looming' Trouble

Back in my office at the Observer Corps again in my regular job, a signals exercise was botched and the Signals Commandant suggested that I was to blame through my well-known superior attitude to such technical matters. I had made some silly jokes about 'looming' when I heard about the exercise, (looming being something to do with laying telephone cables) but I had nothing to do with the exercise as Adjutant. I confirmed this with the Field Signals Company, who assured me that it had nothing to do with me.

I recorded the details and kept a note, in case there were to be any 'questions'.

At that time also the Army was asked to take responsibility for Civil Defence. We pleaded 'too much on our plates' to which the Civil Service happily replied with their own establishment headed by one assistant secretary, two principal officers, four assistant principals and eight higher executive officers.

Another indication of our naïvety was our turning down of half a million pounds of a budget on the grounds that it would not allow us to set up the complete Corps system of controls and underground posts we had planned. We spent about nine years waiting to get some of that back.

We had years of ceaseless verbal battles in the wasteful system of dual administration, where everything we did was mirrored by a man in another office in civilian attire, in the Department of Finance. I made a wall chart, which consisted of a linked series of boxes showing where the estimates were (on whose desk was the paper?) at any given time of the year, in order to avoid the run-around I used to get on the phone when checking on 'progress'. In other words, when could we purchase what was already agreed?

Captain Mick Dagg came up with a 'Crash Plan', an excellent plan but a very much attenuated and cheaper version of our general concept. I heard that this was to be unveiled at a presentation of our submission to the General Staff. We had waited for this opportunity for ages. I felt that if the money-starved General Staff and the money-guarding civil servants were given wind of this it would be good-bye to our major plan and they would only have eyes for, and memory of, the 'Crash Plan'. The 'Crash Plan' was very well presented but I voiced my worry about the wisdom of including it in our presentation. Nobody agreed with me, understandably, and I found myself standing alone. This was the only serious row, if that is the correct word for a respectful disagreement, that I had with the Colonel in my service in the Corps. I felt that I had to apologise for my persistence in the bar before lunch, especially after a hint from John, the head-waiter, who had over-heard.

The Colonel's reply cheered me up: 'Well, Pat old boy, lots of senior people may disagree with you but you are always ready to give an officer-like account of yourself and your opinions.'

With the advent of the five-day week in the commercial world, I had the idea that this would be an excellent way to improve conditions for the men and encourage recruiting without the cost of a pay-rise.

My suggestion met with: 'How can you possibly say that an army can simply stand down on a Saturday?'

'Like it does on Sunday', I would answer, but I knew that it was not acceptable.

We were then working a half-day on a Saturday and in Army HQ officers were allowed to come in civvies. I worked a roster for the NCOS and men to allow a skeleton staff for Saturday and all others off, with the agreement of the CO, who simply said, 'OK, you couldn't sell your idea to anyone else so you are working a form of it yourself. I don't mind, but I'm not agreeing officially. As long as the work gets done on the Saturday, you fix the roster with the CS.'

We fought on for the sinews of our war. A filing system grew and became engraved in stone: a challenge to anyone to try to change it. A fastidious, intelligent sergeant in the orderly room had an excellent appreciation of what was required. But as his ideas came from his service in the Signals Corps, and as we were fed up with hearing how well they did everything there, neither the CS nor myself could see our way to publicly admit the obvious merit in his scheme. Like Topsy, our system just grew and grew. Some things remained the same however: Paschal was promoted to corporal but still called Paschal.

Other 'organisational developments' included my decision to end the growing habit of some to congregate in my office for the coffee break leaving me gasping in the residual smoke. Also, I had acquired a mahogany bookcase, which was superior to any other in the HQ, and I successfully closed my ears to any suggestion that it would be more appropriate in a more senior office.

By then I had started studying in the evenings for a degree in UCD, in economics and philosophy. Contrary to today when cadets do a university course as part of their military education, I had to apply for annual leave to do exams and, to prove that I was still a soldier, give a talk to the staff on the Saturday in-between. I chose 'Bull' (non-productive military activity) as my subject.

Something of which I was not aware and discovered only on the day I was retiring was that I had a reputation of being a biro-robber. Seemingly when I went in to talk to one of the staff I would absent-mindedly pick up a biro from the desk and walk away with it. I had no idea that the decks and desks were automatically cleared of biros on my appearance at the door.

On retiring, I received a very nice pen from the NCO staff, engraved: 'For the Captain, so that he might never have to rob a biro again.'

d. Neutrality

Our problem was, as Col. Johnny Stapleton put it: 'During the Emergency we were caught with our trousers down, now, we haven't even got trousers.'

For a fortnight in October 1962, in the words of Dean Rusk, the super-powers were 'eye-ball to eye-ball', with atomic rockets 90 miles from Florida and Cuba ringed by an American naval blockade. It must have cheered him no end to learn that the Irish Army Observer Corps were at their desks until all hours. Our lack of trousers was partly due to the widespread hope that Ireland would never be at war and even if we were, somebody else would handle it for us. This attitude was now hardening into what has become the 'neutrality lobby' which pretends that our pragmatic 'qualified' neutrality of the Second World War was really due to our idealistic Christianity and is an unchallengeable dogma of Irish political faith.

I remember that in a brief for the German Military Attaché (based in London) that I wrote in 1965, I stated that our 'policy is one of neutrality'. I said that 'we have no military alignment with any foreign power nor do we receive military aid from any power'.

'Ideologically we are firmly opposed to the principles of communism and the sympathies of our people lie with the Western democratic way of life.'

That was what I wrote but, in fact, the release of State papers has since revealed the help we were prepared to give to the Allies, and that we had British observers present on exercises, ready if necessary to come in. The complete indifference of radioactive fallout to the status of neutrality and national borders had to be faced, even by a small country like ours.

The Cold War terms of 'MAD' (Mutually Assured Destruction) and 'Flexible Response' seem to have been attempts to make the nightmare amenable to daylight examination. The unavoidable fact is that, even if we manage to persuade those who are fighting the war that we want out and please leave us alone, the effect of a nuclear explosion anywhere in Europe will have devastating consequences here.

If, by a miracle and favourable meteorological conditions, we escape radioactive fall-out, that would simply mean that in a Europe that was a nuclear wilderness we would be clean safe ground. Ireland would therefore become what armies call 'vital ground' for both sides and we would be in the middle of it, as they struggle for possession. The nuclear question is dragged in to the neutrality argument to frighten people who do not even want to think about it. Nuclear weapons have been invented, they are part of our world and the only way to prevent madmen using them is still, unfortunately, the threat of 'Mutually Assured Destruction'.

Wars are started by people who have high hopes of winning. There is no hope of winning a nuclear war, despite books like Kahn's *On Thermonuclear War* which try to make it seem debatable.

The problem today has escalated to the nightmare threat of terrorists being supplied with nuclear weapons by some rogue state. Does anybody believe that the reptilian mind capable of putting a bomb in a mosque to kill hundreds of praying people, or indeed into a pub full of innocent chatterers, would think twice about neutrality? The strategic 'marginality' of Ireland and the 'military insignificance' of the Irish Army are also regularly offered as argument by the neutrality lobby. Yet the strategic value of Ireland, specifically with regard to the 'Western Approaches' has been well demonstrated by Gen. Hackett in his book *The Third World War*.

The Irish component of the British Army, (a full Army Corps – 10th, 16th and 36th Divisions) played a not insignificant part in the First World War. The strength of the Irish Defence Forces in the Second World War (two divisions, over 50,000 full-time plus nearly 150,000 in the part-time organisations) had to be a factor, also, however minor, in foreign invasion 'estimates'. In Montgomery's *Memoirs* he records that, after Dunkirk, there was 'only sufficient transport and armament' for the one division capable of going overseas. Another pointless observation is that the Irish Army is incapable of preventing an invasion by any other army, because, in fact, none of the powerful European armies are capable, on their own, of defeating a superpower. The State, being Plato's 'individual writ large', can only be expected to live up to its sovereign responsibility of contributing to its own defence in accordance with its material capability.

All that is expected of us is to make our contribution to the European Rapid Reaction Force and to the battle-groups. We would have no difficulty in fitting in with the British Army, with whom we do most of our external training and with whom we have in today's buzzword 'inter-operability'. However, presumably for good 'political' reasons we choose to act in conjunction with the other 'neutral' states, like Sweden, with the inevitable problems of travel cost and language. However, English is an international language and Swedish and Nordic officers generally on foreign tours have no problem. I got on very well with a Swedish colleague and his beautiful lady wife Ulla on a UN tour of duty in Cyprus.

In the interest of functional co-operation between both parts of this island, as a step towards unity, is there any hope that our grandchildren will see an EU Irish Battle-group of Irish soldiers, from units North and South of the Border, who share the same proud military tradition and are entitled to the 'common name of Irishman' as Wolfe Tone would have liked? Gen. Sir Peter de la Billière wrote on the difficulty of fitting an American brigade in with the British division as was considered during the re-subordination question in 'Desert Storm'. He claimed that it would be easier to 'fight the British Division one brigade down' than to reinforce it with an American brigade and 'so introduce all the complications of liaison, communications and different operational concepts'. Our reason for ignoring this bit of military common-sense is political fear of the neutrality lobby.

On the front page of the *Irish Press* of 7 April 1964, large headlines announced a sea-changed Khruschev's praise for the United States for their very reasonable speeches against a war, which could wipe out half of mankind.

Under a four-column picture of a Soviet surface-to-air missile, another headline: 'ARMY CORPS TO KEEP WATCH ON N-WAR HAZARDS.'

This piece outlined the Observer Corps, and stated that 'most of the key command positions have been filled', listing tasks and procedures. It referred to 'deep atom proof' shelters and a tie-up with the American and British Distant Early Warning System. Perhaps, due to the fact that we were still arguing for money with the Civil Service, or maybe due to the reference to a possible sinful (against our sacred neutrality) foreign involvement, fall-out from this report landed on our HQ that morning with grim requests for a 'Leak Inquiry'.

'Sir Humphrey' in the TV sitcom always welcomed one in order to find out what it was that they should cover up, but our equivalent, with boring predictability, simply wanted to know: 'Who spoke to the press?'

Of course, nobody had, or nobody would admit to that courageous decision, so we all signed the bit of civil service paper that cures all ills, to that effect.

The 'Neutrality/Anti-War' lobby continues to swell, in the words of Daniel O'Connell, 'on the exuberance of its own verbosity'. As was their case on the War in Iraq, when undoubtedly, serious mistakes were made, like not putting in the number of troops (500,000) as requested by the Chief of Staff, and bad post-conflict planning, which led to chaos. They seemed to rest their case on the failure to find WMD, but they did not seem to be aware of the elementary fact that no intelligence can ever be 100% trustworthy.

Despite the fact that information is processed into intelligence in six careful stages, including collation with previously recorded items, and rated for importance on a scale of 1-6, and for reliability on a scale of A-F. The provider could have been fooled by a deliberate 'sting' or a forged document, etc. So all intelligence calls for a judgement, bearing in mind the risks if ignored and it turns out to be true. For example, if it turned out that Sadam Hussein, really had WMD and threatened to use them, what would people think of the national leaders who ignored the warning? He had already used them against his own people. Sadam Hussein, the man, was a major factor in the 'intelligence estimate'. Yet, due to fear of the neutrality lobby we dare not say anything officially on the side of the US or the UK intervention.

8
The Military College

a. The Command and Staff School

In order to get them to settle down for the long haul, one College Commandant used to ask the newly arrived Command and Staff School students to look out the lecture hall windows at the trees.

'You will, because you are highly observant, note that some leaves are still green. By the time you finish here they will all have become red or gold, have fallen and indeed will have sprouted fresh and green again.'

We were back, but the sight of the boot-stamped square, the sound of an NCO barking orders, and, even more, the smell of wood smoke in the autumnal air made us feel that we had never left this brown brick island on the sea of pale green grass on the wide Curragh plain. We remembered our cadet years, on returning from leave, feeling that the mists swirling around the Curragh could have been billions of light years in depth.

Having completed a BA (philosophy, economics, English) at UCD, I had hoped to do a Master's. When the Colonel's request that I be allowed to defer my Command & Staff Course, in order to continue study, was refused, I was told informally that the Chief of Staff, my ex-Cadet-master, believed that the C & S Course would be of more use than another university year.

In my later experience I have, in fact, made more practical use of Military College mental drills on 'approaches to problems' and the structuring of reports and analyses than anything I have learned in other educational institutions. Today one can qualify for a Master's on the C & S Course. As it happens, I now know why the Colonel's request failed. I have read his letter in my file in the Officers Archives, in my research for this book, and find that he had made a strong case for me 'facing an exam in the Autumn' and 'all the study' I had been doing. Obviously the Chief could see no reason why I could not do this 'exam' and still go on my C & S Course. I must not have explained exactly what was required. I simply wanted to be left in Dublin, if I could get started on a Master's.

In other armies getting on the 'Staff College' course is something to compete for, but as one of the advantages of a small army, all officers here are given the opportunity of passing the selection tests. Now in our middle thirties, most of our class were married but, as happens on college courses we gradually seemed to revert again to our cadet personae, despite a certain lightening and greying of hair. Night patrols to the Hideout in Kilcullen and deep patrols to country pubs eased the strain. Most of us had been together also for the six months of the Standard Infantry Course. I had also completed the three months Intelligence Course, for which I had volunteered. Now, as captains, we were working for a qualification that should enable us to command a brigade.

The College was very advanced in its methods of training and education and a heavy emphasis was placed on personal work and study. No evening was ever free of study in preparation for the following day's work: our 'cubby-holes' would be full every evening of 'précis' and papers for some future exercise or discussion period. All students were constantly preparing for several things at the same time: a paper on some aspect of military science; a test talk; a contribution to a seminar or more seriously, preparing for one of the regular tests that mile-stoned the course. The system of tests at the end of sub-courses rather than, as at university, the end of the year, was one of the best features of the College approach. A large part of private study time was spent in organising the work of some team of which one had the chair, which had the task of producing some exercise or seminar.

Trying to get all the members to a meeting after hours, when one of them was, in turn, chasing you to attend his work session of a syndicate, of which you were just a member, called for diplomacy and determination. The training objective of this was to produce stress conditions and to give us experience in dealing with a long on-going situation of conflicting demands with fortitude: the 'mental robustness' of which our Cadet-master spoke many years before. The overall objective, as given, was to 'develop the capacity of officers to think and reason logically, to express their ideas effectively in speech and writing, to exercise sound judgement and to make decisions accordingly, and to apply the principles of war, leadership, organisation and command'.

That was the objective, the result depended on the individual student.

b. 'Night Patrol'

The work method in the Command and Staff School was that all 'general background' had to be absorbed from the appropriate *précis* or study material on the night before and class time could therefore be devoted to a discussion of the problems encountered.

Generally speaking this system worked well, but there was also the odd occasion when too late a discussion period in the bar or too deep a 'night patrol' interfered with the sharpness of the following day's contribution in the syndicate room.

We had returned one morning from the Kilkenny Beer Festival as a sunburst was sending cosmic arms of orange and saffron glory across a darkly green landscape. We recognised this as one of the manifestations of the ancient Irish Sun God, symbol of the ancient glory of our country. Were Finn and the Fianna moving in the shadows? We were disappointed not to see wolfhounds and round towers. We had been proud to form the rearguard of the party in Kilkenny Castle, insisting on remaining until the last 'civvy' went home. Surely the Castle belonged to us and not to the accountants or artists, clerks or cobblers? As the last wave of red beer broke in white froth over our glasses, we, the twentieth-century members of the profession of arms were left in possession of the fourteenth-century monument to its glory.

That was all very well but we still had to face the day in the syndicate room without the preparation necessary for comfort.

After a brief rest in bed, shaved and breakfasted, we arrived in class. The now watery sun did nothing to improve our appearance and seemed to throw dark shadows under eyes. We had a hard day's 'cuffing' in front of us. We survived on our thin preparation, but it meant pulling every arrow of technique out of the quiver.

'Any preliminary comment?' The College Staff Officer, leading the discussion, began in the usual way. He looked at Dan, one of our deep patrol to the Kilkenny Beer Festival on the night before, who fielded it brilliantly. He simply moved his head with a quizzical expression towards one of the 'safe' members, who panicked into thinking the question had been for him and that he had been caught off guard. He made an appropriate comment and the discussion leader did not seem to mind the apparent confusion. Maybe he had looked in that direction? Attack being the best defence, I got in a quick look at the bottom of a page in the middle of the *précis* while that was going on, so I was able to get in a worried sounding question, being unhappy about something on the bottom of page nine. This defensive move worked well, but unfortunately it was landed on another of the walking wounded in the form of a direct question apparently demanding a reasonably concrete answer. He played it with commendably officer-like calm, and in a reproachful voice looking at me, who had sounded worried, said, 'I don't see any problem in that'.

Another one of the 'patrol group' was in support immediately. He had time to look and see what was the problem to which I had drawn attention and made a sensible sounding comment. The discussion continued with the healthy members taking up the running and the rest of us tuning in gradually to the general concept because all military knowledge is relative to something else and we had all worked hard and well except for a few nights like the previous one. However, having got the second or third, 'It all depends on the situation', as answers, the syndicate leader asked:

'OK, Goggs, how did last night's patrol go?'

We worked on a military 'appreciation' (if the instructor had completed his Staff Course at Camberley in the UK) or an 'estimate of the situation' (if the instructor were a graduate of the US Staff Course at Fort Leavenworth). Both provided the same sound framework on which a practical analysis of problems could be traced and a solution considered. One always began with the mission, analysed for explicit and implicit tasks. The factors influencing the situation would then be isolated and a deduction as to how each would affect the mission would be arrived at. At that stage, possible courses of action would be listed giving advantages and disadvantages of each. The decision was the final product, which is expected to be as full as possible: who, where, when, how and why. It was a mental drill that once absorbed is never forgotten, that I carried with me to all my subsequent appointments, military and civilian.

c. 'Brigade Commander'

I had my ups (to be remembered) and my downs (to be forgotten). One 'up' was when I was detailed as the Brigade Commander for a three-day exercise. My Brigade HQ was in a room with large-scale maps of the operational area on the walls and teams in adjoining rooms, representing sub-units, sending in messages by phone and radio on their problems and the progress of the 'battle'.

An Infantry Brigade consists of three Infantry Battalions, an Artillery Regiment, a Squadron of Cavalry and companies of Engineers and Supply and Transport as well as a Field Ambulance of the Medical Corps, etc. Their 'commanding officers' and 'staff' would be taking part. All participants wore the appropriate rank markings.

Normally the Cavalry Squadron would be an advance, or flank, guard and the three Infantry Battalions would move on parallel routes with the Artillery Regiment at the rear and military police directing the move. The 'Supply and Transport' Corps petrol points would have to be fixed on the way, with the Field Ambulance ready for action, etc.

I began well by being the first in the exercise room on the first morning and the mixture of reality and play-acting came to my advantage with incoming 'brigade staff' saluting in mock seriousness, including the College 'monitors'. At the stroke of nine, the official start of the exercise, as we waited for the 'sitrep' (situation report), I decided to get started and ordered a 'movement order' for a move South by the brigade to be prepared.

A Brigade Movement Order is a very comprehensive statement of a lot of disparate happenings involving about 600 vehicles and about 3000 men. I reasoned that all exercises are based on realistic expectations and the South coast was the German target area during the Second World War. Also getting the lads on 'my staff' started working, even if wrong, would cost us nothing and would reduce the waiting nervous tension. It would also give me a chance to start issuing orders before being required to do so by the exercise situation, so that I would be more relaxed and off to a running start.

This was a near disaster because while it was sound, it was too sound and the exercise was held up while an investigation was under way to see if there had been a leak from a comrade in one of the other rooms. It was established that no such leak had taken place and my reasoning on the South coast was accepted. The College Commandant, Colonel Rea, cheered me up by apologising for the implied doubt. He was that kind of officer.

The days progressed with my Infantry Battalions getting stuck on various ridges, my Artillery needing supplies of ammo when the trucks were needed by the Engineers to bring up essential bridging equipment, my Signals losing contact with the vanguard at vital moments, etc. I had to continue to call my 'O Group' (Order Group) together for new orders and give decisions as required.

All actions and orders were noted for the three days of the exercise by the monitors. At the end there is a critique in a lecture hall with all the monitors lined up in front. Each member of the 'brigade staff' and the 'commanding officers' of the brigade units had their own monitor, an expert in that area, (Artillery, Cavalry, Engineers and Signals) who reported on their performance. The College Staff Officer, who had acted as my monitor, stood up at the end and simply said:

'The Brigade Commander was in command from start to finish.'

So what? One may truly ask, but on a course like that of almost total physical and mental commitment, it was a very satisfactory feeling.

I was advised at the pre-Christmas assessment to 'keep doing what I was doing', that I was a 'B plus'. I had my scores but, in the overall position, when all the marks for the tests in all the subjects were added up, I was not in the competition for the top place. My successes were specific. Perhaps it was the old story of the 'things I was interested in'? It had echoes of my time in the Cadet School. I was never the kind of student who wanted to 'top a course', whereas it was a matter of personal interest and pride to do well in areas I believed to be important.

d. Tests

Under this heading I have decided to be kind to myself and dredge up any scores that will make me feel good. I will simply wipe the mud or chalk dust off them and wave them around. We owe it to ourselves to do this occasionally. Montgomery would agree, as he believed that morale is built on success. I will not gild the lily. I hope, also, that I will not sound like modern footballers who, on scoring, will turn to the crowd and seem to beg 'clap me', unlike the Paddy Bawns of ancient Kerry fame. I draw a veil over my disasters.

One of the important tests in which I happened to do well was the infamous 'Test Talk' (a forty-minute presentation on some principle of war or campaign). This used to be one of the aspects of the course that reduced some tough-minded officer students to panic. My chosen subject was the Clausewitzian concept of 'War as a Continuation of Politics by Other Means'. I used Orwell's *Nineteen Eighty-Four* and the twisted use of language by dictators and terrorists as central strands. I titled it: 'War is Peace.'

Hitler claimed in a speech that he never asked anything of France or the UK. This was true, but, in fact, whereas he never put it in words, he really asked to be allowed to do what he liked in Europe, in order to create the Thousand Year Reich. Terrorists of all colours and persuasions, Green, Orange and Jihadi, all claim to be fighting for the 'freedom' of the people, whom they cheerfully bomb to bits when 'necessary'.

I was generously given 100% for the first time (I was told) in the history of the College. I gather that that award broke the mould and that others have been awarded since. I understand that the reasoning behind it is now accepted. In practical, sensible terms, how good can anyone do in this exercise? If someone does all the necessary research and produces something that is considered by the College Staff to be worthwhile, then they deserve more or less full marks.

In hindsight, I often wonder how much good did that do me in the long run? Did it simply give me a reputation of being over-confident? Arrogant? Perhaps it makes people feel that the recipient gets things too easily. Anyway I was very pleased and grateful for that encouragement.

At this stage I am afraid that I am conveying an impression of an indoors, lectures and talks, course, whereas the 'C & S Course' has very much an outdoor focus on the hills and valleys of Ireland, over which we may one day have to fight. Tactical exercises assume a major importance as the techniques studied on the sand tables and models in the lecture halls must be put into practice. Hail, rain or snow, as unfortunately in battle, had to be endured, as we tramped up and down hills with our map-boards, deciding where to place our brigades in the best defensive positions or move them in attack.

All likely problems were built in to these tests and I had another one of my slim bag of scores on one. The normal procedures were that we would be given the 'gen' on the 'war situation' and allowed time to 'recce' the area, before returning to announce our individual decisions. If it were an attack exercise, those advocating a right flank attack would stand together, as would the group settling for the left or 'up the middle with smoke'.

On one exercise, a defence operation on the high ground over the lakes of Blessington, I found myself sitting on my shooting stick on a little mound on my own. All groups would be questioned on the basis of their preferred decisions and as the discussion progressed some might change and join other groups. Eventually, in this case all the class more or less settled for a counter-attack of some sort while nobody would join me.

The instructors worked this up into a kind of a good-humoured joke with: 'Well, will anyone at this late stage, join the Goggs on his little mound?'

No takers.

This went on for the afternoon as various aspects of the exercise were teased out until the College Commandant arrived. In a friendly aside to me he pointed out that it was nearly five o'clock and if I gave up we could all get to the Mess bar in time for a beaker before dinner.

Eventually, however, the Chief Instructor said with a laugh: 'I have news for all you guys. The mound was too small to take you all but looking for divisional assistance with immediate artillery support was the correct thing to do. It would have been suicide to get the men out of their trenches for a counter-attack in that situation: even if they were all Robert Emmets.'

As in war, the occasional success makes up for the inevitable disasters. My admiration for the Montgomery-type caution and pragmatism had paid off. I had many entertaining arguments with an ex-British officer, who owned a local hotel, on that question. He had served under Monty and did not like him. He seemed to think that 'Monty' was a bit of a crank, who could have done with more of the American 'gung-ho'. I agreed that it was a tragedy and a prolonging of the war when Montgomery and the Brits failed to persuade Eisenhower and the Americans to go straight for Berlin and not advance on a wide front across Europe.

But I quoted how the foundation for the victory at El Alamein was the promise by Monty to his troops of the Eighth Army that he would not ask them to attack again until he was sure they would win. He achieved this in the battle of Alam Halfa, when his carefully prepared plan, with his tanks in hull-down positions, beat the Desert Fox. This led on to El Alamein and the 'end of the beginning'.

As on all courses, military or civil, tests merely throw light on progress or reveal necessary areas for improvement. I always believed that the principal thing was to find enjoyment in what you had to do, and take satisfaction of the occasional job done well.

e. Certificates

In my day we were awarded course certificates if qualified from the C&S Course. Today students can qualify for a master's degree. At the presentation of the certificates, reference was invariably made to the suitability of such training for civilian management.

Professor Denis Lucey presented this idea in *The Irish Times*, particularly the ability to think strategically. He argued that 'military training and education was a major advantage in today's business world' and 'that Clausewitz's dictum of war as a continuation of politics is equally relevant to commerce'. He pointed out that 'modern business school teaching has borrowed heavily from the military'.

The Chief of Staff, Lieut.-Gen. Sean MacEoin referred to this phenomenon at one presentation saying, 'We tolerate this leakage to civilian employment because we have no resettlement schemes. We do not like it but we accept it.'

The result of the 'leakage' from the Officer Corps is an ex-army 'old boy net' across most sectors of Irish life, public service and private commercial as well as academic. My own Cadet School classmates have held a wide variety of civilian appointments at senior level. For example, glancing down through a list for one of our cadet class reunions: Group Operations Manager Cantwell and Cochrane; Personnel Director Calor-Cosangas; Supply Manager Whittaker Corp, Kuwait; Manager Irish Bloodstock Breeders Association; Personnel Manager MNC Group; Lecturer Maynooth; Director Battersby Auctioneers; Bursar Castleknock

College; Manager Equitation Division, *Bord na gCapall;* Training Executive, Irish Hardware Association.

Of those who took early retirement, the first was as a lieutenant, who became a Jesuit (Fr Michael MacGreil) lecturing in sociology in Maynooth. He produced the Ewart-Biggs prize-winning study *Prejudice and Tolerance in Ireland.* He now says Mass for our cadet class reunions. Fifteen others, as well as myself, retired in our mid-thirties as captains, another one took early retirement as a commandant and the last, as a lieutenant colonel, a total of 18.

In physical as well as mental fitness, the officer is at his best both personally and professionally on his Command and Staff Course. This is partly due to the feeling of competence both physical and psychological that one gets from the satisfactory performance of such a mix of tests, day by day for nine intensive months. It comes like an invigorating cold shower to men, working in grooves for years, waking them up to their real capabilities.

It also comes at that psychological milestone, around the age of 35, when one is forced to think about the future and the length of time, despite senior qualifications, one had, in those days, to wait for promotion. This generally meant in my day, in our peacetime army, in the forties for commandant, which would merely add a few extra increments on a captain's salary and the fifties for lieut.-colonel, a battalion commander, who would really need to be a fit thirty-something. This is therefore the time when those (almost half of our class), who eventually switch to the pin-stripe, begin thinking of such a move. This is not the case, however, today, when the Army offers so many opportunities at home and abroad. If serving today I know that I would find it even harder to leave, despite the possibility of more money in civilian life.

I put in a paper on the course for a career plan whereby the infamous career pyramid with a large number of junior officers at the base going up through various bottlenecks to much smaller numbers at the higher levels, could be redesigned. I suggested that introducing the rank of Warrant Officer could fill a lot of the appointments now filled by junior officers (e.g. assistant quartermaster, or assistant adjutant). Two of the principal features of the plan would be a university segment of an officer's education and an optional outflow at a certain stage into an appropriate level of the public service. A university component was, years afterwards, recognised as part of an officer's education. The civil service unions however objected strongly some years ago when some officers were drafted in to the Department of Finance to help prepare for a special EC regional project.

Another suggestion I offered during the course was that we should visit the battlefields of the Somme. Current classes do so. I had in mind particularly the 16th (Irish) Division and the 36th (Ulster) Division and their combined victory at Ginchy and Messines Ridge. About 30,000 Irish soldiers from both sides of our mental, politico-religious, border fought and won together. The largest Irish Army ever to fight in one battle.

Douglas Gageby (then editor of *The Irish Times*, who had Emergency service) commented in the Mess one evening on my return, something about 'having seen an out-of-focus photograph of me in the *Irish Independent*'. That photograph was the cause of much laughter because we all thought that a well-known and popular Dublin GAA player would be chosen. I had some laughs with Cathal O'Leary about this in later years. Whereas I, an unknown organiser of cushy cross-country runs in the Cadet School, was the student featured in the piece about the presentation of certificates.

9
Peace in Cyprus?

a. The Trumpet Sounds

I draw attention occasionally to my contribution to world peace at the behest of the UN. I firmly hold that the praise lavished on the heads of Dag Hammarskjöld, U Thant, Lieut.-Gen. Sean McKeown and myself is well deserved. (In my case perhaps, not by name, but it is the inference I take from all the relevant speeches about UN peacekeepers.)

Nonetheless, family hands rush to mouths to stifle dramatic yawns and a clever son-in-law did a comic rendition of a photograph of me talking to my grand-daughter, with speech balloons:

'Pappy, did you know that this is Auntie Ursula's birthday?'

'I'm glad you told me that, Reb, because it reminds me of another old army story.'

Clever friends ask: 'Well, did you die anyway?'

Knowing full well, on the evidence available to them that I did not.

Other smart alec questions include:

'How long did you spend doing all that *gaisce* in any case; sure you were only a few months abroad?'

My reaction is, so what? According to P. H. Pearse a real hero has only to live for one day to achieve immortal glory.

By the time the trumpet sounded for me to sort out the situation in Cyprus on behalf of the UN, I had reached my mid-thirties. Despite being qualified for higher levels, with my C & S Course, I was still only half way up the captain's ten year pay scale. I would be crawling up the seniority list for the next twenty years. It was seventeen years that month since I had entered the Cadet School.

Things were sluggish in the Army in the sixties, while the job market outside was improving day by day. An indication of how the situation was exercising military minds is given in an article in *An Cosantoir* of September 1968. In a survey of British Defence Policy, Lieut.-Col. Sean Garvey draws attention to the British 'enlightened efforts to link military service with industry so as to ensure good post-service employment for officers and men'.

He describes it as 'a feature of life which has been ignored or treated lightly', by ourselves, adding that 'experiments in this field will be watched with keen interest'. So, like half of the class, I had started sending applications for 'civvy' jobs.

Nonetheless, I bravely answered the call to duty, in November 1968, hoping that the Cypriots would feel reassured that 'one sword at least their rights would guard'. With the heady feeling of heroic self-sacrifice, like an ancient Greek hero sailing into a golden sunset, I followed the trail of the medieval knights to Cyprus. Late for the summer sun but still very pleasant, the holiday aspect however was reduced by the 'Sandbag Panic' – anything that stood still had sandbags put around it, in anticipation of a Turkish attack. My job was in the UN HQ in Nicosia Airport which had, in my memory, more sandbags than bricks.

After having just put away my Othello studies, here I was in Othello country, in a modern version of his war, with Turkish planes overhead as well, I imagined, as the guns of a Turkish fleet on the horizon. Nicosia Airport would be a number one target. Nothing happened, but I was not disappointed.

There were six armies represented in the Force (UNFICYP, United Nations Force in Cyprus). The British ran the HQ Mess and a British Brigadier, Brig. Harbottle, was Force Commander. A charismatic personality, like Colonels Tony Lawlor or Aiden O'Byrne, while 'on parade' he was the essence of military formality but socially very informal and relaxed at a party.

In routine administration, while being obviously in command, he could be entertainingly individual. As when a phone call from the secretariat interrupted a meeting with a series of complaints about accounts, seemingly he brought the discussion to an end with a classic Blimpish:

'Go away', putting down the phone.

After their '7 to 9' party I met him in the hall on the way out and, perhaps fortified by the few jars, I told him that a British officer at the party had told me that he had written an article for *An Cosantoir* (our defence journal) on his UN service and I asked him if he would consider something like that.

He simply smiled and said, 'Ah, my UN comrade.'

I found my old sparring partner, the Signals commandant from Observer Corps HQ, installed before me. He kindly pretended that I was welcome so I felt that it was time to tear up a defensive note that I had held on to, about a botched Signals exercise. I was told by my predecessor in the appointment, Captain Enda Ryan, that it was the custom that commandants/majors were not saluted or addressed as 'sir' by captains in the HQ. Looking back on it, I think that I may have accepted that a little too enthusiastically, without waiting to be informed by the officers affected, when I could have said something like, 'But I insist.'

Two British officers, a captain and a major, volunteered to show this new kid around the block. We were continuing the briefing patrol in a pub, one day, when, as I was getting to the point of a story, I heard the sound of what seemed to be a heavy truck hitting something close. I continued with my story until I was interrupted, 'Hey, that's our bag, old fellow, blasé, stiff upper lip and all that, ignoring bombs.'

I had not recognised the noise for what it was, but I did not enlighten them.

We continued our journey northwards with me determined not to be over-impressed by Durrell's mountain climbing 'into blue space, topped by mouldering turrets' of the great Crusader castles. Reaching Kyrenia, we entered the Harbour Club, the centrepiece of their presentation: *Bitter Lemons*, etc. I was at the counter when the landlord noticed my Irish Contingent flash.

'Irish?'

'Yes.'

'Dublin?'

'Yes.'

'South Dublin?'

'Yes.'

'Stillorgan?'

'Yes.'

It transpired that his brother, a university lecturer, was a neighbour of mine at home at the time. The two friendly Brits announced that they were resigning as my guides: 'We bring him here to a pub famed in song and story but, of course, he is an old mate of mine host's brother.'

Shortly afterwards we were invited to attend a soccer match in which 'A' Company of Dancon (Danish Contingent), commanded by Major Budde-Lund, with whom I had become friendly, was playing. Our problem was that none of the three of us were fluent in soccer lore. I had never been to a soccer match. In my case Gaelic and Rugby were my limit; the other two had to omit Gaelic from my short list. I had become friendly with that Danish Major after I had sympathised with him on their hard luck at the Battle of Clontarf. I was the only one also to notice that he wore decorations as well as service medals. He explained that he had been equerry to the King. On leaving Cyprus he presented me with his black and red lanyard, which could only be worn if presented and could not be bought.

The Danish Officers' Mess was bright with candles and flowers and the sun shining on the lunch table. We made the usual mistake at the smorgasbord of taking too much of the first course, but with a waiter pouring a schnapps with everything, we had a most pleasant meal. Plunging in their pool fully schnapped, members of the mess staff followed us around with towels.

Their social formality was a lesson to us. I remember on my first invitation to their Mess, standing chatting with the CO before eventually picking up my glass of Danish beer. As I did, so did he, and then the whole group lifted their tankards saying: '*Skol*'. Feeling silly, I realised that they had all been waiting for the guest to begin.

Years afterwards, these memories came back when we enjoyed the wonderful hospitality of a next-door neighbour, the MD of the Danebank: long lunches with Danish beer and schnapps in his garden. He had astonished his Irish guests at his first party when we stood for some time on arrival looking at the bottles, waiting for other guests to arrive before starting. He adapted quickly, however, like his forefathers, who had settled here after many business visits in their longboats, and became 'hibernior hiberniores ipsos'.

A note on our eventful history was also struck at a dinner in McKee Officers' Mess for the officers of a visiting Norwegian naval ship. Their Captain was pleased, as he said in his after-dinner speech, that while we 'once called them Vikings (he pronounced it Wikings) and attacked them coming ashore, we now invite them to dinner'.

b. The Office

There was a serious side, of course, to our life in Cyprus: local and world peace. My job was in logistics. In the HQ organisation, the Lieut.-Colonel (British) was known as 'Logs 1', the Major (Canadian) 'Logs 2', and the Captain (me) 'Logs 3' (re-titled 'Twigs' by Enda). One of my tasks was to be in a position at all hours to inform the Force Commander of the operational situation (location, state of readiness) of a thousand vehicles.

I had a British warrant officer on the staff, addressed as 'Mister'. A large happy man, who was a very impressive soldier, in rank, between an NCO and a commissioned officer, very efficient and helpful to me. He had a wonderfully English way of saying, 'Charming', if someone came bustling in demanding attention without the usual courtesies. He confirmed my view as put in a paper on my C & S Course that the Warrant Officer idea works.

The Lieut.-Colonel was also friendly and helpful, an easy mannered polite man. The Canadian Major was easy to get on with but I remember him having two regular complaints. One was his impatience for his over-due promotion to Lieut.-Col., as he was now 37. This only reminded me of our situation, as I saw no prospect of that rank before my fifties, which was why, of course, I was looking over the hill at civvy-land. The Major's other complaint was usually voiced in mock seriousness: 'What's with this Mr Warrant Officer, anytime I want him to do something, it's the Captain wants this, the Captain said that. Do I count on this ranch?'

At the end of my first fortnight both the Lieut.-Colonel and the Major had to be absent at the same time and the 'Logs' briefing of the incoming regiment, the Royal Green Jackets, fell to me.

'We have full confidence in you,' they lied.

I had picked up information from briefings in the two weeks, with help supplied by the Warrant Officer and our Canadian Sergeant, but I had to begin with:

'Sir, gentlemen, as I have been on the island only a few weeks before you, you may take down all I say and use it in evidence against me.'

The laughter broke the ice and they settled down. I was considerably helped also by the contributions from my 'guide' British Major who would jump up during my briefing saying things like, 'Can I do my bit now?'

It seemed to go down very well, so much so that when an Irish Lieut.-Colonel arrived to give the Engineers briefing, he seemed puzzled at the atmosphere, giving me a hooded look. His own way of livening up proceedings was to throw in the occasional stage-Irish pronunciation.

The Irish and the British generally got on well despite an apparent desire to replay the 1916 match by one or two of ours. They would sing 'Kevin Barry' in response to our attempt at the 'Sash'. While there may have been some occasional subterranean rumblings among some Scots or Welsh, the English officers looked at the problem of the North in very much the same way as ourselves. My father always said that he had socially 'tuned in' to the English, during his service, much more easily than to our fellow Celts. Also, despite their predilection for quoting *Winnie the Pooh* and *Alice in Wonderland* as well as public-schoolboy type boisterous games in the Mess after a few jars (in contrast to our resort to singing and 'philosophical' discussions) the British generally were socially pleasant companions.

I felt very embarrassed one day when confronted by a sergeant-major who reproached me for not turning up in the NCOS' Mess for drinks. I had, like most Irish, taken him to mean, as we would, casually, 'drop in for a jar', but he had intended it to be a formal invitation. I find the act of lying extremely difficult: even at school I could not lie my way out of trouble if something were put to me in concrete terms. Yet I had to invent an excuse on my feet, as the situation became clear to me. I think I succeeded because he remained friendly afterwards: at least in what passes for friendly salutes from sergeant-majors in any army.

On the other hand, Christy had the opposite experience. He went in to the NCOS' Mess one day looking for a sergeant, when he was confronted by the senior NCO present who asked him politely but firmly, 'Have you been invited in here, sir.'

At one drinks party that refused to come to life, the Brits formed a rugby scrum and livened things up by sweeping everyone on their way until they hit a wall of puzzled, stony-faced Finns, without doubt, the most interesting contingent. There were some questions one evening from the Finns at dinner about Othello's Tower in Famagusta. I explained where I saw Othello's place in Shakespeare's forest of tall but fatally flawed leaders. I also recalled my Uncle Joe declaiming:'I kissed thee ere I killed thee', after a visit by the 'fit-ups' of Anew MacMaster to Dingle.

The Finncon Colonel told me that they were very interested in all this but that English came far down their scale of language skills after Russian or German. Their competence with English nonetheless illustrated the international aspect of that language.

I decided to introduce them to our national language. I recited a few stanzas, beginning with:

> 'Oiche dhom go doilig dubhach,
> Cois farraige na dtonn dtrean,'

This in what I imagined was a style of Yeatsian declamation, but, when I could see no nodding of Finnish heads, like our politicians, I continued in our second official language.

They were different, however, in that they did things their own way. One very soldierly young Finnish officer told me that he was studying for the Church. Another explained that he was only just back in the Army after a term in prison (something to do with the damage caused in a crash of an Army Air Corps plane). There is no way, in these islands, that a commissioned officer would be accepted back in those circumstances. A Finnish officer was insulted in a down-town restaurant one night and on the following night the men of his platoon went down and demonstrated their displeasure.

The 'Q' staff complained that Finncon ate the emergency ration packs and had to be constantly supplied with new ones. I was asked to try to 'sort it', as I seemed to get on so well with them and see would I succeed where others had failed. In due course a 'jildy' young Finnish lieutenant arrived in my office, introduced with a flourish by the Warrant Officer: 'A representative of our gallant Finnish allies, sir, he wants to talk of cabbages and kings.'

The young officer saluted: a good military custom to salute when entering someone else's office regardless of rank. I stood up and returned the courtesy, welcomed him, offered him coffee, and had just got into my stride about the rations when the saluting business started again, like pressing the wrong key on a computer.

I think that he must have been acknowledging my instructions. He repeated that he clearly understood and after more pleasant chat and a quick flurry of mutual salutes he left. I called in the Warrant Officer and the Sergeant. I knew that they had been listening and asked them did they think I had succeeded. The Warrant Officer shook his head:

'I'm afraid, sir, that it will take more than Irish diplomacy and a battery of salutes to achieve this.'

He was right. My effort produced no immediate result. I had very shortly afterwards my own problem. I had allowed the Finns a Rover in temporary exchange for one of their cars that had to be sent to base workshops. The Rover had a revolving light on top as it was intended for military police or medical use. If I were to offer them a Silver Ghost 'Roller' instead, I just could not succeed in getting it back.

Whatever unit had it enjoyed going around with the light flashing and held on to it for dear life. Phone calls failed to penetrate the wall of stolid Nordic politeness and repeated assurances that I had nothing to worry about.

We never forgot, however, that the Finns had proved themselves to be top-class soldiers, having taught the Russian Bear a lesson in 1940 that strength was not enough.

They made good, professionally dependable and pleasant, comrades. I enjoyed working with them and the Swedes, and learned to look at old problems in new ways.

They did things their way.

c. International Comrades

Working with an international HQ had its pitfalls in varying interpretations of orders and SOPs. It was pointed out to me that, while the HQ comprised various nationalities, we were essentially one military organisation and that members of our own contingents should not try for short cuts through various procedures by going to their own fellow countryman rather than the appropriate section. This seemed logical and conducive to a smoothly working HQ and initially I tried to maintain the correct attitude. Luckily in a short time my CO, the British Lieut.-Colonel, a calm and sensible officer, commented that one of the advantages in a mixed nationality group was that each contingent had someone in HQ to whom they could go with a problem.

I felt somewhat foolish because I had only just suggested to the Irish QM that he should go directly to the stores section, to sort his problem, rather than through me. I was glad to get back to him and explain the clash of orders. UN Forces tend to suffer from the 'many cooks' syndrome, as was illustrated afterwards in Bosnia.

I heard a Swedish officer say one evening, to a companion, as he looked out a window, 'It must be either the Green Jackets or the Irish, judging by the seriousness of the drill.' The most serious drill on the island however, was performed by the Austrians at the funeral Mass for a comrade-in-arms: Captain Christy McNamara, who brightened any gathering with his songs, often in the *sean-nos*, but who tragically died during his posting. I had had a most enjoyable evening with him over the mountain in Kyrenia during the previous week. After Christy's funeral, I got a lift back to the Mess from our Engineers Lieut.-Colonel.

This was the first friendly contact since the night I was asked by the Provost Marshal (a Canadian colonel), to go down to the table where the Engineers officer was sitting, to let them know that if they wanted the bar to be kept open late it was customary to have a 'whip-around' of a few pounds for the barman.

I was quite happy with this because I liked that particular barman: a cheerful Scotsman, who was gradually picking up an Irish vocabulary, asking me if I wanted a '*toisin*' of whiskey and a drop of '*uisce*' with it. I went over and sat down and waited for an opening to pass on the message. The Engineers officer seemed to have taken a dislike to me since the briefing of the Green Jackets and was not prepared to listen. I could never work out what his problem was. The Provost Marshal was watching so I just shrugged my shoulders like a French Canadian and left.

To me, the French Canadians were a revelation. They were so totally French in accent and manner, despite providing walking evidence of the widespread influence throughout the Commonwealth of the old imperial military standards in their Guards and Black Watch Regiments. On my first evening looking around the Mess bar, a Canadian lieutenant asked, 'Are you looking for the gentlemen from the Emerald Isle? They are usually at that table?'

He pointed down to the other end of the room, but as I was not looking for anyone in particular he said, 'Let's be buddies' and bought me a beer.

I was happy standing and chatting with the mixed crowd of Canadians, Finns and Brits, at the counter. There were just a small number of Irish officers in the HQ and the officers with whom I would have enjoyed socialising were all out in the Infantry Company Group at Xeros, Jimmy Mortel and Tom Stapleton, to name but two.

d. KIA

Christy's funeral Mass was a sad occasion but by then death on foreign service for any reason was becoming a fact of life for Ireland. Apart from the toll of accidents, KIA (killed in action) has appeared on many an operational log.

From the national trauma of the solemn funeral down O'Connell Street of Kevin Gleeson and the other Niemba victims the country had grown up to the realities of world 'peace-keeping' under Chapter VI of the UN Charter. Legislation has since been passed to allow Irish troops to be sent abroad on missions under Chapter VII, peace enforcing, although army lore has it that they have operated for years under Chapter 6 1/2.

Ten men of Lieut. Kevin Gleeson's patrol were killed. One, Private Joseph Fitzpatrick, had survived and returned to the Irish outpost in Niemba. They had been attacked by Balubas, primitive but fierce fighters, who opposed Mr Tschombé's secessionist policy. Diplomatic opinion as reported was that this ambush had created a new situation and made an already explosive situation in the Congo more difficult. Kevin Gleeson was a friend of mine, who had been detailed for the Standard Infantry Course with me and was wearily preparing all the material necessary (for test talks, etc.) On a visit to the Command Adjutant he requested a posting to the Congo battalion (the 33rd Battalion, with Lieut.-Col. Dick Bunworth as CO).

I always remember my last chat with him in the Mess at Clancy Barracks, tall, pale complexioned, sleek hair, and his non-heroic, soldierly comment, half-serious, half-joking: 'Why am I going on this caper? Is it just to dodge the course? I'm now perfectly happy, married, mortgage fixed and, at last, a car; what else do I want?'

I mumbled something about being envious of him going on this military adventure. He looked at me quizzically:

'You could get killed on this kind of a caper.'

The raised arm of that young Irish officer, facing the Balubas with his shout of '*Jambo*' (friend) will haunt the national memory for a long time as a symbol of our innocence and Christian approach, which we have since learned must be tempered with caution. Nonetheless, a lesser-known fact, of which we can also be proud, was the honourable decision not to take punitive action on the spaced-out Balubas by a follow-up patrol under a young officer, who was obviously very suitable, years afterwards, for command of the UN operation on the India-Pakistan Border. (Brigadier General Gerry Enright). The incident inevitably calls to mind the classic military performance of Pte Tom Kenny, stumbling out of the jungle still with two painful arrows, saluting the officer in command of the patrol that found him, Comdt P.D. Hogan: '808457 Pte Kenny, reporting, sir.'

This really was a *Bumper Book for Boys* story brought to life.

There were, of course, many others, notably Lieut. Paddy Riordan, who also died in the Congo, in the battle for the Tunnel, described in a German paper as leading his men as if on parade. I had been a student on an Intelligence Course with Paddy some years before and I do not think that we ever referred to that possible result in any of our 'elegant solutions' to the course problems.

The blood shed for a new Ireland on the world stage was part of our national coming of age.

This has been acknowledged recently in the posthumous award of the Military Star to 38 Defence Forces personnel, including Kevin and Paddy, who died in hostile action overseas.

I have never been closer than at one remove from the glory of *pro patria mori*. Once was as I was going through Nicosia when stopped by what looked like a Turkish FCA lad with a rifle as big as himself.

Small brown round face, little brown cap with a red badge. I was thinking of the line:

'More pandy for the Pallas Battalion.'

I just smiled at him and waved my swagger stick walking past.

Thinking about it afterwards, I realized that it was extremely naïve of me. I knew that he had no reason to stop me but, of course, that need not matter in those circumstances. On the following night he shot at someone else. The Brits were much more wary. One warned me, 'You're too trusting. Never take a chance with any of them.'

e. Life on the Island

Life on the island was quite pleasant, with letters from home on the latest adventures of our three 'babs' and on yet another two ex-Cadet School classmates, who had got 'civvy jobs'. Entertainment consisted largely of the occasional few beakers in the Mess, and, bearing in mind an early start (07.30 hrs in the office) there were not many late nights. I went down town on only a few occasions.

On one of these trips we visited an old wine shop with huge dusty vats on display, giving the impression that here surely lived Bacchus, where, for a few mills, one of the ancient keepers of his shrine brought glasses of golden *'Crème de Banana'* liqueur on a silver tray. A thin bright beam of Greek sun cut through the semi-darkness of the shop and lit an internal fire in the small glass in my hand, as I was shown how to squeeze a section of orange into the liquid to cut the heavy sweetness. This liqueur has been part of the closing ritual of special family dinners ever since: obligatory at occasions like Christmas and the New Year. My sons-in-law (Martin, Ian and Assie) insist on carrying it on to the next generation.

Films in the Canadian Mess, where we sat in armchairs and sipped beer in comfort, were another attraction. For the New Year I went with two Brits to bring the traditional New Year's dawn 'gunfire' of rum to the troops in their billets. Many of them were Irish, who told me, whether in earnest or out of politeness, that they could just as easily have joined the Irish Army.

The UNFICYP operation involved mainly short unaccompanied tours, of months rather than years. Tours with family were for a year. One of the hazards of an unaccompanied tour of duty was the easy move into a 'shacking up' arrangement with someone unattached on the island. I knew that some of our UN comrades were involved. I found myself one evening chatting again with a fair-haired nurse, whom I had found to be pleasant company and had met on a previous social occasion. I was jokingly recounting my youthful day-dreams of rescuing girls from pirates when she smiled, 'Would you like to mind me for a while?'

My response was to continue the conversation at that level and by the time the evening was over I found myself returning to base with the others. It took some time for the penny to drop but then I realised that this was how it happened. However pleasant and easy, this kind of a situation for some, must have led to a first step down a primrose path of disloyalty.

When I first arrived I heard that instead of our usual male orderlies we were to have females looking after us. I wondered if that posed problems for some? No problem. On the following morning she arrived, all in black, carrying her eighty odd years with Mediterranean grace.

The Irish Infantry unit on the island at that time, was stationed at Xeros. The strength had been reduced from battalion to company group. My predecessor, Enda Ryan, informed me that they had invited us to a dinner to celebrate my arrival and his departure. It was a very pleasant affair as these normally are but at a late stage during the night, when the noise was revving up to its closing decibels, Enda, turning to me, jokingly referred, *sotto voce*, to the CO as 'an old bollix'. I saw the CO looking at me. It seemed as if he had heard the remark and thought that I was the one who had made it. This was bad enough but on a later evening I happened to come out from a party given by the police when I saw him in mildly embarrassing circumstances and he turned and saw me looking. Such is the way that the Fates tangle the threads of our occasionally ill-weaved patterns of relationships in our march to the music of time.

My room was under a veranda of greenery facing towards Mount Troodos. One Sunday morning, a Brit called in, 'You're presence is required on the officers' team. We are playing the NCOS and we need every hand,' he said, filling the room with the sound of total fitness.

I wondered was he 'under-trained'. I remembered the lesson I took from our Athletic Coaching Course in the Cadet School: 'Better to be under-trained and full of pep, than over-trained and sluggish.'

I knew that I could claim to be under-trained, but was I really 'full of pep' on that particular morning?

'But I'm not a player and anyhow I'm still in dressing gown and pyjies,' I said, feeling like the original rat.

'Excellent, just the right man to confuse them.'

Thus attired, I joined the motley team dressed in sunglasses and all kinds of gear from swimming trunks to track suits as well as the more conventional football strips. We were not doing too well but we were saved by the arrival of the fire engine. We used its water hose as heavy artillery against the very fit NCOs, who refused to move back and were only finally forced to admit a scoreless draw, when our friends in Army Air Corps helicopters bombed them with what seemed to be bags of flour.

I was on a short unaccompanied tour which I had enjoyed, but I was happy enough to return home, having missed home and the 'babs' more than I had expected. But this meant returning to my effort at getting a civilian appointment and time was running out. Five of my cadet class had already succeeded and if I did not get something soon my job prospects would run into the sands of my forties. Happily, I succeeded in getting an interesting offer soon after coming back. It must have been 'the times that were in it' because conditions outside were good and eventually a high number (18) of our cadet class, succeeded in making the change of career.

Was that a good move? At this stage we can just say that we did well, but those, who soldiered on, did very well indeed, reaching senior rank – two making general level. However, my years patrolling the jobs market turned up, at last, something worthwhile. I had an offer of an appointment, which would allow me to work in an area of interest to me (leadership training) and would double my income, with my salary and pension. Literally an offer I could not refuse.

I enjoyed my service in Cyprus, working and meeting with Brits, Danes, Swedes and Finns.

A Brit said to me: 'It must be the Viking-Irish memory they seem to think that you're one of them.'

As it happens our most recent operation in the Lebanon consists of a combined Irish/Finnish battalion.

After I had left (not because) the problems worsened. Disputes continued between Greeks who owned land and Turks who owned trees on it. Or someone taking a load of stones, (classified as war material), from one place to another, when intervention by the UN would be demanded. 'The quietness, the sense of green beatitude' of which Durrell had written had sadly been shattered by a vicious form of the Northern Ireland tragedy. Where once the villagers had basked in a multi-cultural sun, under various 'trees of idleness', threats and counter threats shattered their peace. However, the cautious Turks waited for five years after I had left to roll 300 tanks and 40,000 men on to the beaches of Cyprus.

The Turks called it a 'peace operation' but, by the time it was over, nearly four and a half thousand people were dead and another one and a half thousand missing. Over 140,000 people were driven from their homes. The Turks brought in over 100,000 settlers from Turkey. There are now more of these than the local Turkish Cypriots for whom the so-called 'peace operation' was waged.

f. Assignments

In a way that may not be easily understood by civilians, I felt bad about being privately glad to be home. Even though I had enjoyed my trip to Cyprus, mainly due to the characters I met there, I am not really a great foreign traveller and I believed that my father and uncles had punched in as much foreign travel as any family needed.

Back in my office, the work of the Observer Corps continued. Unabated, I feel would be the most apt descriptive word. We were determined to ensure that, in a future Emergency, we would, metaphorically speaking, at least have trousers to be caught with down, as well as our flashes and red berets.

On returning, one of the most interesting duties I was given involved taking a visiting Canadian Military Attaché around to meet various senior people in the Eastern Command. At a later date, I did the same for the Zambian Military Attaché, who was kind enough, as I met him at the Shelbourne one day, to suggest returning with him to take a commission in the Zambian Army. He indicated that I would have immediate promotion to major and lieutenant-colonel in a reasonable time.

At that stage however, I had a good prospect of a civvy job and my mind was more or less made up for a job at home. Remembering all the family members, who had made a life abroad and then had to return and take up the threads again, I did not think that this attractive offer was my cup of tea, even though a few of my army comrades had made the move to Zambia and seemed to have done well. An old comrade from the 2nd Infantry Battalion, Captain Leo Walsh, had made the move and established himself very well in the intelligence service of the Kaunda regime. A one-time copper mine manager, with whom we sometimes socialise commented, with a laugh one day: 'people were careful of what they said in Leo's presence'. I took that as a humorous comment as I always remembered that Leo was the one who put in those three little words 'at own request', when I was published in routine orders as leaving the QM's office to take command of a platoon, to make sure that I got fair play.

Ex-Irish officers were welcome, as being considered to have all the advantages of having the English language and all the necessary expertise without the disadvantage, in their view, of being associated with colonialism. Maybe they were really being too kind or conveniently forgetful on that last point. My sister-in-law, Ursula, and her husband David, regrettably no longer with us, ran a business in Ndola and confirmed that visiting Irish officers were very popular.

One of my last assignments, in my regular service, was as a member of a Board set up to make recommendations for the career structure of Military Air Traffic Control. The problem was that, in those days, the most senior appointment in that field was a commandant and it was seen as something of a dead end. In order to arrive at a 'man specification', we visited major military and civilian Air Traffic Control installations, Baldonnel, Shannon and Dublin Airport. The Chairman, Col. O'Brien, laid it down for the other two members (lieut.-colonels) that, while I was designated as Secretary, I was expected equally to contribute.

In my approach to the problem I could see another possibility for the employment of warrant officers at an appropriate level. I had seen how well the efficient and mannerly Warrant Officer in Cyprus fitted in. The problem, I was told, was that it would not be easy in a small army to introduce another grade.

However, another significant aspect of my concept was the idea of a combined interview board for prospective ATC staff. Representatives from the Army and the Department of Transport and Power together could determine if the candidate would be acceptable to both. The officer could then serve up to the time he judged right, and, should he wish to move out, he could transfer to civilian ATC at the appropriate point in the scale. Transport and Power seemed to indicate a positive interest. The Colonel was interested also but said that, in his opinion, while he thought the idea was good, he felt that we would not get it through because he believed that the combined interview board was somewhat ahead of its time.

Around that time, I had an amusing off-duty adventure one evening when I bumped into a British officer, who had served in Cyprus, drinking with an Israeli officer on leave, in the Hibernian Hotel. During a general discussion I referred to some details of Israeli tank battles, principles and SOPs. I was just about to explain that I had delivered a project on this for a course in the College when it occurred to me to say no more. I got the feeling that others found the mix interesting and appeared to be enjoying listening to the Irish officer knowing more about it than the British officer and even surprising the Israeli, who asked, 'Where are you serving?'

I thought on my feet and said:

'Oh, Army HQ.'

This seemed to make my contribution even more interesting and the Israeli spoke to me privately afterwards saying that he never knew that the Irish Army had such an interest in their situation. He mentioned contacts for me and offered to pass on material if I needed it.

When the others decided that they would like to see more of the town and it was suggested that we go on for a few more 'beakers' I went along with them, as it was still early. Unsure of what exactly they wanted to do, we stopped the taxi and to my astonishment, the Israeli called over a garda, who politely listened.

'I'm Colonel ( ) and these are Lieut. ( ) and Captain Goggin and we're looking for whores.'

The garda stood up straight and then slowly bent inwards again to look appealingly at me. I winked and smiled in my state of shock and this seemed to reassure him that he had interpreted our request correctly, so he gave us directions to an hotel on the quays where he knew that we would have no problem getting a few more jars. I eventually escaped.

Our international contacts were now producing visible signs that our army had moved on to a broader stage. There were, for instance, Indian officers staying in the Mess: a Colonel and a Captain. The senior man, a calm, stolid, self-assured man, was a pleasant addition to the social life of the Mess but the handsome Captain was slightly disconcerting, asking members, in the authentic drawl of the Raj, 'Do you play polo?'

Irish troops always seemed to get on well with the Indians, notably in the Congo and years afterwards in Somalia, when an Indian brigade provided the security for our Transport Company.

This was the year also that we had for the first time, the additional

186

educational value of Zambian cadets in the Military College. Now the novelty has worn off. Officers from the British and foreign armies have attended courses in the UN School, which was brought to a very high standard under the command of Colonel Jim Mortell, who, as it happens, was the young officer raising the flag in the early days of RTE. We had a most interesting briefing on the UN School at a recent class-reunion day, as well as briefings on the Cadet School and the Military College today.

I had been flattered once at being offered an appointment in the Cadet School by one of our most gentlemanly of officers, Colonel Cyril Mattimoe. But as it would mean a reorganised domestic routine and with the decision on retirement becoming more urgent, with me now in my middle thirties, I did not take him up on his suggestion. I knew that I would regret that decision, if I were to stay on, having no doubt that the Cadet School must offer the most satisfying work in the Army. However, Harry, an ex-classmate in 'Officers' Records', informed me that it was subsequently decided that I was to be posted regardless. But, by then, I had an offer I could not refuse, for an outside appointment.

In my time, an army officer qualified for a modified pension after twelve years, gradually improving as he serves on. (The pension scheme has now considerably changed.) It took a captain ten years to get to the maximum of his regimental pay scale and I was only halfway up. I was faced in that small army (I could not have known that it was to increase in strength) with spending the next twenty years of my life waiting for promotion to Lieut.-Colonel.

Yet this decision to leave was the hardest in my working life. Changing jobs afterwards was a simple pragmatically inspired move; but, I really do not think that however much I loved the Army I could have said to the family that I was prepared to turn down an offer that could improve our lifestyle to that extent. The improvement was empirically verifiable: central heating installed, a good car purchased that finally merited the approval of our cleaning lady and holidays in Greece.

The Colonel said that he supposed that there was no point in asking me to stay but he guessed why I was going: 'To go to work in the morning and decide things for yourself rather than spend several more years bringing in recommendations to me.'

However, I could not go, it appeared, without one final adventure. A report of a speech in the *The Irish Times* before I had officially applied for retirement, referred to the setting up of a new Leadership Training Section in Macra na Feirme(a rural youth organisation) to be 'headed up by Patrick J. Goggin'.

It had got my middle initial wrong but its meaning was clear. Questions were asked at GHQ. The Colonel, thinking on his feet, informed the Chief of Staff that he already knew about it from discussions with me. I assumed that that would be the end of my military adventures.

10

War in Ireland?

a. Back in the Green

My military adventures were not to be at an end however. In a very short time, once again, like St Patrick, I heard the voice of the Irish people calling on me. At least that was what I took the message to mean from the Adjutant, 2nd Infantry Battalion. That was the unit to which I had been assigned on retirement, having been awarded a commission on the Reserve of Officers (First Line). With the State seal in the centre, it was signed by President Eamon de Valera, Taoiseach Jack Lynch and Minister for Defence Michael Hilliard. It is now framed and on display, more for the famous signature rather than the name in the centre of the parchment.

I was only getting into my stride enjoying my civilian job in the autumn of 1969 when developments in the Northern situation caused the Army to call up the Reserve and turn to me for help. Things were bad: Captain Terence O'Neill had resigned as Prime Minister, despite his being made our 'Man of the Year' some months previously. British troops had arrived, albeit without the bugles of the US Cavalry, but, nonetheless, to the rescue of the beleaguered Catholics, who fed them with apparently endless cups of 'char' and 'wads'.

That ever vigilant, reverend gentleman, Dr Ian Paisley, revealed that he had shocking evidence to prove that the troops had come to 'keep the Catholics happy'. But confirmation of what went tragically wrong afterwards between the people and the Army that came to help them, has been provided by Gerry Adams in his book *Before the Dawn* (1998).

He reveals the response of 'we activists': 'What can we do about the fucking soldiers?'

Now we all know what they were able to do, which was mainly ensure that the soldiers became and remained the enemy. The 'Green' activists got their usual help from the 'Orange' variety with a Junior Orange parade offering the opportunity for 'Green' stone throwing to which a Scottish regiment over-reacted. After that, the picketing of the Army discos by Sinn Fein and the tarring and feathering of local girls who fraternised with the troops, produced the coolness followed by hatred that suited the 'Green' activists.

The Sharrock and Davenport biography gives an interesting sidelight on the situation in Gerry Adams's home area. The local company commander, Major David Hancock, had got on very well until he was warned by a local man, 'I think you'd better go Major, things are going to get rough now'.

Some soldiers did the kind of things also that tired and worried soldiers do and have done since the beginning of time, especially after the murder of comrades. Between them they produced the street dramas of the Northern Troubles. Those sad years have produced some perplexing mysteries. Like, how is it that when trained men fired baton rounds at hundreds of stone and petrol-bomb throwing rioters directly in front of them, they only ever succeeded in hitting innocents on their way home from either evening devotions or visits to sick grandmothers?

When the call to arms was sounded, I knew that I was not going to stand idly by. I equipped myself with map-board, talc and china-graph pencils as well, of course, as my 'wellies'. I headed into Cathal Brugha Barracks with a fond farewell to my family, not knowing when I would see them again. It was not too long however, because when I reported in I found everybody in the bar, and, after a few briefing beakers, was told that I could report in the morning.

On the following day I found myself in the Adjutant's office dealing with regular strength returns and 'parade states' coming in from all the units as their reservists reported for duty. My problem was that they were coming in too often and with too much excitement about 'getting them up to Brigade' usually with only minutes in hands before a deadline.

I was on my way for coffee in the Mess when a corporal in the office said, 'Oh, sir, we have to get this "parade state" in to Brigade in about five minutes.'

'Why?'

'I don't know, sir, but it's what we've been doing.'

I rang Brigade HQ and asked what did they want the frequent reports for? Only to be told that, 'Oh, P, is that yourself back? No, it's not us, it's Command that are screaming for the consolidated brigade report.'

I rang Command only to be given the same story except that it was Army HQ that was making the demands. I rang AHQ.

'Well, the Minister would expect to be updated by lunchtime every day so that he can inform the *Dáil*, if asked what kind of a response we are getting from the Reserve.'

I took some satisfaction in going down the line again with this information and succeeded in calming the flurry of paper.

However, I had hardly time to enjoy that when I was out of the office with an appointment of Second in Command of a new Infantry Company of reservists.

b. Second in Command

In the short time I had been out, company commanders, who used to be captains, were made commandants. The officer commanding this company, a reserve commandant, was just about to retire from the Reserve on age grounds. As 2nd I/C I was given a more or less free hand in the day-to-day running the Company, with a strength of over 150.

Quite a number of the NCOs and men had returned from the UK and showed me the payslips from their jobs, way above the army pay I was passing on to them on pay-day. Most of their firms understood and would keep the jobs open. However, I was told that a few small firms, happy in their ignorance of all things Irish, seemed to think that the men were going to help some kind of an IRA campaign and threatened to sack them if they went.

It was a kind of 'phoney war' for a while after the Taoiseach, Jack Lynch, said that we could not 'stand by'. Were we going to cross the border with or without the agreement of the British Army? We now know about 'Exercise Armageddon' where this was at least considered at GHQ, but armies consider all contingencies all the time.

It is hard now clearly to remember our thoughts at the time but first and foremost we were soldiers and would have gone wherever we were ordered. We guessed that we would provide protection for refugees coming South but wondered if perhaps we should cross the border to defend some Catholic/nationalist area, against loyalist attackers. Were we really going to put a company into Newry despite our lack of air cover, in order to bring in the UN? I saw this as a political use of military force: somewhat like the political use of nuclear weapons in the cold war. Yet it was a kind of a national dream-time, produced by the shock of the savagery revealed in the murders and burnings, as well as the fantasies of some politicians, like Blaney and Boland. In July and August there were 10 deaths, 154 gunshot wounds and 745 other injuries reported.

The Report of the Cameron Commission places much of the blame on Stormont and the RUC. While we were never really sure what we would eventually be doing, I remember that a hint to anyone that not getting in line would mean that they would not be coming with the Company, if we moved, worked wonders for discipline. I remember one hardened soldier from Belfast, almost breaking down in my office, where I had to talk to him about a complaint from his Platoon Commander. He asked, dropping his 'hard man' mask: 'What will my family think, if I'm left here?'

'Well, that's up to you,' I replied 'you're a good soldier and it's only a question of staying out of trouble from now on.'

Manning the 'Thin Green Line' I had three very good young lieutenants as platoon commanders for the three large platoons of the company, but one, the best, had a tendency to take the occasional morning off, on a day's 'Uncle Charlie' (Uncertified Sick Leave). I intercepted his orderly going down to his room one morning and took his breakfast up to him. We laughed but he was commendably embarrassed.

I was pleased to find that I seemed to enjoy the responsibility, but I made a few mistakes. When our old company clerk of 'B' Company, on returning on the Reserve, heard who was in charge, he told the Company

(LEFT–RIGHT) *Ann Foley, me, Muriel and Colman*

With Muriel –
Mulranny, Achill, September 1961

Graduation UCD – 1966

Army Parade for Republic Day 1948
(COURTESY OF IRISH DEFENCE FORCES)

Command and Staff Course, 1966–67.
The author is fifth from the right in the second row from the front.

After command and staff course

Officers' Mess – McKee Barracks

At brother-in-law Ken's wedding – 1967

With Captain Enda Ryan on UN Duty – Cyprus, 1969

Daughters (LEFT–RIGHT) *Erika (6 years), Jennifer (8 years) and Ursula (6 years) – 1970*

Me with Jennifer on her great-grandfather's (David Goggin) tomb

Paddy with his brother, Bernie, at the stone.

Paddy's eldest daughter Jennifer on Jack, County Louth, 2009.

Bust of Paddy Goggin by his daughter, Ursula

Grandchildren (LEFT–RIGHT) *Zach, Stephanie, Rebekah, Ally, Megan and Jordie*

Daughters (LEFT–RIGHT) *Jennifer, Ursula and Erika*

Patrick D. Goggin, Capt.,(rtd)

Sergeant that he had high hopes for a weekend pass, despite being informed that there would be no passes. When he arrived in the office I welcomed him, delighted to see him back. He would give the kind of support needed in the company office. He hinted at problems at home in Belfast with his family and there being no weekend leave available, so I signed a pass for him. I was very busy but I should have gone and explained to the CS. I did not and, as the soldier waved his pass, a fuming CS came in to complain. It was a stupid mistake so early in my relationship with a key NCO, but we soon got over it in the bustle of activity.

Another mistake was when I asked a senior officer from Command HQ, who was visiting barracks, to have a word with the Company. He was an impressive looking and sounding man. I knew him to be an inspirational type, active in the military history field and keen on the achievement of high standards of dress and performance. On that occasion however he must have been in a peculiar mood or in a crank over something. He harangued the men for about fifteen minutes telling them that they were back in the Army now and they would have to buckle down and be good soldiers again: haircuts and more of that unfortunate line. The cold and closed expressions of the men coming off parade spoke volumes. I had expected he would acknowledge their patriotism in returning and make them feel welcome and valued.

I felt that this must have been a replay of the kind of things that were said to the ex-Emergency reservists when they reported back for service post-war. I had heard that this is why the huge reserve practically melted, but I could never believe that the officers at the time could be so short-sighted. Now I knew how it could happen to the best.

I spent some time restoring morale, joking and putting into perspective the performance of that senior officer (of whom I still thought very highly) but I felt that they deserved it.

Now on reflection I am sure that what happened was that he had interpreted my request as indicating that I had found this company of mature experienced soldiers difficult to discipline and like a good headmaster he was giving the class a bollicking for me.

In many ways I did not mind the call-up and was happy enough to be back. But the problem was that I was enjoying the challenge of my civilian appointment, Leadership Training Officer with a national youth organisation, Macra na Feirme. I found them to have a highly intelligent awareness of the requirements and very willing to help and co-operate, especially the General Secretary and the President, Joe Rea, a man of vision and infectious enthusiasm. I was glad to note, after all these years, that they are still going strong with 5,000 attending at their 2011 annual conference in Cork.

I had set up a series of courses around the country booked in to various hotels before the call-up and was very anxious to get on with it. I even called in on my way home in uniform one day to a meeting of the national executive, to ask about progress. One of Macra's principal objectives was to prepare its members for community and farming leadership. During a series of interviews for press and radio, questions tended to come up about the idea of girls in leadership positions. In those days the idea of girls coming in to the Army would have caused severe apprehension. Now, forty years on, they have achieved high levels of professionalism, reaching senior NCO and officer levels. My worry about them then was in terms of combat roles: what if one of them got wounded?

I was to see in Macra the high levels of commitment and effectiveness of girls in responsible positions on committees.

I put in an application to be released from the Reserve and succeeded in getting back to my job after a few months as the situation eased. I was given to understand, however, that I was a soldier 'on call' at any time during the current emergency.

Some others, who had returned to the colours with me, decided to soldier on in full-time service to their retirement.

c. To 'Reason Why?'

By the time I was back once again in the pin-stripe, however, the fog of war had lifted, the mists of emotional 'sneaking-regarderism' had melted to a certain extent and the Army's mission stood starkly clear. It had to defend democracy on this little island. Back at my civilian job, the mother of all the mysteries of that time for me remains the extraordinary response of our government, led by that epitome of reasonableness, Jack Lynch. For us at the time refusing to 'stand by' was exactly what one would have expected, but, why give the impression of threatening military intervention? This simply exacerbated the situation, encouraging the rioters to think that the Irish Army would be shortly in support.

Did some members of the cabinet (Boland? Blaney?) really believe that the only way to help the Catholics was by supplying arms? Why did nobody think of demanding that the British Government intervene to provide real security against Orange extremists for the beleaguered nationalist areas? The British Army was welcomed initially by the people in expectation of this.

Why was there no attempt made to find out exactly what had happened and was happening? The myth of 1969 is still used as an enabling act for continuing on the 'physical force' road. Answers must be found.

The story still lives that Protestants seemed to have gone on a rampage of murderous hate burning out Catholics, for no reason except extreme sectarianism. But, had Catholics spent some hours before that attacking the Springfield Road and Hastings Street police stations? In fact, were shots exchanged under the guidance of the 'activists', who had demanded that action be taken in Belfast to take pressure off the Bogside? Did this simply seem to confirm the widespread belief for unionists in another nationalist rising, based on Republican documents and statements on the fiftieth anniversary of 1916?

Why was there no request from us to our fellow nationalists to stop rioting? Were some of us in the South in high or low places really hoping that this was our big chance to move the political situation forward, using the troubles as an excuse for action? Yet, Malachi O'Doherty, who grew up as a Catholic nationalist in West Belfast, in *The Trouble with Guns* (1998) tears some of the veils of myth from our view of 1969, reminding us that 'most Catholics made no attempt to arm themselves for defence against loyalists and the state'. He confirmed that there were several hours of rioting outside Hastings Street police station before the 'B Specials' came on the scene and the loyalist mob gathered on the Shankill and invaded the Falls.

What help were the republican activists? I cannot remember reading of many situations where they arrived like the US Cavalry to defend their people and beat off the attackers. They seem to have succeeded too often in drawing Loyalist murderers in to defenceless Nationalist areas. John Cole, in his memoirs, writes of the 'conspiracy of fear' recording the plight of a Catholic doctor's family on the Upper Falls.

The 'other side' were certainly not any better. But the Security Forces were so convinced that a nationalist rising was in the air that the army faced towards the Falls waiting for the threatened insurrection rather than towards the rioting Loyalists.

It emerged afterwards that even the Gardai had radios on the border in expectation of the same insurrection after 1966.

As one of the thousands of minor cogs ready to grind into action to help when ordered, I cannot say now that I was asking many of those questions at the time. Our main worry was the Catholic/nationalist areas left defenceless by the British Army whose responsibility it was. As a citizen, as a soldier and as a consumer of what passed for history, I think that the bottom line was that I accepted the situation painted in all its primitive colours and so did the men of my company.

Conor Cruise O'Brien wrote in the *Irish Independent* twenty years afterwards:

'I think we were all in the grip of a visceral tribal Irish Catholic reflex without realising what was happening to us. Several of us were intellectuals who thought of ourselves as tremendously non-sectarian and secular, even agnostic. But whatever we thought we were, our gut reactions were Irish Catholic when the crunch came in 1969.'

I have sometimes wondered about this in the forty years that now separate us from that time, when Ireland teetered on the brink of catastrophe. Did we sail close to the unthinkable in 1969?

In simple terms we must ask ourselves, particularly those at the coalface as practical politicians or academic historians, why did we even come close to such a disaster?

John Healy in *The Irish Times* in the autumn of 1968, with extraordinary prevision, wrote a prescient article warning Jack Lynch about 'throwing verbal grenades across the Border', as in his speech in London about the 'evils of partition'. Healy reminded the politicians of the disastrous 'Anti-Partition Campaign' resulting in the Border campaign of the 1950s.

We now have at least some answers. In 1990 Jack Lynch categorically stated that he had no intention of sending Irish troops over the Border to bring about a UN intervention. He said that it would have resulted in 250,000 people exterminated.

Ostensibly to aid refugees from the North in the field hospitals, the troops also had the capability to observe and take action on any attempt by Green or Orange subversives to threaten the democratic health of this state. Lynch wrote that he had instructed the Chief of Staff to ensure that: 'The Army units on the border should look out for activity of this nature and stop it.'

A small focal point of the ideological position of 'physical force' was still in existence. There was no excuse: the intelligence indications were there in the IRA 'discussion' document found by Gardai in 1966. The situation at the time, when he lived on the Border, has been described by Michael Harding in his column in *The Irish Times*, as Fermanagh 'bleeding to death, farmers being blown to bits at the creamery, policemen being shot dead while going to Mass, and shopkeepers bleeding to death behind their own counters.'

Whereas the general consensus was that 'sneaking-regarderism' existed at times in high as well as low places, how bad was it really? Was Mrs Thatcher's fury with the Irish side understandable in 1979, when she considered 'taking the vote from the Irish' in the UK and 'bringing them fully within the UK's immigration laws'? Humphrey Atkins, the Northern Ireland Secretary, we now know from the archives, wished to persuade Michael O'Kennedy, the Minister for Foreign Affairs, 'to accept the view that the IRA was a terrorist organisation, posing as much a threat to the Irish Republic as to the UK.'

Were things really that bad? We now have confirmation that Jack Lynch agreed with Mrs Thatcher's proposal, after the murder of Lord Mountbatten, to allow over-flights for British Army helicopters on the southern side of the Border. Irish military operations were, in fact, quite impressive. For example, by 1993 (the year before the first cease-fire), the Army had carried out 23,500 Border patrols, checkpoints and other operations. EOD (Explosive Ordnance Disposal) teams took part in 350 operations along the Border. All this took approximately one third of the Defence budget.

Hopefully, that is now history. Now, with the surprising statesmanship of men like Martin McGuinness and Peter Robinson, there is great hope for the future, which could even include a United Ireland if suitable proactive action is taken to show that we really consider the Protestant, English-speaking, Northern Unionists to be as Irish as the constitution describes all who were born on this island. One problem is that they hear all the political guff like that about the Irish language and believe it, assuming therefore that a United Ireland would be a very cold home for them, as some kind of second-class citizens. Could they see themselves aiming at a career in an Irish-speaking Army?

We should now clarify the future hope. What kind of a country would this United Ireland be? Should we now deal with that situation like we dealt with Articles 2 and 3 of the Constitution, with a constitutional amendment giving equality to both languages?

We have made some progress, however, including accepting those men, who joined Irish Regiments of the British Army in the First World War, as the honourable constitutional nationalists that they were. Sinn Fein have shown their willingness to learn from the constitutional Redmondite approach. The Good Friday Agreement has been described by Dermot Meleady in his book, *Redmond the Parnellite* (2008) as 'Redmondism for slow learners'. The 'dreary steeples' need not get drearier.

PART THREE
REFLECTIONS

11

A Late Vocation Civilian

a. Off Parade

It is a truth, but perhaps not universally acknowledged, that the immediate practical value of a regular army, when war threatens, is that the State has a number of men who accept without question that 'on the command "fix", you don't fix.' For whom getting aboard transport at all hours of the day or night and literally going nowhere or, perhaps, somewhere completely different to where they were told, while they hung around waiting, is merely an everyday minor 'crib'. Whose only concern as they head off into the darkness is, are they entitled to 'patrol rations'?

These odd people are soldiers, and they will 'hold the fort' in situations which civilians would find totally baffling and disorienting. As the incoming civilians gradually get the drift of the rules of the game of soldiering, most of these worthy regulars will have been moved up the ranks or be quietly shunted into suitable administrative areas thereby allowing the civilians to fight the enemy civilians in the other army. When the war is over the wise old regular owls can take up the challenge of preparing for the next war or retire and exchange perceptive papers with the old regulars of the other army for each other's military journals.

I enjoyed my experience of military duty and indeed military 'low-life'. The closest I ever came to the high-life was being driven in to a reception in Dublin Castle, when the crowd, pressing around the car, seeing only me wrapped in my cloak, seemed to be only mildly disappointed that I was not Prince Rainier. The closest I came officially to VIPs was acting as ADC to the occasional ambassador. Among others, I remember the Pakistani Ambassador and as usual it meant a day in dress uniform with no other duties because technically I was under his command for the day.

On other occasions I acted as the fourth ADC for President de Valera. Seemingly the idea was that, as a tradition from the old days, when an ambassador entered the country, he would arrive with a certain staff and the host country had to meet him with an equal number of knights escort as he crossed the border. There were three ADCs permanently in the Arus so when they needed a fourth they sent for someone like me.

I was also proud to hand over well-turned out Guards of Honour to various ambassadors. I remember the Icelandic Ambassador because my photograph and the Guard of Honour appeared in the paper on the following day. I especially remember the German Ambassador, because of the way he stopped and asked questions of some of the soldiers, about their flashes or collar badges.

Sometimes, perhaps, I consciously act 'the military buff' for the entertainment of family and friends. Sometimes I am one without acting. Take the matter of clothes. Do the ideas of clothes/uniform we develop in our formative years remain with us to the end of the trail? How come I seem to have a No.1 Dress – blazer, No.2 Dress – lounge suit and No.3 Dress – dinner jacket and a clear idea when each is appropriate? Why should I find the current fashion of open-necked shirt with a semi-formal dark suit so illogical? If I felt that informal dress were appropriate I would wear a sweater or an odd jacket with open-necked shirt, certainly not a suit. Yet after all why not? Just my bias? Why do I feel somewhat uneasy, even now, if I visit the Officers' Mess in anything other than jacket and tie, when these rules have been consigned to the dustbin of history?

Perhaps our 'party piece' performances also contribute to the real 'complete us' over the years? In the same way as famous people eventually begin to resemble their caricatures? How many of our friends of the theatre have 'trod the boards' of life as a walk-on part? Choosing sock or buskin as required?

As reported, I had moved out the main gate marching to 'fresh woods and pastures new' with a 'challenging civilian career' circled as my objective on my personal map-board. I had made a successful re-entry as a late-vocation civilian. But, how does the ex-soldier adjust to this metamorphosis? While a minority seem to detach themselves from their army background and achieve a new identity, as carefully reconstructed civilians, the majority retain echoes of their former selves. The military family is like the Church: once a member, one can disguise oneself, but the soldier remains. 'You can take the man from the bog but you can't take the bog from the man.' The brown bog water that soaks all young soldiers never washes off either.

So what do ex-soldiers do that is different from their civilian friends and neighbours? I have continued in various ways very much in the same social groove. I continue to visit bookshops and book-fairs hunting books in my overlapping areas of interest (political philosophy, Irish and military history).

Like a light from afar on my interests at the time I came across in an old file a list of books that the Army HQ Library was asking back in a memo to me signed by Mr C McGowan, *a/s Leabharlannai*, dated 6 Jan 69. They included: *The Act of Creation, Writers and Politics, Man and the State, Power Politics, The Morale of the Dublin Busmen, Psychology for the Armed Services, Management and Morale.*

I have remained in touch with my old military pastures, but there are occasions when I am reminded of my museum status. Like when I found that the three bars on my dress uniform were looked upon with interest by young officers who had never seen them worn (now all wear pips: one for a 2nd lieutenant, two for a lieutenant and three for a captain).

On another sunny day I returned to the Curragh plain for the 50th Anniversary of Defence Forces Week Shooting Competitions. In the tented village, I quickly found our old .303 SMLE (Short Magazine Lee Enfield) Rifle in the museum exhibition, side by side with flintlock muskets. I tried to explain to the 'jildy' young corporal that it was not a museum piece, that it was our rifle with which we won the All-Army. He helpfully suggested that I might enjoy checking in the Military Archives tent where I found the 1951 Military College Rifle Team in an impressive battery of computer VDUs.

Despite impressive Cavalry and Artillery displays, I found myself drawn to the Target Shooting section and was offered as a volunteer by my confident wife who told the staff that I was a good shot. That had them interested and me embarrassed convinced that I was about to be shown up. But, to my relief, I did very well, and pretended total confidence. (I still have the target.)

Whatever the civilian uniform, pin-stripe or casual, when ex-soldiers meet anywhere, acronyms and abbreviations tend to creep back into their speech like an infestation of ants not totally eliminated from a garden: 'Where's the RV?'

'Ok, FUP the Horseshoe Bar at 17.30 hours; H-hour for the party 19.00.'

'Who is supplying the Tpt?'

'The Sheriff will drive, he'll take Mambo and the Weed.'

Army nicknames still identify. The links that keep the bond alive are things like cadet-class reunion dinners, associate membership of one's old Mess, membership of ARCO (the Association of Retired Commissioned Officers) and clubs that are either military or have military connections. The McKee Officers'Club for retired officers, who have been members of Army HQ Mess, is an example, where the Mess is still used for meetings and functions.

As it happened recently the Club, of which I am a member, had its annual lunch on the same day as one of our class-reunion lunches. They had the main dining room, we had Room 4.

The Military History Society of Ireland also provides opportunities for renewing acquaintance with others, serving and retired, at lectures and field days. It has some ex-officers of the British Army, with Irish connections, as members also. I have met Gen. Sir Eric de Burgh, impressively be-medalled, and Major Henry Harris, author of *The Irish Regiments in the First World War*, among others, at Military History dinners. Major Harris's work is not popular with the purist historians because he argued for the large figure of 500,000, rather than the more widely acceptable, 250,000, of Irish troops in that war. I tend to agree with his position, however, because I feel that all soldiers with Irish names from Irish families, who enlisted in non-Irish units in England, should also be included. Converted by Big Jack Charlton, we all have strong bonds of affection for those Irish soccer heroes with English accents. I always felt the same about regiments like the 'London Irish' and the 'Tyneside Irish'. Another memorable contributor, on the Irish Diaspora, was Dr Micheline Kerney Walsh. She entertained and enlightened us on the Wild Geese in Spain.

An officer of the Council of the Society, Lieut.-Colonel Des Clark, late of the Royal Irish Fusiliers, was very helpful to me in connection with a study project I was planning. His funeral service was well attended by Irish officers and ex-officers remembering his lecture on the 38th (Irish) Brigade at Monte Cassino, and listening to the plaintive notes of the 'Minstrel Boy', played by a military piper.

On a visit to Charles Fort, the seventeenth-century, star-shaped, coastal defence fort, at Kinsale, I was remembering a Military History Weekend many years ago. Once again I felt the ghostly presence of the Munster Fusiliers, stationed there in fairly tough living conditions. At least in their depot, Ballymullen Barracks in Tralee, (my FCA Camp) they had reasonable comfort for the time.

On the previous visit, we were not able to enter the Fort so the lecture took place outside: most sitting on the grass, finishing lunch wine; some already on their shooting sticks, as Col. Hally warmed to his story. The fort had held out for King James but was badly sited, overlooked by high ground. After a description of the sheer physical effort of the Williamite attackers hauling the guns up the slope in the October mud and snow, one of the local men who had drifted in to see what was going on, in the unmistakable lilt of the locality, commented, 'Hardy, boys'.

My other memory of that weekend was of some disagreement between Sir Charles and the 'Pope' (O'Mahoney, not the one of interest to the Revd Ian Paisley). In an 'oil on troubled waters' operation, with Donal Crowley (sadly, RIP, one of the best) I was detailed to volunteer to dine with the 'Pope' in another hotel. We had a most educational and enjoyable dinner, as one would expect in that company, with the Pope ordering only the best wines and liqueurs with the coffee. We tried quietly to fix the bill. But, with an aristocratic wave of the 'papal' hand, our guest produced a large round wad of notes and casually dropped them one by one until the whole bill was covered, laughing uproariously. We knew that nobody would believe our story. We needed several more beakers to restore our equilibrium.

A club that is not military, a 'peace' rather than a 'war' oriented body, is the United Arts Club, to which Muriel as an artist was introduced by my CO, Lieut.-Colonel Tom Gunne.

It has a number of serving and ex-officers on its list, mainly Irish but I have met some ex-British. In fact, I was introduced to a club that meets on Mondays in the Royal St George Yacht Club by a fellow member, an ex-Wing Commander, RAF. We have passed the centenary of the Arts Club and the club memories include some of the most famous as well as some of the most notorious names in Irish history.

In the 1920s, Maurice Headlam, in his *Irish Reminiscences*, recalls joining the Arts Club in order to enter 'a different world', where most of the members had 'strong nationalist sympathies', but those sympathies 'did not obtrude as a rule'.

He was a member of the Kildare Street Club and found that only a small number were members of both. He enjoyed dining at the Arts Club and hearing the 'witty imitations' of Cruise O'Brien, (Conor's father), the 'oratory of Yeats' and the Countess Markievicz in 'a sort of military uniform', 'holding forth' in the company of Captain White.

Today's Ireland has been represented by, among others, the then President Patrick Hillery dining with us. John Hume and Paddy Devlin have risked crossing swords where Headlam reported 'intellectuals assert their personality by contrariness and revolt'. I still remember John Hume's words, which cut through a late night philosophical bar debate, on solutions for the North, like a hot knife through butter: 'I am on the ground'.

In the 1990s the most entertaining writer on the Club was Stan Gebler Davies who boasted that being blackballed from the Arts Club (as he was some years earlier) was 'a distinction rarely extended and much prized'. Perhaps due to that intellectual 'contrariness' a well-known Ambassador was suspended for six months as a result of 'intemperate words' to a guest. Gebler coined the line 'building the past on the ashes of the future' in response to a lecture by Professor Joe Lee on 'The Future of the Irish Past' for the Merriman School who assemble in the Club to 'launch their assault on culture'. Unfortunately, the problems associated with the car-parking, fear of drink-driving, has affected it as well as other inner city clubs.

In my first civilian appointment (Leader Training Officer for Macra na Feirme) I was known as Captain Goggin, largely because I had never known any other identity. After that, the rank was mainly used on formal occasions or for signing 'letters to the editor' as Capt. (rtd), if the subject had a military aspect. As the rank implies military education and training, the expressed opinion may therefore be of some interest. It is, as the publisher of Schull Books wrote in a letter to *The Irish Times*, 'an earned rank', just as much as any academic one.

Officers retiring early, (eighteen of the forty in my cadet class) have no other identity when they find themselves in a civilian job. Even the degree or higher degrees of the young officers of today still does not answer the unspoken question: 'Where were you for the last twenty years?'

Without the rank they could be overgrown school-leavers with no previous worthwhile existence. The rank of Captain is the first military title, which the holder can carry for life. It originally signified someone who commanded an army and most captains would see some merit in that. Napoleon advised young officers to 'read and re-read the lives of the Great Captains'. (Could he have had this book in mind?)

Ward, writing in the seventeenth century, puts the ambitious officer on a dodgy knife-edge:

'A Captain ought to carry himself in such a way that his soldiers may both fear and love him. Too much familiarity breeds contempt and too stern a carriage breeds hatred.'

In the 1840s in the British Army a Captain's commission fetched between £1,800 and £4,800, depending on the smartness of the regiment. The system had significant advantages. The money invested as an ensign could grow as promotion followed, either by years of service or on the battlefield, so that when the officer had to retire he had a reasonable nest-egg. Also, as a commission cost money only those of 'gentle' birth or closet robbers could apply for one, both very suitable to the profession.

However, Captain Sir Thomas Bartlet's journal subverts all the serious writings of previous centuries on the responsibilities of his rank in his service with the BEF, politely waiting for the German Army in France in May 1940. He records his difficulties in moving their Mess in response to the demands of the 'war' and complains that, 'The officer is really an easy-going creature in peace time and doesn't take kindly to all the work that's suddenly expected of him now.'

To me, when I left the Army, the rank was just myself and I never thought anything about it. I have had only one odd experience when a father corrected his son for referring to me as Captain:

'There are no Captains in this house.'

The rank of captain can now usually be reached at a young age. But if normal early retirement has to be in one's thirties, then that is the rank with which one retires. That is then the outward sign, or souvenir, of one's army service, just as significant to the individual as the rank of colonel at sixty.

In any case, all officers consider that the most important thing they have in common is the President's commission.

b. Military Diary

Choosing my notes for 1997 as my example military diary, reminds me of the nearly twenty years of note-making, reading, checking and asking questions that have resulted in this book. Even though it is simply my story, my memories, opinions and responses to circumstances, I hope that it will throw some light behind the military walls for interested civilians and especially for young school-leavers thinking about a military career, in which the challenges and rewards have greatly improved.

Perhaps my 'military diary' for this year, a particularly active year, might illustrate some of the activities that keep old soldiers together.

January	Chief of Staff's talk to Officers' Club, McKee Barracks.
May	May Ball, Baldonnel Officers' Mess.
July	Military Pilgrimage, Lourdes.
August	Baldonnel International Air Show.
September	Three-day Seminar on the Civil War, Military History Society.
October	Band Concert for Army Benevolent Fund.
November	Cadet Class Reunion Dinner.

The Chief of Staff's talk to the McKee Officers' Club, usually January, is really a briefing (operations, equipment, personnel) on the year that has passed and on possible future developments. It is greatly appreciated by the members and is always taken to be information given 'in lodge'. The evidence that this is so is quite simply the fact that items of a confidential nature have never been leaked to the media.

On an International Military Pilgrimage to Lourdes, I travelled with my brother-in-law, Lieut.-Col. Kenneth Hilser-Byrne. I was impressed by the cadets, who were staying in our hotel. They will command our Army and Air Corps in the twenty-first century. They approached their officers for a few friendly words in the evenings, even with the occasional pint glass in view, indicating a social self-confidence and a more mature relationship than we had. They were all on parade at 07.00 hours every morning and, as they marched to Mass, swung up their arms as only cadets do, behind the Colour Party and the Pipe Band.

There was a class of Air Corps Apprentices also in the contingent who had the experience of living for the week in a French Army camp. Being the same age-group as the cadets, they all added up to a very impressive marching body and were duly commented on by tourists on the route. I was proud to be marching, albeit in panama and linen jacket, with the old soldiers (Generals O'Callaghan, Berry and O'Connor, *inter alia*) behind them. A foreign gentleman, looking at the flag, asked: 'Are you the IRA?'

In a local school, the teachers had arranged an 'Irish Day', with the children in Irish costumes. All wanted to do Irish dancing with the Pipe Band, some 'playing' the drums, the boys wearing the soldier's caps. I felt that we were ensuring some enthusiastic future recruits for the French Army.

The popularity of the Pipe Band (the Air Corps Pipe Band, reinforced by Army pipers with a Pipe Major displaying an impressively large curling moustache) was evident even among other members of the 19,000 international military brotherhood. In the hotel, where we sat in the evenings, when the Pipe Band was heard arriving a Swiss Army group with gentle sounding musical instruments would quietly stash them away before the flood of pipe and drum sound started bounding off the walls and washing through the room.

The British contingent included a good representation from the Royal Irish Regiment. Groups of them hugely entertained the international gathering in the hotel in high-spirited good humour, by lining up and marking time to the tunes of our Pipe Band as they returned to the bar for refreshments from time to time. Some also occasionally 'fell in' at the rear of our Mass parades, responded to the Irish words of command, and marched with us.

It was a very moving experience, apart from the simplicity of the candle-lit ceremonies, to be part of that huge military expression of Christianity.

The French Foreign Legion with their distinctive loping cadence of 88 paces to the minute must have reminded most men of their boyhood reading. The Italians, Spanish, Portuguese, Germans and Nordic representatives, along with the new armies of the Baltic States and the Balkans, including the dramatically uniformed Croatians, all added to the international military colour. The Flags of all the participating countries are blessed individually, but the most moving moment was the ring of selected soldiers from all the armies joining hands in peace.

There was one memorably silly moment during a delay over some organisational problem. The feeling of total droop from the massed soldiery was palpable, almost at pre-mutiny level, when a British NCO ran out in front of the pews of the British contingent waving them all to stand. They stood, generals and their warriors to a man. Then he waved them to sit, which they did. Then he ran in front of the pews of the other contingents in turn, including us, waving madly 'up', 'down', and being obeyed, continuing this madcap performance until he had everybody in the basilica in uproar, all boredom forgotten.

The outside world impinged in small ways, like when I noticed the Northern Ireland service medal worn by the British chaplain in front of whom I ended up in the general confession ceremony.

The town of Lourdes looked like what any French town behind the lines must have looked like in the First World War, with a mix of uniforms. Somehow the discreet charm of the 'Queen Alexandra's' reminded us of the ultimate result of real war. I saw another cameo of the brotherhood of arms one day when one of our cadets, walking in front of us, saluted a German cadet who returned his salute, tapping his white cadet epaulette.

Another pleasant experience of the international military mix was at an Air Show at Baldonnel where airmen from several countries, including our own 'Silver Swallows', under the command of Captain Graeme Martin, a son of an old army comrade, Captain John Martin, gave heart stopping acrobatic displays. The RAF 'Red Arrows' provided a spectacular performance, forcing me, as an old infantryman, to ask the

Air Chief Marshal, in the interests of balance, if he knew what their rifle shooting was like? It would appear that his ADC did not have the relevant score sheets to hand.

More serious notes were struck at a Civil War Seminar run by the Military History Society and the Military Archives, in Cathal Brugha Barracks. Despite the impressive new buildings housing Eastern Command HQ, I sometimes see shadowy figures of a parading 'B' Company and a CO of the 2nd Infantry Battalion doing his level best to beam, resting on his stick, when I pass this square. On looking in the windows I wonder was that where the famous 2nd Battalion Sports Meetings really used to be held?

If truth shades into entertaining memory at this short remove, how difficult is it to determine the real truth of the Civil War? At the seminar, four professors, (Tom Garvin, Joe Lee, Eunan O'Halpin, Dermot Keogh), as well as Tim Pat Coogan, Dr Michael Hopkinson and Mr Mark Seaman of the Imperial War Museum, fired salvoes of information and opinion at the hundred strong attendance. When the big guns fell silent, there was some sporadic shooting from the floor.

Some wondered at the logic of the assumption that as a Republic had been 'declared' in the GPO, by an unrepresentative minority, that therefore it existed, and was an acceptable *causus belli* for a civil war. If a monarchy had been 'declared' by Pearse in the GPO after his deliberations on the possibility of a German king, would there be men now willing to kill for it?

I asked Ms Ann Matthews, who spoke of 'Women and the Civil War', if she had come across evidence of Madame Markievicz's war crimes (e.g. the killing of an unarmed policeman) as recorded against her in popular history. She said that she was continuing her research in that area.

We examined motivations and problems of historiography, but not the actual fighting. So that it still remains a puzzle to me why the Dublin Guards did what they did at Ballyseedy. They left anti-army mines buried in people's memories all over Kerry.

The Civil War like all wars had its share of myths. The barracks in which

211

the seminar was held, Cathal Brugha, was in itself a reminder of another piece of history disputed in the memoirs of Sergeant John Pinkman, (Liverpool IRA and National Army soldier). According to Dorothy Macardle, the 'small smoke-blackened figure' of Cathal Brugha, coming out of the Gresham Hotel, 'a revolver in each hand raised against the levelled rifles of the troops' fell 'amid a volley of shots'. Pinkman claims, however, that he was, in fact, shot in the thigh by a sniper as he was escaping out the back across Thomas' Lane and bled to death in hospital.

If one test of a good theory is whether it inspires further research, a test of a good seminar seems to be, does it provoke good arguments? If the sounds of discussion in the bar after each session were anything to go on, the Civil War was re-fought with vigour.

Serving and ex-officers also meet at the annual Band Concert in aid of the Army Benevolent Fund in the National Concert Hall every October, which is a most entertaining evening for a good cause. The Army Bands and the Pipe Bands play a variety of the tunes of glory. My memories include pieces in remembrance of the Irish Divisions in the First World War, a virtuoso performance on the kettledrums by the youngest soldier in the band and a line of silver drums with a sergeant in charge whose drumsticks seemed to perform with his benign encouragement. Old comrades meet serving officers home on leave from foreign service in one of the thirty odd countries of the Irish UN Military Empire on which the sun truly never sets. An old soldier does not really have to abandon his old military woods and pastures when he finally sheathes his sword.

c. Home-base

In the Army I was one of 'The Dublin Soldiers' (as titled by our comrades down the country). I served in an Infantry Battalion at platoon, company and battalion staff level, in an AOC Command Unit and with the Directorate, with the Department of Defence

Company in McKee Barracks, and, at Parkgate, with the Observer Corps, without once having to leave Dublin. In the Western and Southern Commands officers 'met themselves coming back', as they moved from one unit to another or one level of operations to another, on promotion or transfer, with all the trauma for the families that that entailed. We had it 'cushy' in comparison.

I still claim my Dingle roots, although my brother Bernie, a retired publisher and naturalist, is the only family left there. But for my daughters however, even by their Wesley disco years, the idea of being proud of being from anywhere was considered to be unbearably 'uncool'. On one occasion, when they were small, proudly showing them the beauty of their ancestral territory, we stopped at the Connor Pass outside Dingle. Ursula ran to see the promised panorama, but a mist had obscured the magnificent view. We heard:'Very poor reception.' They also seemed to believe that nature could be helped. Once sitting at the edge of the gently lapping sea, out the 'Banks', as the beach outside Dingle is called, Jennifer shouted: 'Turn on the hot tap, Dad'.

One abiding memory is of an Easter picnic with our friends Bob and Colette Hurley and their children. It had started snowing shortly after arriving so we retreated to the cars to decide on our move. Later, on wiping condensation off the car window, to our astonishment, the children were still sitting in their anoraks eating sandwiches with pink frozen fingers. I can still see Erika chatting, oblivious of the snow falling on her hood.

I have a lot to thank God for but I remember one day holding a photograph of my three golden-haired little girls and feeling a tear sting my eyes as I sat in the gloaming looking at their happy childish expressions, knowing that I would never see them again. The 'babs' were gone.

I was still sitting there when three 'sophisticated' young ladies bounded in with Erika, asking:'Dad, will you drive us to Wesley tonight?'

Now they, in turn, are gone and replaced by three young mothers and six intelligent grandchildren, who see the point in my jokes.

The happiest outcome was that they all had two each, so there is no competition. Jennifer and Martin have Stephanie and Megan. Ursula and Assie have Jordan and Zachary (called Zach). Erika and Ian have Rebekah and Alexandra (called Ally).

Now, in our house, as at the beginning, there are just the two of us, myself and she, to whom my mother always gave the title of my 'Life's Companion'. As a member of the Watercolour Society of Ireland, she works on her entries for the Society's Exhibition, when she is not nursing the shrubs that owe their existence to her.

Some years after leaving the Army we changed house, thinking that this would be the final closing of a chapter, the military one, of my old life. The new house is in a cul-de-sac in a small estate and I soon discovered that a neighbour had a cousin whose desk I took over on one of my army postings and that a retired Army Medical Corps colonel lived around the corner. The then American Military Attaché told me that he was thinking of buying the house opposite me, but it had just been sold. At that time the Garda sentry box in front of another of the neighbour's houses (the then British Military Attaché, Brigadier Peter Robinson's) added to the military feel. People joked about the possibility of flags but the only one ever in the area was once by neighbours Knut and Selma Heindorf, some years afterwards, who had a Danish Flag for some special occasion.

We were made very welcome by the 'early settlers' and had a great 'warming up' period. In that first Christmas we had parties in most of the houses in the cul-de-sac within the twelve days.

For some years for our New Year's Eve dinner, all the men were ex-soldiers: my brother Colman, my brother-in-law Kenneth and my old comrade-in-arms John Martin. John's charming lady wife Joyce, as a sister of my friend Bob, ties in the Dingle connection.

Brig. Peter Robinson made a profound change in my life: he converted me to Bushmills, rightly pointing out that my little drop of Scotch made me feel unpatriotic and that as Bushmills was on this island I would have the double pleasure of enjoying the product and the patriotism. On a holiday in the North, I have since metaphorically burned incense at the shrine of Bushmills Distillery where they kindly presented me with a parchment testifying to my sound whiskey judgement. (I had been offered as a volunteer by Muriel as the one to undergo the test with sixteen little drops of different whiskies to judge.) On that visit we witnessed one of their traditional band parades and to me they seemed to be simply the villages on parade: young, old, tall, small, fat and thin citizens of Causeway, Ballintoy and all the other townlands that make up that pleasant landscape. I wondered about the antics of one or two of the 'big drum' performers, but that might have been my nationalist prejudice breaking out.

Peter was kind enough to obtain a record of the Pipe Band of the Irish Guards for me. The ladies used to object to my playing the music loudly and I do not know any other way to play that beautiful Irish music. On the other hand there was no objection to the Panzer Grenadiers foot-stamping version of 'Erika' in the Mess at top volume at Erika's wedding. Looking back, I did not help in Anglo-Irish relations either when I had to send Peter's son Tim home one night when he came calling with Bishop Willoughby's son to see my twin daughters, Erika and Ursula, who had been instructed to finish their homework. It was taken in good spirit by the lads who accepted that parents had duties. In passing it must be said that a now retired British Military Attaché, Col. Sean Lambe has the added distinction of starting his military career in the FCA. I had that privilege also but it did not seem to produce the same result for me.

My other daughter Jennifer was, and still is, horse mad, and I had endless entertainment going around with her as she was purchasing her first horse, listening to all the stories about 'cold backs' and other horsey problems, reminiscent of the Resident Magistrate yarns. She is lucky to have found a son-in-law in Martin for me, who joins her in this affliction. Her enthusiasm has never waned and eventually took her to the committee of the Louth Hunt.

I had the pleasure of meeting Richard Filgate (Past Master) in Jennifer's house: a jovial, entertaining conversationalist, who presented us with a brace of pheasant. They were very welcome, as I had not been shooting for years. We now depend on my brother-in-law Ken to invite us to the occasional 'duck dinner'. Richard told me something that I love to believe. I had said that in my shooting days I shot up to the last until the birds set out on their long migration to Africa. He said that in these years he was in Africa waiting for them. I wondered at the feelings of those birds having escaped one Irishman on the home island only to meet another on their chosen new ground.

One of the sad threads in the tapestry of my life is that so many of the friends of my youth did not live to be the friends of my retirement. My childhood friend, Joe Moriarty, died young in an accident. My Cadet School room-mate, Jack Spillane, was killed in a car crash, as a lieutenant. Bob Hurley failed to make his planned early retirement from the bank. Intimations of mortality are underlined as members of one's own age cohort in life fall in the advance across the various age report lines.

My first ever Church of Ireland service was for the 'Thanksgiving for the Life' of Peter Robinson's wife Shirley in St Pauls in Glenageary. We were very moved by the homily given by Bishop Willoughby who referred to all her work for the local Christmas carol singing evenings when the choir from our church, St Michael's, joined with St Paul's. Mrs O'Donoghue provided the lanterns for the singers and wine for the supporters. We were at one such carol singing evening in the early 1980s when the word arrived to Peter of the break in the dreadful hunger-strike. The carol became a prayer of thanks.

We have since attended Church of Ireland and Methodist church ceremonies as well as a Peace Service in the local Presbyterian Church. But I remember when an officer sword-guard for their Commander in Chief, President Douglas Hyde, had to sheathe their swords and wait outside the door of the cathedral until the funeral service was over. I remember also telling a school friend, who failed to bring in the sixpence for the catechism, that it was because his aunt, Mrs Benner of the hotel, was a Protestant. If he did tell her it must have been received with amusement because at his birthday party she insisted on hearing my imitation of her husky voice calling for her dog Jacko.

The President, Mrs Mary McAleese, taking Holy Communion with the other Christian tradition has put down a pointer. When my daughter Erika was getting married, her future mother-in-law requested permission from the Archbishop to take Holy Communion but she was refused, as being Church of Ireland. I remembered Father Des Connell as a helpful, open-minded, easy mannered, pleasant and witty lecturer in UCD. (Witty? metaphysics? yet, as in his references to 'Epistemology for All' books, he kept us entertained and involved.) He was in this case, as Archbishop, confined in the man-made prison compound of Canon Law and could give no other answer. I was very sorry for him, and others I knew, when the story broke of wide-spread clerical criminality. I believe that he felt trapped by the fear of serious scandal and the voice of Rome. At least we now know that he tried hard for the removal of one serious criminal.

Why can Holy Communion not be symbolically in commemoration of Him as He requested, in the plain words of the Bible? Why can't we simply join Jesus at the Last Supper, at the fringe of a party of billions lasting two thousand years? Christians of all denominations on this island receiving Holy Communion together could heal our self-inflicted wounds in partaking of a two thousand year long supper in union with Christ. The President's bridge building (perhaps the long shadow of the future reaching our time?) augurs well for religion in Ireland in the new century.

When it comes to the most profound elements of our faith, the impenetrable mysteries, like the unfathomable mystery of transubstantiation, in which language can only be used analogously, we do not believe that any amount of education in such matters can bring one nearer the truth. A bit like the difference between looking at the moon from the ground and looking at it standing on an orange box.

I was an enthusiastic 'peace marcher'. I remember being allowed to push my grand-daughter Rebekah in her pram, her woolly hat falling over her eyes, for a big rally after the Warrington tragedy. I believed that we were offering a very significant non-verbal prayer for peace. We, the Irish people, were asking that the killings in our name should stop. Our prayers eventually started to be answered in the Good Friday Agreement, bringing us closer to our hope of an 'Agreed Ireland'.

12

The Profession of Arms

a. Officers and Gentlemen?

As a child I used to hear my father telling stories about his days at sea serving on a British Indian Line troopship, towards the end of the First World War. Their army officer 'guests' in the wardroom plunged them into a strange military world, which seemed to affect them in funny ways. Their Captain suddenly became known as the 'Commander' and started to wear a sword, even if he had to wear it on the other side. He insisted that his officers equip themselves with mess jackets to balance the military officers' mess kits at dinner. The ship's officers were not commissioned officers being Merchant Navy but they then found themselves in that strange territory of standards and symbols, which ring with clear meanings to the initiated, but perplex strangers.

This experience seemed to have left him with a strong inclination to do things in a regimental way. He put a little silver bell on the table to ring for the maid who was just outside the door in the kitchen and could easily hear every request. Uncle Joe, who preferred the hills and rivers to the streets, described the short-lived addition as 'a relic of old decency'. As a child I solved the problem by damaging the bell. I still have it.

My father's memories included official growls when he was seen to buy a Chinese sailor a drink and worst of all when he was observed washing a handkerchief in a sink. Not accepted as 'officer-like' behaviour. He had my sympathy up to a point until I heard another story. One day a friend and himself tried to slip unobtrusively past some senior naval brass without attracting attention, on the reasonable grounds that they did not feel really part of that side of operations.

They were quickly brought to heel and ordered to salute the Admiral.

As a sword-carrying 'gang' leader, with 'Leftenant' on my paper badge of rank, I wondered at his lack of discipline. I thought that he must never have read stories about how officers maintained standards even in the desert or the jungle. I never had to wonder what officers were. I knew. They were like the knights of old. Duty was their religion. Duty to their country and their men regardless of cost to self.

Commissions, once reserved for the sons of the aristocracy, are now awarded to a mainly middle-class profession. However, a kind of DIY 'caste system' is still considered essential for military discipline. For General de Gaulle (quoted by Gen. Sir A. Farrar-Hockley in *The Edge of the Sword)* 'authority requires prestige, and prestige requires remoteness'. Somewhat like the idea of royalty, which depends for its acceptance on a sort of social magic that the natural contempt bred by familiarity could undermine.

A young 2nd Lieutenant holds the President's commission just like any other member of the Officer Corps, regardless of seniority, and is saluted by senior NCOS, even those with twenty years experience. Lieut.-Col. Dave Grossman, a US Army psychologist, commissioned from the ranks, has written that, in his early days, with his wife and children, he had experienced the military class structure and the social distance that goes with it: separate social functions, separate housing areas. He concludes rather dramatically that this distance, this insulation against too warm and personal a human relationship between officers and men provides a denial mechanism that allows leaders to order men to their deaths.

As well as a wide and deep professional education and training, the effectiveness of the Officer Corps rests on twin pillars that support a leadership capable of calling on men not just to work harder and, say, make more boxes, but to risk life or limb. One pillar is the acceptance by the group that orders from officers come from a higher plane, from outside the unit, from the Sovereign State. Therefore boys, and today girls, must be taken into the military novitiate to be imbued with a sense of responsibility and apartness: a quasi-aristocratic sense of identification with the State, expressed in the military ideals of 'duty, honour, country'. The second pillar on which the concept rests is that the officer is, in fact, also seen not only to be in, and of, the unit but to be the most dedicated soldier in it. He is expected to give the good example of that sense of service, once associated with the aristocracy because they owned the country for which they were fighting.

It is a truism that soldiers fight and die for their comrades, so that the person of the officer then becomes the essential junction point between the needs of the group and the requirements of the State. The rather old-fashioned formality used to protect this apartness is not a pretension to be an aristocracy. It is a translation of the aristocratic ideal into a practical professional life, expressed in the international phrase 'officer and gentleman'. This implies a selfless, non-money/prestige seeking, 'decent skin', who can be trusted to be fair and just, as well as being an effective professional soldier.

Yet the concept of 'officer', in most armies, seems to be a quantum leap up from term 'compassionate professional', which describes a good senior NCO. Among other leadership qualities, there seems to be what could almost be described as a theatrical dimension in terms of personal presentation, like a good barrister.

Attempts have been made to get around it, in, for instance, the Chinese Army and also the old Soviet Army, excellently outlined by Captain Liddell-Hart in his book *The Red Army*. All the uniforms and rank markings of the Russian officers were abolished and soldiers wore something like one stripe for a corporal, two for a sergeant, three for a warrant officer, four for a lieutenant, five for a captain, etc. Their inglorious movement through the 1940 Finnish campaign produced a snow-bound sea change resulting in a return to the acceptance of the military necessity of an Officer Corps, despite their strong socio-political considerations against it. Hence the return to the outward forms and trappings of the old Russian Tsarist Imperial Army, with shoulder boards, military courtesy and indeed servants for their officers and pay to match.

There have been well-documented cases also of allowing the concept of the 'Officer' to melt away. As in the US Army in Korea, where the behaviour of the American troops in POW camps compared poorly with the other armies whose officer's sense of officer-like duty remained discernible through dirt and rags (as romanticised in *Bridge on the River Kwai*). Too many US officers, when POWs, seemed to have abdicated responsibility for their men, who, in any case, did not seem to have gleaned from their training or experience an expectation of anything more from them. In the *Marine Corps Gazette*, Dr Tanham wrote that 'our national aims were not sufficiently clear to motivate our soldiers to do their best, nor did military discipline and spirit compensate for this lack'.

Prompted by the disaffection of American prisoners in Korea, President Eisenhower issued the famous 'Code of Conduct for Members of American Forces'. I asked the US Military Attaché after a talk in the Military College to bring us up to date on this, but apparently it was outside his brief.

The modern soldier in these islands is very different from his Boer War forefathers. Educated, intelligent, articulate and discerning, he demands a much higher standard from his officers.

The old formalities can remain but any misuse of powers or any unprofessional attitude will not be tolerated. Commanding Officers and PDFORRA (the Permanent Defence Forces Other Ranks Representative Association) seem to have achieved mutual respect.

A sour note is struck by 'Andy McNab' (SAS) in his book *Immediate Action*. He refers to all officers as 'Ruperts' in what seems to be almost a class distaste and appears to resent the fact that experienced NCOS help them gain practical skills for their eventual appointments as Squadron Commanders. He claims that officers were not necessary as Troop Commanders in 'The Regiment'.

In those small-group operations perhaps he is right, but there is a lot more to running a war than the SAS CTRs (close tactical recces) and CQBs (close quarter battles). Without the 'green army' they would be useless.

In my day army pay just could not compete with civilian levels, which, combined with the modified early pension allowed, for myself and about half my cadet class, for a career change in our thirties. RACO (the Representative Association of Commissioned Officers) is now demanding an expectation of reasonable returns for a life of dedication. It sees itself as having, peculiar to itself, a corpus of technical and doctrinal knowledge in the management of military force, vital to national security. The Army as a career has vastly improved today, with new opportunities through the UN and the EU. In my day there were 600 interviewed for the 40 places. Recently there were over 2,700 applications for cadetships. We discovered at a recent cadet class reunion in the Military College that in a cadet class of 36 there were 24 graduates with four masters, as well as some foreign cadets.

The 'Ruperts', as they are called in the British Army, (newly commissioned straight from Sandhurst) will, I trust, continue to be accepted as a trial of the men's patriotism, and get the help and guidance that my generation got from our senior NCOS.

b. A Soldier's Soldier

'Dulce et decorum est pro patria mori', but it can also be 'decorum' and reasonably 'dulce' to live for the fatherland in its military service. The single officer lives in an Officers' Mess that provides a comfortable room, a pleasant dining-room, a good selection of newspapers in the anteroom and a bar across the hall.

In my day the batman-orderly added considerably to that comfort, as he tended the fire, kept the buttons and leathers polished and looked after the normal requirements of his officer. In battle he would perform necessary tasks to ensure that the officer could concentrate his whole attention on the battle and the needs of his men. In the old British Army an officer had a servant and a groom. In the old Soviet Army a senior officer did not have just a batman, he had a staff of servants.

Today buttons do not need polishing, Sam Browne belts are not normally worn except for ceremonial, knee-high field boots are history and all officer's rooms have central heating, so that the virtual disappearance of the orderly, as I knew him, does not matter very much in purely practical terms. There are, of course, mess staff, who do what is necessary, but mention of personal orderlies today is something like mentioning maids in civilian life. In the early fifties, soldier's pay was very low so that the monthly tip to the orderly of ten shillings was not too bad and the 'cushy' appointment was welcomed by many. A red ten-shilling note in the 1950s was worth something in those days as it bought at least five pints, which today would cost over twenty euro.

Money was scarce for all and that was one of the reasons why on returning after a Christmas leave a detective called. (As an old J.B. Priestley reader I would like to be able to say that he was an inspector.) He had my cavalry twill coat over his arm and I identified it. It seems that my orderly had arrived in a pawnshop with the coat and the manager assumed that a soldier was unlikely to have his coat tailored in Callaghans of Dame Street, as he learned from my name tag in the inside pocket, so he informed the Gardai.

'Thanks,' I said to the detective, 'I'll have a word with him, but I don't want anything done about it.'

'Too late now,' he said, 'the case has to go ahead.'

I knew that it was something that just went wrong and that he would have had the coat back in the wardrobe before I returned from leave. In court, I painted a picture of friendly familiarity indicating that it would be something that the orderly would expect me to allow, and that I trusted him fully: on active service I would have to trust him with my life.

The judge looked at both of us quizzically and asked would he lose his appointment.

'If he were convicted,' I said, 'he would have to be dismissed.'

He was given the benefit of the Probation Act.

Back in the Mess he surprised me with a salute saying, 'Jasus, sir, you played a blinder, getting us off.'

On the following day, he brought in a reading lamp for the room, as a present from his wife, saying, 'It was spare. I never liked it but it's better than the oul' one you have.'

He was very dependable (I know) but inclined to be cranky over the fact that I did not have a radio in my room like the other officers:

'I dunno how you do without a radio. Those oul' books of yours need a lot of patience to read them.'

The most unforgettable character I ever had as an orderly was an old soldier who lived in married quarters but was quite happy to get his meals in the Mess kitchen. He had service in the British Army and was at the army age of forty when he became my 'gentleman's gentleman' (soldier's soldier?) although his chronological age was probably in the sixties, and his weather-beaten hardiness looked more in the seventies.

I did not believe him when he said that he never learned how to light a fire: 'We never bothered with them in India'.

On a morning after a Mess party he would arrive down to my room with tea and toast saying, 'It's a damp oul day outside, sir, you hadn't a day's uncertified for ages.'

His age finally caught up with him when he reached his army records age of forty-five. I explained, 'You're on three months pre-discharged leave now, you don't have to come here anymore, you're off duty, permanently.'

'Am I, sir, I see.'

Like our maid Hanna at home, after being 'sacked' once again, he arrived down with the hot water the following morning: his only concession to his civvy status was his tweed cap. He continued until the three months were up and even then, it was somehow sadly difficult enough to get this across.

I was finally promoted into one of the first floor, large windowed, rooms in McKee Officers' Mess. Before that I lived on the snow line, with dormer windows looking out over a ledge. I invariably banged my door and left the key inside so that to get back into my room I had to climb out another window and walk along the extremely narrow ledge on the roof to reach my own window. I could only perform that

225

feat with at least three pints or small whiskies inside. On visiting the Mess now I look up and shudder.

My last room as a single officer therefore was one of the best but it caused me much embarrassment when, on a morning that I had decided to take a day's uncertified sick leave, I asked my orderly, who had brought in tea and toast, 'What time is it?'

He leaned out the window to see the barrack clock and shouted in at me, 'Jaysus, sir, it's all of nine o'clock, you'd want to be getting out of bed if you're getting up.'

On the front steps, a few feet below, the General Staff stood waiting to assemble for a conference.

c. Mess Life

Mess meetings are held once a month and attended by all members of the Mess with an equal vote regardless of rank. The only officers with precedence are the Mess President and the Officer Commanding the Mess. Sometime in the nineteenth century there was a dispute in a British mess between a senior officer and an aristocratic junior officer, who refused to bow to the wisdom of the senior man in the argument. The Duke of York ruled that, in the Mess, seniority would allow a correction on the part of a senior officer on purely military professional grounds only. This seems to be the accepted practice today, at least on these islands.

I still have my copy of the Mess Rules issued in the 1950s, listing the duties of the Mess Committee (Mess Secretary, Mess Treasurer and the quaintly titled, Wines Bar Officer). It outlines precedence in the Mess as: *At Official Dinners the Commanding Officer will preside. Other members seat themselves as convenience and hospitality dictates. At ordinary meals the Mess President shall preside.*

'There would be no saluting between members of the Mess on Mess premises.'

(The good old Duke of York?) but: *'When the CO first enters the Ante-room all will rise'*, pointing out sensibly that this applied to sitting officers only.

Ladies were viewed with some suspicion. There were six detailed paragraphs outlining the battle drill for dealing with them. Apart from official functions they were allowed in the Mess ('with the sanction of the CO') only *between 10.00 hours and 17.00 hours*. Apart from an immediate notification of the Orderly Officer of any breaches of this code, the bad news would, of course, have to be broken to the CO, as if he did not have enough on his plate already. Whatever about lady visitors (and I remember some being served by the barman as they sat in cars outside the Mess) dogs were dealt with more curtly:

'Dogs will not be allowed inside the Mess premises.'

The sheer relief of writing that after the verbal athletics of the ladies paragraphs. I can see a weary Mess Committee sitting back, smiling at the simplicity of it. These paragraphs must provide amusement to any of our distinguished lady officer members of the Mess today, if anyone is rude enough to point them out. The Mess President today of McKee Officers' Mess is a charming lady commandant. Ladies and dogs having been dealt with, there followed a stern reminder: *'Children and servants, other than orderlies, must not be sent to the Mess on messages'.*

Gambling in the Mess was forbidden. Our poker games never took place. But, in case I had any ideas about changing anything, the final paragraph reminded the reader that: *'These rules are compiled in accordance with Defence Force Regulation A/13 dated 26th July 1944.'* It warned that *'failure to hand up this Book of Mess Rules on transfer from the barracks would incur a charge of five shillings'.*

As I still have the document, I wonder was I ever charged that amount on my mess bill? I would surely have been aware of the heavy extra expense.

As a 2nd Lieutenant, at a meeting of AHQ Officers' Mess, I rose my one bar on my thin figure, topped with more wavy hair than was considered really military, above the assembled portly senior members saying, 'I suggest that the Army Headquarters Annual Military Ball be held in Dublin Castle. It seems more suitable than the Metropole.'

This would be the good old Cadet School idea: stand up, say what you think when the opportunity is presented if you have convictions; you will be expected to have views even if they are rejected. I expected that my suggestion would most likely be rejected, and I hated drawing attention to myself but, like calling the soldier in O'Connell Street to his military courtesy, I believed that it was my duty to follow through. Perhaps someone else would think about it and act on it at a later stage. Luckily the implied criticism of their previous efforts produced mainly an amused surprise. I blushed a few years ago to discover that the evidence is still in the Mess Minutes Book.

For single 'living-in' officers the Mess staff contributed to making the Mess a 'home from home'. Mess barmen were trusted to speak and be spoken to as 'in lodge' there was never a question of broken confidences. For married 'living-out' officers the Mess was a club to which they could call in on the occasional evening for a few 'quiet beakers' and a chat.

d. Clothes and the Man

I asked one orderly/batman early in my career, why did he join the Army? He replied:'The Army seemed more interesting, sir. I like being a soldier, so far.' He was selected for a Cooks Course before I could reconcile that statement with the fact that he told me that he had been working as a valet to a well-known man of the theatre. He also occasionally embarrassed me by asking questions like: 'What suit do you want for this evening, sir?'

I could find only one, as, except for the occasional cocktail party, when I aired the charcoal grey, I lived either in uniform or a sports jacket, with leather patches on the elbows and edges of the sleeves. I returned this jacket once again on one occasion to Callaghans for two matching leather strips. I had torn one sleeve on a briar while out shooting on leave.

Bill Kelly, the tailoring manager, held it up.

'I'm looking forward to the day when you will be coming in for tweed patches on your leather jacket.'

All my uniforms were tailored in Callaghans of Dame Street, as well as my civvies. I simply went in and ordered, got measured or took away, without today's essential requirement of money changing hands. Monthly bills would arrive with various coloured stickers getting less diplomatically friendly to the stage when they actually hinted that they were owed money. I would eventually lodge an amount and, in this way, I dressed to the standard required of an 'officer and gentleman'. I remember handing in ten pounds (mega bucks) on occasions to the Callaghan's stand at the Horse Show, but I knew that the world was changing when one day I happened to hear another customer being asked for a deposit.

In those days officers' uniforms consisted of:

Battle-dress: helmet, web equipment, map case, revolver, boots, 'bulls-wool' uniform

Service dress: green cap, tunic, slacks; Sam Browne belt; brown gloves and shoes.

Ceremonial uniform: green cap, tunic; cavalry twill breeches; field boots/knee-high leggings; Sam Browne belt; gloves; sword.

Dress uniform: black cap (gold thread cap badge), tunic, (gold thread rank insignia), slacks (with red stripe); gold lanyard; white gloves; black tie, long for day, black bow for evening or white bow with wing collar.

Modern battle-dress as well as the sweater and summer shirt-sleeves dress came in later. The old 'Ruritanian' full dress uniform with the shako, high neck and much braid, was gone, but I had arranged to buy an Infantry one (dark blue, silver braid) from a retiring officer. All corps had different forms of the old dress uniforms (e.g. black for Artillery, sky blue for the Air Corps.) The long black cloak with velvet collar and red satin lining was, however, still accepted as regulation wear with the new dress uniform for some years. The new dress uniform came in at that same time so the officer (Captain John O'Carroll, retiring to take up a civilian appointment) very kindly took it back. He told me some years afterwards, at a meeting of the McKee Officers' Club, that he had presented it to the Military Museum in Collins Barracks. I have since also presented the cloak to the Director.

The new dress uniform, still in use, came in about 1957. I ordered mine as we left on the Brigade Concentration Exercise in Youghal. The problem with the 'new' dress uniform is that it is intended to suit two very different situations, social and ceremonial. It is adequate for both but falls somewhat short in comfort for one and formality for the other. The vulgarly titled 'bum-freezer', that allows for comfort of tummies expanding with food and drink, has been accepted by the Naval Service and the Air Corps.

e. A Soldier's Friend

The ability to stand up and say what one believed, regardless of expected opposition or criticism, was acknowledged as an 'officer-like' quality, despite tight military discipline. This probably helped in another sector of that wide operational area that is an officer's professional life. In those days, on courts-martial, while the prosecuting officer was a qualified barrister, the defending officer for a soldier was often simply one chosen by the soldier to be what was quaintly titled 'the soldier's friend'.

How the soldier made this selection was entirely a matter for himself and depended on what officers he knew and trusted. Any officer so nominated was bound to accept the task, if available, regardless of his unit.

Our court-martial system first saw the light of day in the Defence Forces (Temporary Provisions) Act, 1923. According to Colonel W.B. Moran, the relevant legislation was copied rather than drafted, as an almost complete copy of the one then existing in the British Army. Even by the passing of a Permanent Defence Act in 1955 there were very few changes. (A Courts-Martial Appeal Court since is a major improvement).

The members of the court-martial are officers, one of whom will preside. The members undertake the functions and duties of both judge and jury, deciding on all questions of law and fact. To assist them they have the services of a Judge Advocate who will advise them on matters of law and sum up the evidence. I remember being the junior member of a court martial once and as such had the awesome responsibility of giving the product of my deliberation first in the course of the private discussion.

I also found myself being asked to perform the duty of the 'soldier's friend' on a number of occasions and I had some successes. One case was of a soldier charged, according to my notes, under Section 126 (a) of the Defence Act, 1954, with sleeping on his post when acting as sentry. The very type that I would normally feel like hanging, but my only hope then was to get as light a sentence as I could. I did this by making a long-winded speech on the condition of the soldier after a previous sleepless night, on the summer heat, the small sentry box with the very small windows, etc.

As I expected, the prosecuting officer smiled and said what a lot of vague emotional rot or something to that effect, and could they please have facts. At this the court requested me to be more specific and the prosecuting officer laughed and complimented me on my theatrical performance. I then produced drawings and specific measurements taken by the Barrack Foreman of Works of the box, the size of the windows and the temperature of the night as recorded by the Met Office. This did not get him off but in the silence that followed I hoped that it went some distance to help in reducing his sentence. Evelyn Waugh, as a captain in the Royal Marines, records in his diary for August 1940 that he was faced with a similar task. He tried a medical approach but failed like I did to get the man off.

I had more success in having a charge of 'desertion', under Section 135 (1) of the Act, which was very serious, reduced to 'absence without leave'. This was for a soldier who had been absent for way over the 21 days (after which absence becomes 'desertion' and would carry heavy penalties even in peacetime). A young soldier, I listened to his story and found him in a high state of fear as he realised the seriousness of the charge. I wrote to the Vincent de Paul and the Legion of Mary who knew the man's family.

While accepting desertion as a very serious crime, but that we could not then establish beyond reasonable doubt that he had a real intention to desert, I suggested that we could, by examining what happened on a step by step basis, see his situation as a series of wrong but comparatively minor decisions. Beginning with 'breaking barracks' after being refused to be allowed out by the PA at the gate because of his black narrow-trousered suit which, in the opinion of the gate policeman was too much like a Teddy boy outfit. Then arriving home to find a family problem, which made him stay out for the weekend, and which dragged on and ended with a visit to England to help sort the problem with some relations.

The best bit was a report from a prison in London where he had been detained for a month after getting into trouble with some friends. This was provided confidentially with the help of a member of the staff of Garda HQ. When he returned home he gave himself up. Not the ideal soldier but at least not a deserter and I had the charge reduced to AWOL, as was my duty to him.

The irony of it was that I had in my possession a document that would have 'hung him', where he told someone in England that he had 'deserted from the Irish Army'. While the 'soldier's friend' might not be as free as a civilian barrister in the conduct of his defence, I felt that it was my duty to him to withhold that piece of paper. I was convinced that he used the word 'deserted' in an ignorant and casual way, devoid of the full weight of meaning as in military law. I did a detailed petition against the sentence, as was his entitlement, but I have no record of the result in the file.

These experiences were of value to me in that they gave me practice in putting my own feelings aside and focusing on the needs of the individual, even if I sometimes felt like falling-in a firing squad.

f. Days of Wine and Roses

It may be simply stressing the obvious, but it is true that thoughts on the military profession invariably bring with them dark echoes of 'death or glory'. Yet also, it seems to be internationally accepted, that, even if only for the professional health of the practitioners, much energy is expended on the light side.

Entertainment in the Mess was mainly in the bar or the occasional 'small game' of poker. On a Saturday night it would not be unusual to be invited for 'a few quick hands of poker' and at twelve o'clock to be having 'the last ace-pot', standing-up. I remember on one memorable occasion seeing five 'living-in' officers going straight to Mass in the Garrison Church on a Sunday after an all-night game.

There were billiards rooms but people's ideas of progress meant that all over the Army the billiards tables were let go to make room for extended bars. This is now accepted as a mistake, but mess meetings at the time voted for the change enthusiastically. After the restraints of the Emergency, extended bars seemed to fit in with the national mood. Anthony Cronin and Nuala O'Faolain have painted entertainingly colourful but stark pictures of literary Dublin, of the life of the pub and the pint, of the drinking Bohemia: the 'Catacombs' in the flagged floor basements of Dublin's Edwardiana and of course, McDaids.

Ulick O'Connor quotes a Stephens line: 'a nose-red city half as old as time.'

Nuala O'Faolain wrote that 'for every real writer around there were ten literary minded people like me. The culture was terribly dependent on drink'.

Military drinking seems to be practised with equal enthusiasm by all armies: the Tsar's Cossacks standing on window ledges challenging danger with vodka to the strains of the balalaika; the British mess horseplay, after which everybody at the party pays for any damage. Also the story of the great Stonewall Jackson being reported to Lincoln for drinking too much wine and the President's suggestion that some of his less lucky generals should try it.

The military establishment tends to be an internationally recognisable type of social institution, which can become isolated from society in general. It tends to be self-sufficient, mobile and all-embracing: military barracks are hotels, schools, workplaces and recreation centres, where soldiers of all ranks eat, sleep, work, rest and play. The 'what's down town' attitude of the old army has, of course, been dead for some time as more married officers live normal suburban lives rather than in the big old houses of the married quarters, which left them facing the awesome task of purchasing a house on retirement.

Our bachelor group did not break off for many individual 'dates', although I had the pleasure of taking the most beautiful model in town, Hannah Jorgenson, to the Cavalry Ball, and in my last single year I was invited to organise a group of Irish officers who were to escort American débutantes on part of their world tour. They had met academics in Berlin and lawyers in London. We, God between us and all harm, were to be their 'Irish experience'. Our 'team list' ended up decorated by a series of rings all over it as it had been produced for improvement on innumerable bar counters. We had a great week: hunt balls and cocktail parties in Count O'Kelly's and Toddy O'Sullivan's penthouse on top of the Gresham.

There were other occasions when we were called on to serve our country by only standing and waiting as at receptions in Dublin Castle for, in my case, a famous cardinal and most memorably for Princess Grace. I remember standing on my own once, as there was a crush at the drinks, when a waitress came out with a silver tray and asked me what I wanted.

A white haired old gentleman came over and said mysteriously:

'A gentleman will always be served.'

I remember this particular night because I had got to know Brian Lenihan and when the party was over we decided that a few extra jars would be nice, so we headed down town: Brian in white tie and tails, myself in cloak and dress uniform. As it was very late we knocked at the door of Groomes. A garda loomed into view:

'Ah, you won't have any trouble there.'

My special memory of that night was of hearing Brian winding up a conversation with someone who came to him with a request for help with, 'No problem'.

This was afterwards misused by John Healy, who conveyed the impression (albeit humorously) in his column (Backbencher) that Brian meant that no problem existed (as in – 'what crisis?') This is very different from the meaning clearly understood by me that Brian fully accepted that the man had a personal problem but was emphasising that he had no problem about helping him, in that, regardless of obstacles, he would do his best to solve the man's difficulty. He was one of those whose sheer transparent decency went a long way to balance the sleaze factor in Irish politics.

I remember being in a discussion on separatism with him in the Prince of Wales Hotel in Athlone and saying in response to a sensible point on federalism he had made, 'That's all very well, Brian, but I doubt very much if you would say something like that in public.'

He was on a visit to England the following week and was interviewed by the *Daily Telegraph* during which he repeated his view that the Scots seemed to be moving OK at their own pace. That did not do him any good with the loud separatist element in his party.

Pubs, we visited on a Friday or Saturday night, usually were the Wicklow Hotel, the Old Stand or Neary's, but never McDaids, which seemed to attract a (to us) peculiar crowd of the then fashionable 'literary left' intellectuals. (My happiest memory of Dublin pubs after I had retired was meeting the widely admired Con Houlihan on occasional lunchtimes, who christened me 'the first yuppie', presumably as I would be in my customary pin-stripe. Con was a word wizard, who had started his journalism in the *Kerryman*.)

We were never really part of literary Dublin with exceptions like Captain Alan Simpson (Pike Theatre and the 'Rose Tattoo' case) and people like Captain Seamus Kelly who was Quidnunc of *The Irish Times*. Alan once invited some of us in the Bailey to a party and as we were not quite sure of the address we pulled up in the open MG Sports (owned by a young but wealthy Trinity student) to enquire at a block of flats. The response was that we had a bucket of water thrown at the car for some obscure reason. The student foolishly got out to deal with the perpetrator, a rough-looking character, who was immediately joined by what seemed like a dozen others. The result was that he got a blow on the lip by someone wearing a large ring which marked him with an X. I rang the Gardai from a call box but by the time he arrived, on a bicycle, we were driving away. When we arrived at the party, Alan's wife Carolyn took the walking wounded away for treatment.

It was Alan also who invited me to a party in a mews across the lane from the Pike. I met the (afterwards famous) Paddy Gallagher there and he told me of his decision to join the 'electronic media'. Years afterwards, meeting him at book-fairs, he always reminded me, with a laugh, of our arguments that night, when having first taken me to be 'the quintessential, unreconstructed Free State Officer', he was surprised at my 'liberal ideas'.

I got my all-time greatest social put-down at the same party, at which we were warned by a priest, pulling pints, that we should stay near the wall as the floor was wobbly. I had got chatting with an attractive foreign student and thought that I had got on well. When the party was over, not long before the dawn, as we were leaving, I addressed her: 'My beautiful Danish sculptress.' Cutting through the remains of the party air, I heard: 'I am not a sculptress, I am a sculptor, I am not Danish, I am Norwegian and I am not yours yet.' I made some face-saving response like: 'Well, at least you admit to being beautiful', before escaping.

We liked the Horseshoe Bar at the Shelbourne or the upstairs bar in the Gresham, where we once complained of the lack of Guinness. Toddy O'Sullivan informed us that any time we wanted to order in advance he would ensure that it was stocked for us. I do not remember if we ever took him up on that. He always welcomed officers in dress uniform at the Saturday dress hops. Tickets were made available.

On one occasion, on our way, we dined in Jammet's, with its Edwardian echoes in dark wood, mirrors and marble. I had no idea then of its status as a watering hole for national and international literati. As the impressive custodian of the door took my cloak to put away, I apologised: 'Sorry about this nuisance.'

'Not at all, sir, you lend tone to the occasion.'

As well as orderlies, the mess staff in the bar and the dining-room added considerably to the quality of life. In quiet moments in a few hints and smiles an experienced barman (like Corporal 'Peggy' O'Neill, the equivalent of a British Army 'King's Corporal') would let one in on his knowledge. It never went any further: talking in the bar was talking 'in lodge' and the barman felt equally part of it.

Also, in McKee Officers' Mess the sight of the tall, silver-haired, white-moustached, distinguished looking head waiter, John, in impeccable black, had the effect of reducing the chaos of a bar session group of noisy young officers into the order of the dining-room. Standing inside the tall windows, lording it over his panelled domain, he was at one with the oil paintings of the Chiefs of Staff looking down from the walls. He once signalled me out of trouble as I held forth on the joys of soldiering in an Infantry unit as being more rewarding than a desk job to my seniors in a staff section. They were getting somewhat miffed that I did not appreciate the honour of serving with them.

Another memory of John is a sad one, as he knew the family of a soldier who died in Cyprus and accompanied the chaplain and me to the house in Ballyfermot to convey the bad news. Another one of the officer's jobs that everybody dreads. The thought of what I had to do had me looking somewhat green about the gills and, when we arrived, a hint from John had the woman of the house pour a drop of whiskey for me. I still remember the incongruity of them standing around me, saying things like, 'Ah, the young officer is taking this hard'.

They said that, when they saw the chaplain and myself arriving, they did not need to be told.

In Cathal Brugha Officers' Mess there was a waiter, Jim, with a marvellous flow of Dublinese: 'Have you had an elegant sufficiency, sir?' He took a part-time job in a Dublin hotel but he did not last: his bustling repartee was too much. I was present one night in that hotel when I heard him call to the barman: 'Two more brandies for the couple in the corner.' Everybody in the lounge looked around to see a pair of octogenarians, trying to fade into the carpet.

Our cadet class was asked for volunteers for the Equitation Course. I did not apply because I was sensible enough to realise that I was unlikely to be one of the 'stars' and therefore could find myself posted down the country far from my pleasant berth, if I failed to make the top few. My ex-cadet-school classmate, Captain Des Ringrose, did and made excellent progress. Even though he complained once about the sun blinding him facing a double bank in the Aga Khan Cup competition. Des as usual took it in his stride.

His brother, Colonel Billy Ringrose, became Chef d'Equipe and is a past President of the RDS, who once kindly asked me if I was interested in joining a committee. The team and its individuals had some marvellous successes which makes for puzzling reading in Colonel Sir Mike Ansell's book that since his friend Colonel Dan Corry and the other famous names from the thirties retired, the Irish team did not seem to do so well.

I have some good memories of one Horse Show Week as, at a hunt ball in the Gresham, when some young English guests at our table started throwing bread-rolls, I insisted that they cease as I was an officer in uniform and could not be party to that behaviour. They responded and we had no more trouble.

Seemingly I had been overheard by a waitress commenting, 'To tell the truth I always prefer soup rather than these cold starters.'

She went off and returned with a bowl of soup for me, alone of all the guests, saying, 'You deserve it, we were proud of you.'

Later that night I was approached by an officer of an Irish regiment in the British Army.

'How about a bicycle race across the floor for the first time in the history of our two armies?'

I reluctantly turned down the idea as he was in civvies and I was in uniform. There seemed to be a much more easy-going tolerance at British Army parties than in ours provided that everybody was on parade on the following morning. Looking back, I think that I was wrong, but he understood my concern and we had a philosophical beaker instead. However, a distraction arrived in a young man whose father was a Marquis, (not exactly pronounced marquee but we wondered if he should be titled the 'bivvy' i.e. small tent) who put a clockwork spider walking on the ceiling and, when the wind ran out, it fell and scattered ladies at the unlucky table.

Looking back over my annals of military lowlife, it would be true to say, that, from time to time, the adjective '*aoibhin*' (pleasant) could qualify the life of the officer as much as '*an scolaire*' (the student). Like when I was sent as a young 2nd Lieutenant with my platoon as an advance party to prepare for a Battalion Camp in the Glen of Imaal. I had Coolmooney House (used as the Officers' Mess) all to myself: a charming old house dating from the early 1800s, complete with haunted room, large windows and banks of colourful rhododendrons. It had its share of legends. One was that Nelly, a young maid made pregnant, either was thrown from an upstairs window or committed suicide in despair. Her ghost was reputed to haunt a room in the house. An officer went to sleep in the room once to prove his bravery and disprove the legend. After a late jar session, one of his brother officers went outside to a tub of icy water and held his hands in this to freezing point. He went to the room and put his hands on the sleeping officer's face. The result was as expected.

Based in Coolmooney House, I was Monarch of the Glen for a while with the kind of staff that made life very comfortable: my orderly to look after my room, a driver to take me to Mass, a chef to cook my meals and a waiter to ensure my comfort at table. I thought, perhaps this is what army life is really all about (I was wrong). My perception, and indeed the paper position, was that I was the Commanding Officer, the boss. The reality was that the Sergeant did what was necessary with the platoon in preparing the camp and the chef ran the Mess. I heard him once giving instructions to my orderly. My Sergeant's main concern was keeping my enthusiasm within bounds, like when he persuaded me to drop the idea that as we were in the country I could organise some tactical exercise for the troops.

My 'warts and all' presentation of the silly side of the young officer's life is of something that exists side by side with the determination to do one's serious duty at all times. The idea of 'work hard, play hard' was a constant. All armies accept that for young officers to spend all their time focused on the 'death or glory' aspect of their profession would result in an unhealthy distortion of vision that could produce fanaticism. The 'amateurism' of the old British Army, was intended to keep the army as the servant of the people and not a breeding ground for another Cromwell. This resulted in times of danger, as in Northern Ireland, that thankfully there was no rush for instant glory, despite some very serious mistakes.

One of the most serious mistakes, of course, was that the backlash as well as the millions spent on Bloody Sunday inquiries could have been avoided. Most of the soldiers in the unit involved either did not fire or fired only one round. It would seem from the reports since that three soldiers (Corporal 'F', Soldiers 'G' and 'H') killed seven, and seven others killed one each. They could have been identified when they came in to return unused rounds, asked to explain why they fired and charged if necessary.

In those years the Irish Army drew support from its honourable tradition in the service of the people, ready to do what an Army's got to do. We now know that the Taoiseach, Jack Lynch, had a very clear concept of the necessary military action to counter the security threat and that he issued clear orders.

But what exactly is that military tradition, within which the Irish Officer has his being?

g. Our Military Tradition, a shared inheritance?

I had a picture of the Irish Guards 'trooping the colour', cut from some magazine, in my room in the Officers' Mess. On being informed of a proposed visit by the Chief of Staff to our quarters, hints were given by someone to remove it. Being the type that I was in my 'boy-scout' days, there was no way that I would hide anything I believed in, or pretend to believe other than I did. I believed that Irish regiments in other armies shared the inheritance of the Irish military tradition, even if its heart was in Ireland. I also believed that the people of Ireland, of the whole island, had inherited that tradition, in the same way that they inherited the Irish literary and musical traditions, which could not be said to end at an artificial border.

President Mary McAleese has since called for a 'shared commemoration' of the First World War, that milestone in the family histories of so many,

North and South, Catholic and Protestant. Brian Cowan, when Taoiseach, went further and called for a mutual commemoration of all our historical milestones, nationalist and unionist. He reminded us that:

'In homes and schools across this island, we grew up knowing and hearing only one set of stories, singing only one set of songs.'

With this we seem to have reached a turning point in our sad history, something that future historians will acknowledge. This could be an important step on the road to John Hume's 'Agreed Ireland' and an acceptance by all on this island of 'the common name of Irishman', as hoped for by Wolfe Tone.

This has always been my hope and belief, and I find support in most of the books on my bookshelves. However, looking back across the years to that picture, I realise that I could on numerous occasions have made life easier for myself. Yet when General McKeown reached my room, after looking at my bookshelves and seeing the picture, he simply smiled and said, 'Have we reached that standard in our ceremonial?'

He had been my Cadet-master and the first graduate of the Cadet School to be appointed Chief of Staff. Some wondered what would have been the reaction of 'one of the old crowd'. From what I learned from my father-in-law, Commandant Charles Byrne, afterwards, they would not have been any different.

Shortly afterwards I submitted an article to *An Cosantóir* suggesting the idea of a ceremonial battalion with four companies each representing a province, with appropriate flash, for example, the Ulster one having the 'red hand'. In those post-Emergency, pre-UN service days of the 1950s I was concerned, after my occasional duties as recruiting officer in the barracks, about the boring image of the Army and its negative effect on recruitment.

In the course of the paper I must have enthused over the ceremonial of the Brigade of Guards I had seen on a visit to London. For whatever reason, it was indicated that, whereas the journal was not official opinion, nonetheless it would be taken to be a reflection of that. Perhaps my idea could wait until the 'force was with me'? I wrote that 'we have a tradition in the profession of arms equalled by few, yet very little use is made of it and consequently we lose the boosting effect on our morale'. This was accepted at coffee-time conversations about the picture afterwards. The problem is that when one gets one fly out of that particular ointment, the next fly in a long queue jumps in.

For instance, who owns a military tradition? Is it something that can only belong to a separate independent state, or is it something that belongs to the people of a nation regardless of how they are politically organised? The Irish military tradition includes the honourable record of its soldiers in foreign armies, like the Regiment of Ultonia in Spain. The Irish Brigade in France was well covered by J.C. O'Callaghan in his 1869 book. Even though honourable soldiers they could, of course, be described as mercenaries. However, Captain D.P. Conyngham, wounded in 1864 at the battle of Resaca, wrote in *The Irish Brigade and its Campaigns* that the Irish soldier 'had just the same right to fight for America as the native American had'. He was a 'patriot and no mercenary'.

The Irish regiments of the British Army contributed significantly also to enriching our military tradition. Their memory, in human individual dignity, has been very well served by Myles Dungan, in *Irish Voices from the Great War* but his suggestion that 'Ireland has no great military tradition of its own', because Irish soldiers 'were merely an adjunct to the army of its near neighbour', simply misses the point. They mainly lived and fought, however, in Irish regiments and were recognised as being Irish by friends and enemies. John Devoy, (*Recollections of an Irish Rebel*), recalls 'bloody fights between Irish and English regiments.Irishmen in the British Army were men of fine physique' and many had 'a good primary education'. General Godley, in his *Life of an Irish Soldier*, remembers dinners during the First World War with 'two Ulster Orangemen of the Black North' (36th Division, General Oliver Nugent and Captain Somerset Saunderson) and 'two Southern Home-Rulers' (16th Division, Captains Stephen Gwynn and Willie Redmond). The talk 'would at times get rather heated; but I need hardly say that they . . . were in reality the best of friends'.

The Germans recognised and tried to subvert Irish regiments.

Unlike India on independence, however, due to our particular 'narrow ground' we did not retain the militarily priceless regimental names that Irish soldiers had honoured with their sweat and blood. My brother, Lieut.-Colonel Colman Goggin, visited some comrades on duty on the India/Pakistan Border, where they were entertained in the Officers' Mess of the Khyber Rifles, whose name and traditions live on. The 'Dubs' and the 'Munsters' were as dead to us as the bodies under the waves of 'V' Beach at Gallipoli, when it was not possible to see the bodies on the sea floor because of the blood in the water. We were not able to see them for the bad blood of our distorted 'history'. Irish soldiers gallantly contributed their blood but the Irish people were not allowed to wear the pride.

The Military Heritage of Ireland Trust under the chairmanship of Maj Gen. P.F. Nowlan offers help for research in this field. Groups like the Royal Dublin Fusiliers Association are also doing much good work to bring those men in from the political cold, and to improve mutual understanding. Their memory was too uncomfortable a reminder to the 'physical force' ideologues of the other great tradition in Irish politics, constitutional nationalism, handed down from O'Connell through Parnell to Redmond. This proud tradition, in my youth, rarely got the star treatment given to the gunmen by teachers, writers or politicians.

President Mary McAleese, in the Daniel O'Connell Memorial Lecture, said, 'We acknowledge him as the Liberator . . . the man who cranked up on these islands a slow-burning momentum towards democracy... that has at last paid off in the peace we share on this island today.'

In the First World War the constitutional nationalist soldiers had bravely followed their political leader's call. There were over 200,000 volunteers from the island of Ireland and with the 300,000 Irish emigrants, who served, add up to half a million men, with an estimated dead of between 35,000 and 48,000. These are huge figures for this small island and, taking the families into account, add up to a significant proportion of the population and a significant part of what we were. The pay and family allowances are given by some commentators as the reason for this level of recruitment, but Bartlett and Jeffery in *A Military History of Ireland* reject the 'crass reductionism' of this explanation. 'Enlistment has always been a private matter.' David Fitzpatrick in *The Two Irelands* wrote that this approach cannot explain why so many took that 'dangerous, uncomfortable and ultimately irrational decision'. The poverty paradigm seems designed to devalue the honourable political basis for their enlistment and to degrade their sense of honour and loyalty as soldiers. Yet, in the misery of a POW Camp (Limburg) in Germany about 3,000 Irish soldiers were given the opportunity to desert their comrades to freedom, money and good food.

The American Ambassador, J.W. Gerard (*My Four Years in Germany*) reported in 1917 that Sir Roger Casement 'tried to get these Irishmen to desert their flag and join the Germans. He finally discontinued his visits after obtaining about thirty recruits, because the remaining Irishmen chased him out of the camp'. Ironically, René MacColl (*Roger Casement*) noted that Casement had complained in 1900 of an attempt by the Boers which 'was, of course, futile' to 'seduce' 1,078 Irish POWs to be 'false to their own allegiance' and to 'dishonour their oaths'. In both cases, the 'traditional pride of the Irish regiments asserted itself to an extent that none had foreseen'. In fact, evidence of the political consciousness and commitment of these men is quoted by Peter Hart in *The IRA and its Enemies*. 'Of 66 accidentally spoiled soldier's and sailor's ballots in Cork in 1918 only six votes went to Sinn Fein and 56 of these men cast both their votes for the Parliamentary Party.'

Bartlett and Jeffery, remind us that 'with statehood North and South the Irish military tradition has largely retreated from the public view'. Yet, our Constitution now recognises that our nation is defined by the people on this island, who claim Irish nationality. So it seems to be equally sensible to allow the people of this island to claim ownership of the Irish military tradition. We suffer from a confusion of traditions. We mix up the clean sharp blade of a military tradition, which is an effective instrument of war, in that it contributes to the achievement of military objectives, with our two politico-religious traditions which are more like nail-studded clubs with which civilians beat each other.

The Russian Army, as the Workers and Peasants Red Army, looked to its Tsarist tradition for inspiration after its disastrous Finnish adventure and reintroduced military titles and all the discarded insignia of the old Tsarist Officer Corps. The American Army came through a heart-rending civil war but its soldiers now look back with pride on all its previous heroes in blue or grey. The British seem more aware of its value than we have been. The 38th (Irish) Brigade of the British Army in the battle for Monte Casino in the Second World War had as its motto '*Ubique et semper fidelis*' taken from the Irish Brigade in the service of France. We had an informative and entertaining lecture on this in the Military History Society. It seems that soldiers in other Irish regiments were very keen to be taken in to that Irish Brigade.

We Irish Nationalists of the South share our military tradition with our currently separated Northern brethren whether they are Nationalist or Unionist, Catholic or Protestant, who enriched it together. Just as nobody would pretend that our music, dance or literary traditions belong solely to the people of the twenty-six counties. The Irish military tradition is indivisible and this island will someday provide an Irish EU Battle-group consisting of battalions from North and South, who have already worked side by side on UN operations. In fact, as my ex-classmate, Col. Mick Moriarty, records in his *Diary of an Irish Soldier*, a troop of the Life Guards, part of the British contingent in Cyprus, was put under the command of the CO of the Irish 41st Battalion, providing an escort for arriving Turkish soldiers.

The other big fly that jumps in to a discussion of this question can be put as follows: Contrary to all the above was the military tradition of the modern Irish State not born until sometime in the period 1916-1921? Is the true salt of the Irish earth, racy of the Irish soil, military tradition really merely a paramilitary one?

Bartlett and Jeffery, add a question mark on what seems to them the 'ambiguities' of 'An Irish military tradition?' They refer to 'a recent history of the Irish Army' which 'traces its origins no further back than the setting up of the Irish Volunteers in 1913'. Yet while in Colonel

J.P.Duggan's impeccable research in *A History of the Irish Army* it is possible to trace human links in that way, an army is greater than the sum of its parts or its recruitment material.

It was of course, politically useful for the founding National Army to insist on its centrality in the military campaign that achieved the current level of freedom. As David Fitzpatrick wrote: the 'evolution of the national army was tortuous since Mulcahy and his staff continued to claim allegiance from the IRA and assert their continuity with the volunteers . . .' The really surprising thing about this ploy was its longevity. Long after it was serving any purpose it lived on in public discourse. Despite the Free State Army being obviously a constitutional, law and order army, which took on the 'physical force' element.

We owe our democracy today to the founding fathers when they came to accept that military force should be used only on the orders of the elected representatives of the people and not at the nod of a millenarian conspiratorial elite. Having taken that defining decision, the founding National Army became the inheritor of Ireland's long and honourable military tradition. It had its baptism of fire in the tragic Civil War and faced previous comrades as deadly enemies. This was a double test. But the Army has maintained its professional integrity ever since. Noel Conway commented in *The Bloods* (3rd Infantry Battalion)that, during the Emergency, they were 'neither pro-German nor anti-British'.

In fact, over 5,000 deserted the Irish Army to fight with the British. We had no doubt on which side we were, with British officers observing exercises. For those who were harshly punished for desertion the sad aspect of it is that the Irish regiments they served in shared our military tradition. According to research by Joseph Quinn, Captain Peadar Cowan, defending deserters at a court-martial, quoted the definition of desertion as 'leaving a post of danger for a post of safety', drawing attention to their heroism in leaving a post of safety for one of danger. I contributed an 'Irishman's Diary' in *The Irish Times* during a debate on the letters page on this subject.

We handed over the legacy of the Somme to the Unionists. This suited the extremists on both sides, allowing the Northern Unionists to have pride in the Somme as their defining symbol and us the GPO. No mention of honourable Southern soldiers was going to spoil either party. However, hopes for reconciliation have now been acknowledged in Clare County Library, the Athy Heritage Centre and the Tralee Great War Exhibition.

Alex Maskey, when Sinn Fein Lord Mayor of Belfast broke the sectarian mould by commemorating these Irish soldiers. The UK Branch of ONE (Organisation of National Ex-servicemen) participated in the Combined Irish Regiments' London Parade. Pupils from the Christian Brothers in West Belfast visited the Somme Exhibition. Danny Morrison of Sinn Fein, reviewing Myles Dungan's *Irish Voices from the Great War*, admitted that: 'Until I read this book I had only the vaguest comprehension of the extent of Irish involvement and the magnitude of the sacrifices.'

He noted that 'the CO of the 6th Connaughts asked would they be considered saints or traitors, little knowing that they wouldn't even be considered'.

In the Island of Ireland Peace Park the Army honoured, *inter alia*, the constitutional nationalists of the 16th (Irish) Division. We can commemorate their heroism with our unionist fellow Irishmen commemorating those of the 36th (Ulster) Division, in an ecumenical service of remembrance. Just as those two divisions fought side by side to victory on Messines Ridge, we can celebrate side by side what we have in common. While not wearing the green as requested by Redmond, nonetheless they were patriotic Irishmen and an honourable part of the Irish military tradition.

The shared heritage of the Irish military tradition is an invaluable bridge between the two political traditions, and was one of the important objectives of Mary McAleese's Presidency. It also provides a step on the road to John Hume's 'Agreed Ireland'.

At a reception in *Arus an Uactaran* I was given the opportunity of expressing my admiration for the President, joining Queen Elizabeth at Messines at the joint British/Irish memorial. They have since made history on a visit to The Irish War Memorial Garden at Islandbridge.

I had always admired those constitutional nationalist Irishmen who answered their political leader's call in the First World War and felt that they were unfairly brushed under the historical carpet by the militant republicans who had won at home. I felt that the least I could do was to wear the Poppy in their remembrance, and offer the occasional contribution in the form of a letter to *The Irish Times* at Poppy time in November. As a means of making some small response, also, some years afterwards I joined the Dublin Fusiliers Association enjoying their Saturday afternoon lectures.

I believe that our constitutional nationalist tradition from O'Connell through Parnell to Redmond has, until 2012, never been given the credit it is due and that includes our proud military tradition. All my life I have heard from school, pulpit and political platform all praise for militant republicanism and we wonder how 'dissidents' remain and Omagh happened. At last with editorials in *The Irish Times*, like 'Redmond's moment' and articles by people like John Bruton, 'Redmond was a realist', the State is finally recognising our national debt to Redmond and the significance of the centenary of the Third Home Rule Bill.

The modern Irish Army has a history of less than a century but it has earned its place in the pride of the people. It defended our democracy in the Civil War and our neutrality in the Second World War. It has provided a bulwark against subversion at intervals throughout the twentieth century. It also has an honourable record in defence of world peace in at least twenty-seven countries.

It has inherited a military tradition second to none.

Kipling's words sum up its position:

> *'We're not so old on the Army list,*
> *But we're not so new in the ring.'*

Epilogue

On Dun Laoghaire pier, on my daily walk, especially on one of those bright blue days when sea and sky light up the world, I realise how privileged I am to be living within walking distance of the sea again. The sea provided light and sound for my youth but apart from one round of Dublin Bay from the Royal Irish Yacht Club with Captain John Martin, an ex-Army comrade, I am happy to 'walk on by'. Thinking of the demolished Victorian train shed, on Carlisle Pier, I feel the presence of the ghosts of emigrants, who left from there, Michael Collins leaving for the Treaty negotiations and the final embarkation of the British Army. As the sea gently sucks on the great granite blocks taken down from Dalkey Hill, I think of the waves beating on the rocks at the harbour's mouth in Dingle, as *an Seabhac* wrote, '*gan stad, gan staonadh*'. I try to remember an onomatopoeic line in Virgil that Brother Barry said reproduced the smooth, sibilant sweep of the incoming tide. The oldest sound in European history.

In this peaceful place questions tend to come. Why is there something rather than nothing? Where are we going? Have we made progress in my lifetime? Have I succeeded in bringing any measure of order out of chaos in my own little patch? All our human lives seem to be a series of questions. I question therefore I am?

The philosophical task of each generation seems to be to question the assumptions of the previous one. I have asked questions all my life. I continued to ask questions having been privileged to serve in two national organisations (Macra na Feirme and the Irish Hardware Association) and two of our great departments of state, after my retirement from the Army.

All history for Collingwood was the search for self-knowledge. We must now fight for freedom from the tyranny of the dead, freedom to

249

clarify and define the relevant political concepts of our own time in accordance with our knowledge of today's world and do our historic duty as a generation. This is history's categorical imperative.

Yet in questioning the national philosophy I have discovered that great care has to be exercised when our pantheon of secular saints, whose philosophy is written in the blood of martyrs, comes under scrutiny. To some people, mainly those who are simply not interested in reading or thinking about history, any questioning of someone like Patrick Pearse seems to be taken as a personal family insult. One such, with normal education and level of intelligence told me, one day, that my trouble was that 'I read too many books', implying that he knew all that was necessary and did not need to seek answers.

As I listen to the sound of a boat engine coming over the water it brings me back to where I came from. The old walled town of Dingle had a charter from Queen Elizabeth 1, when it was incorporated with a Sovereign, ten Burgesses and a number of Freemen, its jurisdiction being a circle of land and sea with the Church of Saint John as its centre. With the great Atlantic waves beating to the south outside the placid little harbour and the sheltering hills to the north, Dingle in my youth had remained a fossilised relic of its medieval self. Now it is so cosmopolitan that one could improve one's German, French or Dutch in the pubs. This seems appropriate in a town which in the Middle Ages had a population of over five thousand and a booming wine trade with Spain and Portugal. Crests of Spanish traders still adorn the walls of some of the old houses. An old Irish saying has it that 'the people go but the hills remain'. Mr O'Cuiv's may come and go but the name 'Dingle' remains. It had remained largely uncontaminated by outside communication until my friend John Joe Sheehy and the Dingle Development Committee launched it into the twentieth century with booster rockets of sea angling festivals. That decent girl Ryan's Daughter also helped to open the town to the world tourist market.

Looking at Dun Laoghaire from the head of the pier it seems like Dingle writ large with a Dart: a townscape gently folded against a backdrop of hills. On my left rises the gentle wooded slopes of Dalkey Hill with its castle and Killiney Hill crowned with the obelisk to Queen Victoria. To the right the large bare sheltering slopes descend to complete the semi-circle guarding the town. Its 'forward defended localities' are held by four yacht clubs and the start of the sea-bridge to the other island. As I head back, a conical-topped hill in the distance starts to sink behind the sea-front houses. The stubby tower of the Town Hall thrusting skywards asserts temporal power amidst the proud spires of the churches. All of the Christian family, none of them strange to me in this new age: Roman Catholic, Church of Ireland, Presbyterian, and Methodist. I have been in every one: peace services, weddings, christenings and simple ecumenical prayers.

The Martello tower on the flank is a reminder of the arrival of the advance guard of my family clan to Dingle, with look-out-posts on the hills waiting for Napoleon's invading ships. I pass the granite memorial in memory of the heroism of Captain J.McNeill Boyd, RN, who drowned here attempting to rescue others. I'm glad that a memorial has at last been unveiled to the 501 Irish people who lost their lives on the torpedoed RMS *Leinster* in 1918. Was the eighty years delay due to the fact that half of them were in khaki? Also on my left the 'Forty Foot', a reminder of the sporting soldiers of the Fortieth Foot who probably did swim in the currently accepted dress of this informal club.

As I move closer to the shore, that large aquatic animal, Dalkey Island, with its tower cap, begins to swim around the headland and vanish completely by the time I pass the bandstand, now restored, where the bandsmen of two armies have entertained summer crowds. I wonder if, as in the 2nd Infantry Battalion in my day, did some of the grandfathers of the present army bands play on that bandstand in the other uniform?

The moored yachts float into my consciousness, as now without the power of engine or sail, they line and sway in response to the commands of wind and wave. I note the aggressive self-assertive names of the reds (*Firestorm, Live Wire, Red Arrow*) and the relaxed, laid-back self-effacing names of the whites and blues (*Solstice, Sunfish, Enchantress,*

Nyala, Santa Fe). Approaching the town, ghosts of the imperial past rise up around me. The 'Queens Hotel' on a gable; the Royal National Lifeboat Institute, the Royal Marine Hotel, once HQ for the port and the Officers' Mess; Haigh Terrace. Reminders of part of what we were.

Yet, the well-rewarded Protestant Ascendancy, with some notable exceptions, (e.g. Lord Powerscourt, Irish Volunteer officer, then Captain Dublin Fusiliers) failed in its historic mission. Why? Self-centred selfishness? Biased education? Or simply like the French aristocracy, failing to recognise that the rulers are part of the body politic, not, a separate nation within? They kept the people at arm's length instead of encouraging them to take pride in their holdings and share in the running of the country. In the words of Yeats, they were no petty people, producing top-class soldiers and administrators in foreign countries. But they had to be stripped of their political, financial and social, power in Ireland, as they were by the constitutional revolution that produced Catholic Emancipation and ended with the Local Government and Land Acts, restoring local political power and land to the people. In reaction to their exclusiveness, we seem to have narrowed the definition of 'Irishman', to a Catholic, Irish-speaking, *ceilidhe*-dancing, hurler. I often think that there was only one real Irishman ever in this country, the 'bould Thady Quill'.

When will this history end? Are ex-soldiers more conscious of it than civilians? This undeclared, long civil war, illustrated by the confrontation of English-speaking Irishmen with pikes on Vinegar Hill by Gaelic-speaking Irishmen in red militia tunics whose loyalty to their officers and regiments was duly commended.

Was the IRB inspired rising of 1916, in the words of Maureen Wall, 'as much a revolt against the Irish Parliamentary Party as against British rule in Ireland'? Irishmen in the Free State Army put down the anti-democratic attempt in 1922 to defy the people.

The Emergency Army faced the double threat, external and internal. The drastically reduced post-war Army helped to block attempts to subvert the State in the 1950s and again stood by democracy in 1969 in a very thin green line.

Do the peoples on these islands really belong together? We speak forms of the same language: we move freely in and out of each other's homes and cities. Is it possible that we on Newman's 'Isles of the North' will one day agree to an arrangement that will allow the four tribes to report to a confederate government as a sector of the European Union?

We were part of the Advance Guard from these islands in Europe, when Irish monks prayed in isolated European monasteries and the blood of the Irish Brigades watered its rolling plains.

Our financial mess at the start of the new century provides us with two pointers to our current state. One, depressing, is the so-called 'sub-prime' lending that would have been unthinkable to my friend Bob and his father, both bank managers. The other offering hope for new relations, was the mannerly, neighbourly way the British Prime Minister announced their contribution to our 'bail-out'. This book is mainly an observation of the political and military *mores* of the mid-twentieth century as seen through the prism of one Irishman's place in the ranks, yet it is important to know who is reporting these ideas.

Entering George's Street, I pass the new Post Office, showing its newness in its title of just 'POST'. This eliminates one small difference between us and our English neighbours, who will always say 'POST Office' while we persist in 'Post OFFICE'.

I pay a quick visit to a local bookshop in the hope of a bargain, my principal means of adding to my book collection since I escaped into retirement. Then, up through Royal Terrace, interestingly translated as '*Ardan an Ri*', when, they could have rendered it neutral as '*Ardan Rioga*', but in historical terms correctly referring to the visit of King Edward VII.

I start to wonder how much longer will the rearguard be attending Class Reunions of the cadet class that first paraded in 1950? The memory swims into my mind that the old Infantry full-dress uniform that I once had was now in the Military Museum with my old dress cloak. I wonder should I be in there also with my old Lee Enfield Rifle? Wordsworth's words sometimes come to me in this mood.

'Who is the happy warrior, who is he that every man in arms should wish to be?'

Have I ever met him or is he still part of my never-ending research into the military being?

Do all paths of glory really lead but to the museum? Yet why did the Bugler Walsh always sound 'Reveille' after the 'Last Post', if it was not to do with the soldier having to fall in on that big square in the sky for the final 'check parade'? When the bugle sounds for me in the underground post that will be my final resting-place, I hope some old comrade will order, like Othello:

'Call all my sad Captains. Let us have one more gaudy night.'

Appendix A

Clippings that may throw some light on my story

Dingle Shooting Competition

Nephew and Uncle are Successful Marksmen

The final of the shooting competition in which hundreds participated during the week for a valuable silver cup, presented by the Dingle Carnival Committee, took place at the close of the Dingle Carnival on Sunday night.

The following qualified for the final, having no less than 40 points out of 50: Cpl. Paddy Goggin, Dingle Batt. F.C.A.; Coleman [*sic*] Goggin, Dingle P.O.; Bernie Goggin, do; J. Foley, do; P. McNamara, Upper Main St., Dingle; Dion O'Connor, do; J. Begley, Dygegate St., Dingle; P. Sugrue, Burnham, Dingle; J. Brosnan, Ballybowler; George Foley, Oakpark, Tralee.

The final results were as follows:—Cpl. Paddy Goggin, Dingle F.C.A., 1st, 47 points out of 50; 2nd, his brother Coleman [*sic*] Goggin, 46, and their uncle, Mr. Joe Foley, P.O., Dingle, with a score of 45, was third.

Rev. Father J.J. Beasley, C.C., Dingle, Chairman of the Dingle Carnival Committee, on presenting the cup to the winner, congratulated him and remarked that Mr. Everett, Minister for Posts and Telegraphs, should have been present, as there were five from Dingle post office in the final out of the ten who qualified.

Those in charge of the competition were Lieut. M.E. Burke, Lieut. J. O'Sullivan, and Sergt. P.J. O'Riordan, D.A.O. Q.M.R., all of Dingle Batt., F.C.A.

Rev. J.J. Beasley presided and acted as judge.

Military unit visits Carlingford area

A fully-armed mobile military unit, accompanied by Civic Guards, visited Greenore, Co. Louth, and other areas of Carlingford Lough, yesterday afternoon. Reports say that the unit appeared to be reconnoitring the area rather than patrolling it.

It was the first time in recent years that a military unit has been seen in daylight in the area, although units are known to have been in the district patrolling the area after dark.

Dingle Batt. F.C.A. Cup Winner

At Ballymullen Barracks, Tralee, on Sunday last, the final of the .22 Miniature Range Competition was concluded when Corporal P. Goggin, of Dingle Coy., won the F.C.A. trophy, a valuable silver cup which was presented by the Battalion for the best shot.

The men from each of the following F.C.A. Companies competed: Dingle, Lispole, Annascaul, Camp Castlegregory and Cloghane.

At a dinner given in the Officers' Quarters, Captain J. Long, Asst. Area Officer, presented the cup to Corporal P. Goggin and a silver medal to the runner-up, Sergt. P. Driscoll, Camp Coy.

Capt. Long congratulated the winners and each man of the Battalion who competed.

Macra to get new training programme

The President of Macra na Feirme, Mr. Joe Rea, yesterday announced the setting up of a new division of the association's headquarters with the responsibility of supervising a continuous programme of leadership training.

Mr. Rea, who was speaking at the formal opening of the courses for Macra officers at the Association's headquarters in Dublin, said that the new division would be responsible also for the development of a whole range of publications, documentation and instruction manuals.

"It will aslo keep in close touch with the latest techniques in leadership training in Europe and the United States," he said, "so that the very latest information will be at the disposal of our members."

The new leadership division, he said, would go into operation in January. Mr. Patrick J. [sic] Goggin had been appointed as Leadership Training Officer and would head the new department.

Dr. Tom Walsh, director of An Foras Taluntais, said: "Matters of vital significance in farming in future will be covered in the course—group leadership, co-operation, management, industrialisation, programme planning, officer duties and tourism. I am especially glad that co-operation has been included."

College Wins Rifle Team Championship

Marksmen of the Military College gave a grand display of shooting when winning the rifle team championship test in the all-Army tests, which continued at the Curragh yesterday. Out of a possible 630 points the college team scored a total of 538 points, 15 points more than the 12th Batt. team, which finished second with 523 points. First Brigade headquarters were third with 521 points. Although they scored well in the early practices, the college team struck top form in the finals, the difficult rapid and snap shooting tests. Here they established clear superiority, and, with each member of the six-man team shooting with brilliant accuracy, the team drew further ahead to an impressive victory over 27 rival teams.

Twelfth Batt., winners of the light machine-gun championship on Monday, yesterday captured the Marksman Cup, for combined rifle and light machine-gun. Their teams scored a total of 898 points out of a possible 1,060. Military College were second with 872. The Motor Squadron was third with 826. In the heavy machine-gun championship Third Batt. won the team event with a total of 470 points, and 13th Batt., 441.

The Individual Machin-Gun title was won by Pte. T. Irwin, 3rd Batt., 255 points, with Cadets O'Neill and Kelly, both of the Military College, filling the minor placings.

The All-Weapons Cup competition for combined rifle light machine-gun and heavy machine-gun was won by the Military College with a total of 1,340 points; 3rd Batt. was second with 1,326 points, and 12th Batt. third with 1,308 points.

Members of the Military College team which won the rifle championship were Captain P. Keane, Coy. Sergeant Peter O'Connor. Sergeant P. O'Sullivan, Cadet P. Goggin, Cadet J. McNulty, Private C. McQuillan.

The championships will continue with the sniper test today, and will end with the individual rifle championship tomorrow.

Appendix B
Some of the Books in my Life

I add a selection of books from my bookshelves, because I remember an old saying: 'See a man's bookshelves, know the man'. I enjoy reading, and as John McGahern wrote, 'Reading and writing are as close as they are separate'. Or as C. Gilbert Wren put it: 'Basic to my being-in-the-world is a wide range of reading'. I hope that I have succeeded in passing on my love of books to my grandchildren.

One of the best things that happened to me as a child was a present from my Aunt Noreen of a book about Rupert, the bear with the scarf.

I still remember a line –

'"Oh", cried Rupert in alarm.'

This got me started reading, so that, when I was learning to read at school, I was off to a head start to the amusement of the teacher.

I eventually moved on to the popular books of boy's stories that seemed to offer models of behaviour.

Today, looking for presents for grandchildren, what is on offer seems to be mainly horror and fantasy.

There was great respect for the printed word in our house. I still remember my childish pleasure in taking down one of the large illustrated volumes of a children's encyclopaedia, *Cassell's Books of Knowledge*.

My grand-uncle Maurice was a co-founder of the *Kerryman* and afterwards my uncle Paddy was editor and my uncle Brendan was the Dingle reporter – 'Dingle Doings'.

Another relation from further back wrote a slim volume of local history. His manuscript of another book on local customs and folklore was left in Dublin at an interesting time, April 1916. It, like much more, went up in flames.

My brother Bernie is a retired publisher (Brandon Books).

My books are listed in appropriate categories on my computer.

I add three of these in the following pages –
(1) 1916 – The Easter Rising.
(2) Irish Army.
(3) Irish Soldiers in other armies.

1916 – THE EASTER RISING

Archives, Brit. Parl., *The Irish Uprising 1914-21*. London, 2000

Augusteijn, J. (Ed.), *The Irish Revolution 1913-1923*. Basingstoke, 2002

Barton. B., *From Behind a Closed Door: Secret Court Martial Records of the 1916 Rising*. Belfast, 2002

Bell, J. Bowyer, *The Secret Army: The IRA 1916–1979*. Dublin, 1979

Bolger, D., *'16 on 16' Letters from the New Island*. Dublin, 1988

Boyce, D.G. (Ed.), *The Revolution in Ireland 1879– 1923*. London, 1988

Bromage, M.C., *De Valera and the March of a Nation*. London, 1967

Cardozo, N., *Maud Gonne: Lucky Eyes and a Happy Heart*. London, 1979

Carroll, F.M., *American Opinion and the Irish Question 1910–1923*. Dublin, 1978

Carty, X., *In Bloody Protest – The Tragedy of Patrick Pearse*. Dublin, 1978

Caulfield, M., *The Easter Rebellion*. London, 1964

Coates, T.(Ed.), *The Irish Uprising 1914–1921*. (British Archives) London, 2000

Coffey, T.M., *Agony at Easter: The 1916 Irish Rising*. London, 1969

Collins, P.(Ed.), *Nationalism and Unionism, Conflict in Ireland 1885-1921*. Belfast, 1994

Coogan, T.P., *1916: The Easter Rising*. London, n/d

Coogan, T.P., *De Valera, Long Fellow, Long Shadow*. London, 1993

Cronin, S., *The McGarrity Papers*. Tralee, 1972

Cronin, S., *Our Own Red Blood: The Story of the Easter Rising*. Dublin, 1966

Cronin, S., *The Revolutionaries: The Story of 12 Great Irishmen*. Dublin, 1971

Davis, R., *Arthur Griffith and Non-violent Sinn Fein*. Tralee, u/d

de Valera, T., *A Memoir*. Dublin, 2004

Devoy, J., *Recollections of an Irish Rebel*. New York, 1929

Dicey, A .V., *England's Case Against Home Rule*. Richmond,1973

Doherty, G. (&)(Eds.), 1916 *The Long Revolution*. Cork, 2007

Donnelly, M. (Ed.), *The Last Post*. Dublin, 1994

Dorgan, T. (&) (Eds.), *Revising the Rising.* Derry, 1991

Drury, P. J. (Ed.), *Anglo-Irish Studies* II 1976 & IV 1977. Cambridge 1976

Ebenezer, L., *Fron-Goch.* Llanrwst 2006

Edwards, R.D., *James Connolly.* Dublin, 1981

Edwards, R. D., *Patrick Pearse: The Triumph of Failure.* London, 1979

Ferriter, D., *Judging Dev.* Dublin, 2007

Figgis, D., *A Chronicle of Jail.* Dublin, 1917

Fitzhenry, E .C. (Ed.), *Nineteen Sixteen: An Anthology.* Dublin, 1935

Fitzpatrick, D., *Politics and Irish Life 1913–1921: Provincial Experience of War and Revolution.* Dublin, 1977

Fitzpatrick, D., *The Two Irelands 1912–1939.* Oxford,1998

Foy, M. & Barton, B., *The Easter Rising.* Stroud, 2000

Glynn, A., *High upon the Gallows Tree.* Tralee, 1967

Golway, T., *Irish Rebel: John Devoy and America's fight for Irish Freedom.* New York, 1999

Greaves, C. D., *1916 as History: The Myth of the Blood Sacrifice.* Dublin, 1991

Griffith, K. & O'Grady, T., *Curious Journey: An Oral History of Ireland's Unfinished Revolution.* London, 1982

Gwynn, D., *The Life and Death of Roger Casement.* London, 1930

Gwynn, D.,*The Life of John Redmond.* London, 1932

Hart, P.,*The IRA at War 1916–1923.* Oxford, 2003

Henry, R. M., *The Evolution of Sinn Fein.* London, 1970

Henry, W., *Supreme Sacrifice: The Story of Eamonn Ceannt 1881–1916.* Cork, 2005

Hopkinson, M. (Ed.), *Frank Henderson's Easter Rising.* Cork, 1998

Horgan, J.J., *Parnell to Pearse.* Dublin, 1948

Irish Times, The Weekly, *1916 Rebellion Handbook.* Dublin, 1998

Jeffrey, K., *The GPO and the Easter Rising.* Dublin, 2006

Jeffrey, K. (Ed.), *The Sinn Fein Rebellion as They Saw It* (The Norway reports). Dublin, 1999

Joy, S., *The IRA in Kerry 1916–1921.* Cork, 2005

Kerryman, The, *Kerry's Fighting Story.* Tralee, n/d

Le Roux, L.N., *Patrick H. Pearse.* Dublin,1932?

Le Roux, L.N., *Tom Clarke and the Irish Freedom Movement.* Dublin, 1936

Levenson, S., *Maude Gonne*. London, 1977

Litt, E., *The Political Imagination*. Glenview1966

Longford, Lord & O'Neill, Thomas P., *Eamon De Valera*. London, 1974

Lynch, D. & O'Donoghue, F. (Ed.), *The IRB and the 1916 Insurrection*. Cork, 1957

MacAonghusa, P., *Quotations from P.H. Pearse*. Cork, 1979

MacAonghusa, P. & Ó Réagáin, L, *The Best of Pearse*. Cork, 1967

MacAtasney, G., *Sean MacDiarmada: The Mind of the Revolution*. Nure, 2004

MacCarthy, Col .J.M., *Limerick's Fighting Story: From 1916 to the Truce with Britain*. Tralee, n/d

MacColl, R., *Roger Casement*. London, 1965

MacManus, M. J., *Eamon De Valera*. Dublin, 1945

Mansergh, M., *The Legacy of History*. Cork, 2003

Mansergh, N., *The Irish Question 1840–1921*. London, 1975

Marreco, A., *The Rebel Countess, The Life and Times of Constance Markievicz*. London, 2000

Maume, P., *The Long Gestation: Irish National Life 1891–1918*.Dublin, 1999

McBride, L.W., *The Greening of Dublin Castle*. Washington DC

McGarry, F., *The Rising Ireland: Easter 1916*. Oxford, 2010

McGee, O., *The IRB: The IRB from the Land League to Sinn Fein*. Dublin, 2005

McNally, M., *Easter Rising 1916: Birth of the Irish Republic*. Oxford, 2007

Mitchell, A. & Ó Snodaigh, P. (Eds.), *Irish Political Documents, 1916–1949*. Dublin, 1985.

Monteith, Capt. R., *Casement's Last Adventure*. Dublin, 1953

Moran, S.F, *Patrick Pearse and the Politics of Redemption*. Washington DC, 1994

Murphy, B.P., *Patrick Pearse and the Lost Republican Ideal*. Dublin, 1991

National Gallery, *Cuimhneachan 1916*. Dublin, 1966

Nevin, D., *James Connolly: A Full Life*. Dublin, 2005

Norman, D., *Terrible Beauty: A Life of Constance Markievicz*. Dublin, 1991

Norstedt, J., *Thomas MacDonagh*, Virginia,1980

Nowlan, K.B. (Ed.), *The Making of 1916*. Dublin, 1969

O'Broin, L., *The Chief Secretary Augustine Birrell in Ireland.* Connecticut 1970

O'Broin, L., *Dublin Castle and the 1916 Rising: The Story of Sir M. Nathan.* Dublin, 1966

O'Brolchain, H. (Ed.), *All in the Blood.* Dublin, 2006

O'Buachalla, S., *The Letters of P. H. Pearse.* Gerrards Cross,1980

O'Connor, F., *The Big Fellow.* Dublin, 1979

O'Cuinneagain, M., *On the Arm of Time.* Donegal, 1992

O'Faolain, S., *The Life Story of Eamon De Valera.* Dublin, 1933

O'Keefe, J.O'H., *Recollections of 1916 and its Aftermath.* Tralee, 2005

O'Mahoney, S., *Fron-Goch: University of Revolution.* Dublin, 1991

O'Mahoney, T.P., *The Politics of Dishonour: Ireland 1916–1977.* Dublin, 1977

O'Mordha, Col. M., *Tus agus Fas Oclaigh na hEireann 1913–1917.* Dublin, 1936

O'Rahilly, A., *Winding the Clock: O'Rahilly and the 1916 Rising.* Dublin, 1991

O'Siochain, P.A., *Ireland: Journey to Freedom* (a portrait of D.D. Sheehan, MP, 1901–18). Kells, 1990

O'Snodaigh, P., *The Godfathers of Revisionism.* Dublin, 1991

Pearse, P.H., *Political Writings and Speeches.* Dublin, 1966

Pearse, P.H., *The Sovereign People* (Pamphlet 4). Dublin, 1972

Phillips, W.A., *The Revolution in Ireland, 1906–1923,* London, 1926

Rafter, K., *Sinn Fein 1905–2005: In the Shadow of Gunmen.* Dublin, 2005

Reilly, T., *Joe Stanley: Printer to the Rising.* Dingle, 2005

Roper, Esther (Ed.), *The Prison Letters of Countess Markievicz.* London, 1987

Ryan, A., *Witnesses Inside the Easter Rising.* Dublin, 2005

Ryan, D., *Remembering Sion.* London, 1934

Ryan, D., *The Rising.* Dublin, 1949

Shea, P., *Voices and the Sound of Guns.* Belfast,1983

Sisson, E., *Pearse's Patriots: St. Enda's and the Cult of Boyhood.* Cork, 2004

Smith, A.D., *Myths and Memories of the Easter Rising.* Dublin, 2006

Spinder, K .Capt., *The Mystery of the Casement Ship.* Tralee, 1965

Stephens, J., *The Insurrection in Dublin.* Gerrards Cross, 1978

Taillon, R., *The Women of 1916.* Belfast, 1999

Thompson, W. I., *At the Edge of History*. New York, 1971

Thompson, W. I., *The Imagination of an Insurrection: Dublin Easter 1916*. Mass., 1982

Townshend, C., *Easter 1916: The Easter Rebellion*. London, 2005

Warwick Haller, (Ed.), *Letters from Dublin, Easter 1916: Alfred Fanning's Diary of the Rising*. Dublin, 1995

Weale, A., *Patriot Traitors: Roger Casement, John Amery and the Real Meaning of Treason*. London, 2001

White, G. & O'Shea, B., *Baptised In Blood: The Formation of the Cork Brigade of Irish Volunteers 1913–1916*. Cork, 2005

Williams, D., (Ed.), *The Irish Struggle 1916–1926*. London, 1968

Wrench, J.E., *Struggle 1914–1920*. London, 1935

THE IRISH ARMY

Bartlett, T. & Jeffrey, K. (Eds.), *A Military History of Ireland*. Cambridge 1996

Bredin, Brig. A.E.C., *A History of the Irish Soldier*. Belfast, 1987

Brophy, K.T., *Walking the Line: Scenes from an Army Childhood*. Edinburgh, 1994

Carroll, J.T., *Ireland in the War Years 1939–1945*. Newton Abbot, 1975

Conway, N., *The First Fifty Years of the Third Infantry Battalion*. Curragh, 1973

Duggan, Lt.-Col. J.P., *A History of the Irish Army*. Dublin, 1991

Fisk, R., *In Time of War: Ireland, Ulster and the Price of Neutrality*. Dingle, 1983

Fitzgerald, W., *Irish Unification and NATO*. Dublin, 1982

Flynn, B., *Soldiers of Folly: The IRA Border Campaign 1956–1962*. Cork, 2009

Gray, T., *The Lost Years: The Emergency in Ireland 1939–45*. London, 1998

Harvey, Comdt D., *Peacemakers: Irish Soldiers in the Lebanon*. Dublin, 2001

Harvey, D. & White, G., *The Barracks: A History of Victoria/Collins Barracks, Cork*. Cork, 1997

Hayes-McCoy, (Ed.) *The Irish at War: Thomas Davis Lectures*. Cork, 1964

Keatinge, P., *A Singular Stance: Irish Neutrality in the 1980s*. Dublin, 1984

Kelly, J., *Orders for the Captain*. Author, 1971

Kennedy, M. & Laing, V. (Eds.), *The Irish Defence Forces 1940–1949 The Chief of Staff Reports*. Dublin, 2011

Malone, M., *The Lebanon Diaries: An Irish Soldier's Diaries*. Dunshaughlin, 2006

McCaughren, T., *The Peacemakers of Niemba*. Dublin, 1966

McDonald, H., *Irishbatt: The Story of Ireland's Blue Berets in the Lebanon*. Dublin, 1993

McSweeney, B.(Ed.), *Ireland and the Threat of Nuclear War*. Dublin, 1985

Moriarty, M., *An Irish Soldier's Diaries*. Cork, 2010

Nowlan, K.B. & Williams, K. (Eds.), *Ireland in the War Years and After, 1939–51*. Dublin, 1969

Power, D., *The Siege at Jadotville: The Irish Army's Forgotten Battle*. Dunsaughlin 2005

Quigley, A.A., *Green is my Sky*. Dublin, 1983

Smith, R., *Under the Blue Flag*. Dublin, 1980

Wood, I.S., *Ireland during the Second World War*. London, 2002

IRISH SOLDIERS IN OTHER ARMIES

Babington, A., *The Devil to Pay: The Mutiny of the Connaught Rangers, India July 1920*. London,1991

Beaudot, W.J.K. & Herdegen, L.J., *An Irishman in the Iron Brigade: The Civil War Memoirs of James P. Sullivan*. New York

Beckett, I.F.W., *The Army and the Curragh Incident, 1914*. London, 1986

Bourke, J., *The Misfit Soldier: Edward Casey's War Story, 1914-1918*. Cork, 1999

Bowman, T., *Irish Regiments in the Great War: Discipline and Morale*. Manchester 2003

Burke, T.S., *The 2nd Battalion Royal Dublin Fusiliers and the Tragedy of Mouse Trap Farm: April and May 1915*. Dublin, 2004

Conyngham, D. Capt., *The Irish Brigade and its Campaigns*. London, u/d

Cooper, B., *The Tenth (Irish) Division in Gallipoli*. Dublin, 1993

Denman, T., *Ireland's Unknown Soldiers: The 16th (Irish) Division in the Great War*. Dublin, 1992

Denman, T., *A Lonely Grave: The Life and Death of William Redmond*. Dublin, 1995

Doherty, R., *Clear the Way*. Dublin, 1993

Doherty, R., *Irish Generals*. Belfast,1993

Doherty, R., *Irish Men and Women in the Second World War*. Dublin, 1999

Doherty, R. & Truesdale, D., *Irish Winners of the Victoria Cross*. Dublin, 2000

Dooley, T.P., *Irishmen or English Soldiers?* Liverpool,1995

Dungan, M., *Distant Drums: Irish Soldiers in Foreign Armies*. Belfast,1993

Dungan, M., *Irish Voices from the Great War*. Dublin, 1995

Dungan, M., *They Shall not Grow Old: Irish Soldiers and the Great War*. Dublin, 1997

Falls, Capt. C., *The History of the 36th Ulster Division*. London, 1996

Fergusson, Sir J., *The Curragh Incident*. London, 1964

Fitzpatrick, D. (Ed.), *Ireland and the First World War*. Dublin, 1986

Gerard, J. W., *My Four Years in Germany*. London, 1917

Godley, Gen. Sir A., *Life of an Irish Soldier*. London, 1939

Greacen, L., *Chink: A Biography*. London, 1991

Gregory, A. & Peseta, S. (Eds.), *Ireland and the Great War*. Manchester, 2002

Gunner, C.J. & Larkin, P. (Ed.), *Front of the Line: Adventures with the Irish Brigade*. Antrim, 1991

Hall, D., *The Unreturned Army: County Louth Dead in the Great War*. Dundalk, 2005

Hanly, B., *A Guide to Irish Military Heritage*. Dublin, 2004

Harris, Maj. H.E.D., *The Irish Regiments in the First World War*. Cork, 1968

Harris, Maj. H.E.D., *The Royal Irish Fusiliers*. London, 1972

Harris, R .G. & Wilson, H.R.G., *The Irish Regiments 1683-1999*. Staplehurst, 1999

Harris, S .L., *Duffy's War: Irish Fighting 69th in World War One*. Washington, 2006

Hennessy, M. N., *The Wild Geese: the Irish Soldier in Exile*. Connecticut, 1973

Henry, W., *Galway and the Great War*. Cork, 2006

Hogarty, P., *The Old Toughs: from Milton to Mons and the Western Front 1911-1918. A Brief History of the Royal Dublin Fusiliers, 2nd Battalion*. Dublin, 2001

James, R.R., *Gallipoli*. London, 1984

Jeffery, K., *Ireland and the Great War*. Cambridge, 2000

Johnston, K., *Home or Away: The Great War and the Irish Revolution*. Dublin, 2010

Johnstone, T., *Orange, Green and Khaki: The Story of the Irish Regiments in the Great War*. Dublin, 1992

Kennealy, I., *Courage and Conflict: Forgotten Stories of the Irish at War*. Cork, 2009

Kettle, T., *The Open Secret of Ireland*. London, 1912

Kettle, T., *The Day's Burden and Other Essays*. Dublin, 1968

Kilfeather, T. P., *The Connaught Rangers*. Tralee, 1969

King, C., *The Orange and the Green*. London, 1967

Kipling, R., *The Irish Guards in the Great War: The First Battalion* Staplehurst, 1997

Kipling, R., *The Irish Guards in the Great War: The Second Battalion*. Staplehurst, 1997

Lavery, F. (Ed.), *Irish Heroes in the War*. London, 1917

Lucy, J. F., *There's a Devil in the Drum*. London, 1992

Lyons, J. B., *The Enigma of Tom Kettle: Irish Patriot, Essayist, Poet, British Soldier, 1880–1916*. Dublin, 1983

MacCarthy, Dr C., *Archdeacon Tom Duggan: In Peace and in War*. Dublin, 1994

MacDonagh, M., *The Irish at the Front*. London, 1916

MacFhionngaile, N., *Donegal, Ireland and the First World War*. Letterkenny, 1987

Magnus, P., *Kitchener: Portrait of an Imperialist*. London, 1961

McCance, Capt. S., *History of the Royal Munster Fusiliers*. Schull, 1995

McCourt, E., *Remember Butler: the story of Sir William Butler*. London, 1967

McNamara, P.J., *The Widow's Penny*. Limerick, 2000

Moore, Maj.-Gen. D.G., *The North Irish Brigade*. Eglinton, n/d

Murphy, D., *The Irish Brigades, 1685-2006*. Dublin, 2007

Newark, T., *The Fighting Irish: The Story of the Extraordinary Irish Soldier*. London, 2012

O'Brien, M. J., *The Irish at Bunker Hill*. Dublin, 1962

O'Callaghan, J. C., *History of the Irish Brigades in the Service of France.* London, 1869

O'Rahilly, Prof. A., *Father William Doyle S.J.: A Spiritual Study.* London, 1925

Orr, P., *Field of Bones.* Dublin, 2006

Orr, P., *The Road to the Somme: Men of the Ulster Division tell their Story.* Belfast, 1987

Passingham, Ian, *Pillars of Fire: The Battle of Messines Ridge June 1917.* Stroud, 1998

Pollock, S., *Mutiny for a Cause.* London, 1969

Redmond, Maj. W.M.P., *Trench Pictures form France.* London, 1917

Richardson, N., *A Coward if I Return, A Hero if I Fall: Stories of Irishmen in World War I.* Dubllin, 2010

Robinson, L., *Bryan Cooper.* London, 1931

Romer, Maj. C., & Mainwaring, A.E., *The Second Battalion Royal Dublin Fusiliers in the South African War.* London, 1908

Ross, P., *All Valiant Dust: An Irishman Abroad.* Dublin, 1992

Taylor, J.W., *The Royal Irish Rifles in the Great War.* Dublin, 2002

Verney, P., *The Micks: The Story of the Irish Guards.* London, 1973

Wicklow, The Earl of, *Fireside Fusilier.* Derby, 1970

Wylly, Col. H.C., *Neill's Blue Caps: 1914-1922* Vols. 1, 2 & 3. Schull, 1996

Appendix C
The 25th Cadet Class (1950-1952)

Berry, Sean

Bergin, Noel

Buckley, Ray

Coffey, Dermott

Considine, Mick

Corbett, Jerry

Daly, Dan

Daly, Harry

Daly, Kevin

Dobey, Barney

Duffy, Kevin

Fitzgerald, Nial

Gillespie, Mick

Goggin, Paddy

Healy, Jerry

Heaslip, Johnny

Hegarty, Nicky

Houston, Dinny

Kelliher, Pat

Kenny, Gerry

Manning, Gerry

Moriarty, Mick

Moriarty, Tom

MacNiocaill, Sean

McGreal. Mick

McNally, Billy

McMahon, Mick

O'Donovan, Bernie

O'Donovan, Frank

O'Farrell, Mick

O'Farrell, Padraigh

O'Hora, Tony

O'Regan, Dave

Phillips, Willie

Ringrose, Des

Ryan, Tommy

Smyth, Brendan

Spillane, Jack

Tumulty, Ray

Whelan, Kieran

Maguire, Brian